JCB

Pu... Writing Worktext

Public Relations Writing Worktext provides the fundamental knowledge and the basic preparation required for the professional practice of public relations writing. This textbook introduces readers to public relations and writing, providing an overview of the four-step public relations process, in addition to defining and detailing the writing activities involved. It presents in-depth information on the writing formats and approaches used in implementing strategic public relations plans, and offers instruction for developing all types of writing assignments, starting with memos, proposals, and news releases, and moving on to the more complex tasks of advocacy writing, newsletters, and digital communication and social media. Examples accompany the assignments, providing guidance and structure for the varied writing activities.

Retaining the approach of the second edition, this text incorporates numerous changes and updates, making it suitable for use as a primary course text. Updates include:

- increased focus on writing for the Web, blogs, and electronic media, including information on writing social media releases and a new chapter entitled "New and Social Media";
- a new planning outline to help writers develop more effective messages;
- expanded checklists for writers to reference when working on assignments;
- additional examples of effective public relations writing by leading companies in a variety of organizational settings, including Travelers, UPS, Burger King, Xerox, Frito-Lay, and many more;
- new assignments based on topics, issues, and problems that public relations professionals in all sectors face today;
- restructured content for improved writing flow and consistency.

Authors Joseph M. Zappala and Ann R. Carden offer a clear and engaging introduction to the writing activities involved in public relations practice, resulting in a valuable resource for professionals as well as a practical classroom text for students planning careers in public relations.

Joseph M. Zappala, APR, is Chief Communications Officer for Cornell University's ILR School. He has over 25 years of public relations experience and is a former college professor.

Ann R. Carden, APR, Fellow PRSA, is an associate professor of communication at the State University of New York at Fredonia, where she teaches public relations. She has over 25 years' experience managing public relations and 11 years' experience in broadcast journalism.

Public Relations Writing Worktext

A Practical Guide for the Profession

Third Edition

Joseph M. Zappala

Ann R. Carden

Routledge
Taylor & Francis Group

NEW YORK AND LONDON

First edition published 1996
by NTC/Contemporary Publishing Company

Second edition published 2004
by Lawrence Erlbaum Associates

This edition published 2010
by Routledge
270 Madison Ave, New York, NY 10016

Simultaneously published in the UK
by Routledge
2 Park Square, Milton Park, Abingdon, Oxon OX14 4RN

Routledge is an imprint of the Taylor & Francis Group, an informa business

Typeset in Times New Roman PS and Helvetica by
Florence Production Ltd, Stoodleigh, Devon
Printed and bound in the United States of America on acid-free paper by
Edwards Brothers, Inc.

Library of Congress Cataloging in Publication Data
Zappala, Joseph M.
   Public relations writing worktext: a practical guide for the profession/
   by Joseph M. Zappala, Ann R. Carden.—3rd ed.
      p. cm.
    Rev. ed. of: Public relations worktext: a writing and planning
    resource. 2nd ed.
    Includes index.
   1. Public relations. 2. Business writing. I. Carden, Ann R.
   II. Zappala, Joseph M. Public relations worktext. III. Title.
   HM1221.Z37 2009
   659.2—dc22   2009013211

ISBN10: 0–415–99753–4 (hbk)
ISBN10: 0–415–99754–2 (pbk)
ISBN10: 0–203–87163–4 (ebk)

ISBN13: 978–0–415–99753–9 (hbk)
ISBN13: 978–0–415–99754–6 (pbk)
ISBN13: 978–0–203–87163–8 (ebk)

Brief Contents

Contents

Exhibits

Preface

About the Book

What's been happening in public relations since the last edition of our book in 2004? That's a question we had to answer as we began work last year on the third edition, now titled *Public Relations Writing Worktext*. Of course, technology has continued to have an impact, with the explosion of digital, new, and social media. The strategic role that public relations plays in organizations also keeps evolving. But one thing remains constant—the need for public relations professionals to write well. And that remains at the core of our book. In fact, in this edition, we've made some changes that put even greater focus on writing and the writing process.

The third edition of the book has the same "how-to" format we've been using in the past two editions: introductory text that explains the subject in an easy-to-understand, practical way, along with examples of professionally written materials and a variety of assignments that give students hands-on experience writing public relations materials that are used in practice today. This format seems to work; faculty members and students, as well as professionals using the book as a refresher or reference, tell us that the worktext is a great learning tool and resource. You'll also see changes that we believe make the third edition even stronger:

- expanded text sections with more detailed content on subjects such as research, planning, sales letters, proposals, advocacy writing, and legal considerations;
- more focus on writing for the Web, blogs, and electronic media, including information on writing social media releases and a new chapter entitled "Web Sites and Social Media";
- a new planning outline to help writers develop more effective messages;
- expanded checklists for writers to reference when working on assignments—one of the most popular features in the second edition;
- more and updated examples and reprints of effective public relations writing by leading companies in a variety of organizational settings, including Travelers, UPS, Burger King, Xerox, Frito-Lay, and many more;
- restructured content for better writing flow and consistency;
- new assignments based on topics, issues, and problems that public relations professionals in all sectors might find themselves facing today.

The parts of the book have been restructured to better reflect the public relations process:

Part One provides an "An Introduction to the Basics." Chapter 1 includes information on public relations as compared to marketing and advertising and introduces the different forms of public relations writing, as well as the concepts of communication and persuasion. Chapter 2 focuses on the basics of writing—spelling, punctuation, grammar, and style—as well as ethical and legal considerations. Chapter 3 introduces the four-step public relations process.

Part Two focuses on research. Chapter 4 reviews the importance of research and the various methods used.

Part Three provides an overview of the planning process. Chapter 5 includes a detailed look at developing public relations messages.

Part Four provides in-depth information on the various writing formats and techniques used in implementing strategic public relations plans, from news releases (chapter 6) and features (chapter 8) to business correspondence (chapter 10) and promotional publications (chapter 13).

Part Five completes the public relations process with a comprehensive look at evaluation methods in chapter 14.

Our Vision

This book provides students with the fundamental knowledge required for public relations writing, as well as the critical writing practice they need, allowing them to make mistakes in the classroom and receive feedback on written pieces before they enter a professional setting. Without this experience, students will have difficulty succeeding in field assignments and in that first job. Internship supervisors and employers want students and graduates who can "hit the ground running," and that means having the ability to write a variety of public relations materials competently and with minimal direction. We think this book will give students basic writing preparation to get started in their careers and be a useful resource "down the road" when they need a refresher on some aspect of public relations writing.

Although this book is primarily targeted to college students, we kept another audience in mind while preparing the text—the many people who, with little or no training, have found themselves in the position of performing public relations tasks. Before organizations make the decision to hire a public relations practitioner, they often turn to other people within the organization to write a news release, design a flier, or plan a special event. Nonprofit organizations often ask volunteers to complete public relations tasks. Although we do not suggest that this book replaces proper training in the field, it is hoped that it will provide some professional guidance to people who find themselves in these situations.

Acknowledgments

No book is assembled by the authors alone. There are many people involved in the writing process from beginning to end, and many people to thank for their contributions.

We are grateful to NTC/Contemporary Publishing Company and Lawrence Erlbaum Associates, Inc., who published the first two editions of the book, our new publisher, Routledge, of the Taylor & Francis Group, for seeing the value of publishing a third edition; to our editor, Linda Bathgate, for her direction and flexibility; and to other members of the publishing team at Routledge, including Katherine Ghezzi, Senior Editorial Assistant and Gail Newton, Production Editor; to Louise Smith, our capable copy-editor; and the production house, Florence Production Ltd, where Senior Project Manager Fiona Isaac oversaw the production process that made this book a reality.

We are grateful for the time and comments of practitioners and educators throughout the country who generously agreed to review the proposal for the third edition.

We recognize the contributions of the many practitioners and educators who have developed, and continue to develop, a body of knowledge for public relations through books of their own, other publications, research, and practice. Their work, listed under "References and Suggested Reading" following each chapter, serves as a basis of this text as well as future works in the field of public relations.

This edition of *Public Relations Writing Worktext* includes dozens of excellent, and often award-winning, examples and reprints from leading companies. We thank these companies for providing access to their work and for their willingness to share.

Of course, there would be no book at all without readers. We are grateful to the instructors who selected the first and second editions of *Public Relations Writing Worktext* for use in their classrooms and expressed interest in a third edition. We appreciate their confidence in the material presented in the text and thank them, as well as future instructors and students, who will use the book.

On a Personal Note . . .

Some years ago, when I was teaching full time at Utica College of Syracuse University, I began work on the second edition of our book. After completing the manuscript, I was faced with "publisher limbo." The original publisher decided to sell its college text division, and it was unclear if the second edition would find a publishing home.

When I finally learned, almost two years later, that a publisher had purchased the rights to this book, it was truly a day of celebration. At that same time, I made a major life and career change. After 13 years as a college professor, I decided to return to practice and accepted a position as a senior communications professional with Cornell University. When it came time to revisit the book and get the second edition completed, I have to admit, I started to panic, just a little. Working 50+ hours a week, plus juggling other commitments, I knew this would be an almost impossible task on my own. Fortunately, some colleagues connected me with Ann R. Carden, and here we are, now having finished our third edition. It has been interesting to complete the second, and now third, edition of the book as a practitioner, as I apply concepts shared in the book each and every day on the job—whether I am writing a high-level senior management correspondence, consulting with staff on Web and social media strategy and content, or working on a communications plan.

There are several people I need to acknowledge and whose guidance and support made it possible for me to complete this project. First, legendary PR educator Ray Simon, someone to whom I owe a debt of gratitude. When Ray asked me to assist him with the first edition, I was deeply honored, and a little scared. But his confidence in me made a huge difference, and I am thankful to him for all he did for me, both as a mentor and a friend. To this day, Ray's influence and his wise advice continue to shape my work as a professional and the way in which I relate to people and solve problems. I'm lucky that I had the chance to learn from him during my time at UC.

My co-author, Ann R. Carden, is an outstanding collaborator. There were many times that I lagged behind on a deadline, or when the demands of my job made it difficult to focus on the book. Ann was always there to keep the project on track and to pick up the slack when things got a bit crazy on my end, without complaint. This is the best possible co-author relationship, working with someone who has been successful in the field, but who also knows "what works" in the classroom right now. I couldn't ask for a better writing partner.

I also want to thank my former colleagues at Utica College, especially Kim Landon and Cecilia Friend, who saw me through both the first edition and the first draft of the second edition, and whose friendship meant a lot to me during those Utica years. I miss seeing them every day. And, of course, my thanks goes to all the students I have taught over the years, some of whom still keep in touch with me and still insist on calling me "professor." (At this point in time, I let them know that "Joe" is just fine.) I learned a lot from my students, both inside and outside the classroom. I hope this book proves to be a useful learning tool for the next generation of public relations students.

Finally, I want say thanks to my family and my parents for all their support through the years and three editions. I'd like to dedicate the book to them, and to my partner who saw me through many evenings and weekends trying to get this project done. He showed great patience and understanding when I had to devote "us" time to work on the book, and when stress levels got a bit high. Thanks, Billy. Much love to you and Olivia!

—J.Z.

I would not be writing this section had it not been for my co-author, Joseph M. Zappala, who graciously invited—with only a reference from a mutual friend to go on—a stranger to help with the second, and now third, edition of his textbook. Thank you, Joe, for your confidence in me and especially for your willingness to let me be a full partner in the writing process, which can be a deeply personal thing for the original author. While my co-author was leaving academe to return to the professional world, I was leaving daily practice to enter academe—and much has changed in the field since then! Joe was instrumental in making sure this edition included the most up-to-date and realistic information for today's public relations students and practitioners.

It has been my lifelong dream to teach at the college level and to someday publish a writing text. Knowing how important writing is to the practice of public relations, I wanted to do my part to ensure that future public relations practitioners developed strong writing skills. It is an area I'm passionate about, to which my students, both former and present, will attest. I thank them for letting me know (eventually) that, although I demanded much from them and made grade deductions for misspellings and poor grammar, they are now better writers.

My deep appreciation goes to my faculty colleagues in the Department of Communication at the State University of New York at Fredonia, who always expressed an interest in how the book was going, even though they must have gotten tired of my frenzied "I'm on deadline!" banter. Thank you for your support and indulgence.

My path to this point is the culmination of varied experiences and many influences along the way, and it is my honor to acknowledge them, beginning with my high school English teacher who talked me out of studying nursing in college because she thought I had a talent for writing. My thoughts on the practice of public relations have been honed through the years by every organization for which I have worked, by each co-worker in those organizations, and especially others in the public relations field. Whether it was a formal presentation, casual conversation, or a discussion over lunch (and there were many of those), I have learned much from my colleagues and am grateful to the members of the Buffalo/Niagara chapter of the Public Relations Society of America for sharing their expertise. Special thanks go to Ronald D. Smith, APR; Stanton H. Hudson, Jr., APR, Fellow PRSA; Donald J. Goralski, APR; and Bill Sledzik, APR, Fellow PRSA.

Lastly, I dedicate this book to my family and friends, who have been so supportive during a time of great transition in my life, and especially to my father, T. Guy Reynolds Jr., who instilled in me a strong work ethic, a thirst for knowledge, the belief that job satisfaction comes before money, and the attitude that there wasn't anything I couldn't do—all attributes that allowed me to stretch my wings and try new things; my sister, Vanda White, who has shown me what faith and courage really look like; and, my children, Maggie and Stephen. I love you and am so proud of the adults you have become.

—A.R.C.

An Invitation

A textbook is much like a snapshot in time. Different trends develop, theories evolve, and new case studies are introduced almost as soon as the book is published. With this in mind, we encourage our readers to provide us with feedback on the text so we may continue to develop it into a useful tool in the future. Please send your comments to:

Joseph M. Zappala, APR
Chief Communications Officer
ILR School
Cornell University
403 Dolgen Hall
Ithaca, NY 14850
jz76@cornell.edu

Ann R. Carden, APR, Fellow PRSA
Associate Professor
Communication
SUNY Fredonia
304 McEwen Hall
Fredonia, NY 14063
ann.carden@fredonia.edu

AN INTRODUCTION TO THE BASICS

What is Public Relations Writing?

A song that sounds simple is just not that easy to write.

—Sheryl Crow[1]

I don't know what real childbirth is like, but writing songs seems as close as I'm going to come.

—Billy Joel

You may think that songwriters and public relations writers have little in common. But songwriters, poets, novelists, and other writers, including public relations writers, will tell you that writing is hard, even painful. Most writers know the frustration of staring at an empty computer screen or a blank sheet of paper, waiting for the right words to come, and public relations writers are no exception.

The songwriter faced with writer's block might take a long drive or meditate to stimulate the writing process. As a public relations writer, you don't always have that luxury. In a crisis, when you need to communicate quickly and accurately about a threatening situation, there's little time for leisurely drives or meditation. Consider, as well, that public relations professionals write for many different audiences, for many different media, and in many different forms and styles, sometimes all in the same day. This is no easy task.

Songwriters, like poets, novelists, sculptors, and other artists, often create works that are deeply personal; they are not always creating a work of art to please someone else, but more so to express something important they need to say. This is not so for public relations writers. Public relations writing has an organizational purpose. You must write with the interests of a specific group of people in mind, and balance that with the interests of the organization you represent. Public relations writing succeeds when people respond by doing something your organization wants them to do, whether that be learning something you want them to learn, adopting an attitude or position you want them to adopt, taking a positive action you want them to take, or simply thinking good thoughts about the organization. In the public relations world, writing without such a purpose is a waste of time.

As a public relations writer, you are not aiming to create works of art. Don't make the mistake of thinking that good public relations writing is like a song, or like poetry or prose, full of descriptive phrasing and obscure thoughts. There are times when creative writing is necessary, but creativity should never overshadow what's most important about a public relations message: its ability to communicate information in a way that people will understand. It's about simple words and clear messages that inspire a desired change in thinking or behavior.

While those brochures and news releases you write may not be on the artistic level of a classic novel or an Academy Award-winning film script, they do require special skill and finesse. And that makes public relations writing a fine art.

What is Public Relations?

Before discussing the role of a public relations writer, it's important to give that role some perspective by first defining the public relations function, and then explaining how public relations differs from and integrates with marketing and advertising (as illustrated in Exhibit 1.1). While each of these functions has a distinct purpose, they also work together and share the common goal of helping an organization communicate to its publics—groups that are critical to the organization's survival.

Exhibit 1.2 presents some of the classic definitions of public relations by some of the industry's most respected educators and professionals. In sum, public relations is a strategic function that manages and builds relationships with an organization's publics through two-way communication. Public relations professionals promote two-way communication by providing an open flow of idea exchange, feedback, and information between an organization and its publics. They counsel management on how to best shape policy and establish programs that are mutually beneficial and sensitive to public concerns. Public relations builds goodwill and an understanding of organizational goals among various internal and external publics to help the organization operate smoothly and conduct its business in a cooperative, conflict-free environment.

The goal of *marketing*, by contrast, is to develop, maintain, and improve a product's market share; attract and satisfy customers; and cause a transaction in order to build profitability. Public relations professionals support marketing staff by providing promotional services. One common marketing communications activity is *publicity*, which may involve placing news stories in the media about products and services. The most common form of publicity is the news release, an announcement from an organization written in news style.

If a newspaper publishes your product news release, it does so at no cost to you. Once your publicity material is received by the media, however, you lose control of the content. The media is free to use it in any form they choose, or they can decide not to use it. This differs from *advertising*, which is paid promotional messages that you can control. When you supply an advertisement to the media, they run it as you've written it. Advertising copy has a creative flair, with language and phrasing designed for the "hard sell." Publicity materials are more subtle and read more like news articles. To illustrate the difference, look at the lead from a product news release that appeared on the Verizon Wireless Web site and the opening of a commercial for the same product:

Exhibit 1.1

The Integration of Public Relations, Marketing, and Advertising

Public relations is a strategic function that manages and builds relationships with an organizations publics through two-way communication.

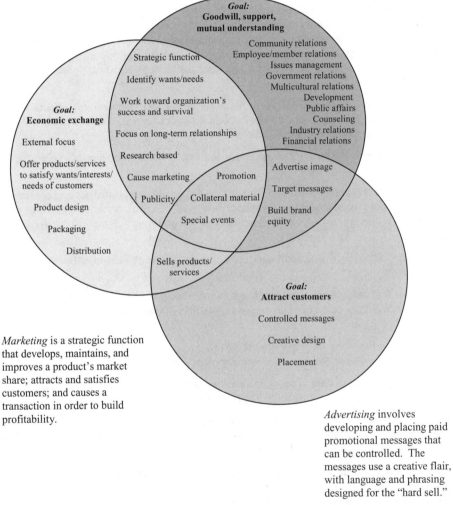

Goal:
Goodwill, support,
mutual understanding

Community relations
Employee/member relations
Issues management
Government relations
Multicultural relations
Development
Public affairs
Counseling
Industry relations
Financial relations

Strategic function

Identify wants/needs

Work toward organization's success and survival

Focus on long-term relationships

Research based

Goal:
Economic exchange

External focus

Offer products/services to satisfy wants/interests/needs of customers

Product design

Packaging

Distribution

Cause marketing

Publicity

Promotion

Collateral material

Special events

Advertise image

Target messages

Build brand equity

Sells products/services

Goal:
Attract customers

Controlled messages

Creative design

Placement

Marketing is a strategic function that develops, maintains, and improves a product's market share; attracts and satisfies customers; and causes a transaction in order to build profitability.

Advertising involves developing and placing paid promotional messages that can be controlled. The messages use a creative flair, with language and phrasing designed for the "hard sell."

Note: Reprinted with permission of *PR Reporter*, Ragan Communications, Inc.

Exhibit 1.2

Defining Public Relations

"Public relations practice is the art and science of analyzing trends, predicting their consequences, counseling organization leaders, and implementing planned programs of action which will serve both the organization's and the public interest."—First World Assembly of Public Relations Associations and the First World Forum of Public Relations

"Public relations is a distinctive management function which helps establish and maintain mutual lines of communication, understanding, acceptance and cooperation between an organization and its publics; involves the management of problems or issues; helps management keep informed on and responsive to public opinion; defines and emphasizes the responsibility of management to serve the public interest; helps management keep abreast of and effectively utilize change, serving as an early warning system to help anticipate trends; and uses research and sound ethical communication techniques as its principal tools."—Harlow, "Building a Public Relations Definition," *Public Relations Review*

"Public relations helps our complex, pluralistic society to reach decisions and function more effectively by contributing to mutual understanding among groups and institutions. It serves to bring private and public policies into harmony."—PRSA Official Statement on Public Relations

"Management of communication between an organization and its publics."—Grunig and Hunt, *Managing Public Relations*

"(1) Management function, (2) relationships between an organization and its publics, (3) analysis and evaluation through research, (4) management counseling, (5) implementation and execution of a planned program of action, communication and evaluation through research, and (6) achievement of goodwill."—Simon, *Public Relations Concepts and Practices*

"Public relations deals primarily with advice on action, based on social responsibility."—Bernays, *The Later Years: 1956–1986*

"The management function that establishes and maintains mutually beneficial relationships between an organization and publics on whom its success or failure depends."—Cutlip, Center, and Broom, *Effective Public Relations*

"(1) deliberate, (2) planned, (3) performance, (4) public interest, (5) two-way communication, and (6) management function."—Wilcox, Ault and Agee, *Public Relations Strategies and Tactics*

"PR involves responsibility and responsiveness in policy and information to the best interests of the organization and its publics."—Newsom, Scott, and Turk, *This is PR: The Realities of Public Relations*

"Public relations is the management function which evaluates public attitudes, identifies the policies and procedures of an individual or an organization with the public interest, and plans and executes a program of action to earn public understanding and acceptance."—*Public Relations News*

"Public relations (PR) is the practice of managing the flow of information between an organization and its publics."—Wikipedia

Product News Release:

The BlackBerry® Storm™ (model 9530) from Research In Motion (NASDAQ: RIMM)—the first touch screen BlackBerry smartphone with the world's first "clickable" touch screen—will be available beginning Nov. 21 in Verizon Wireless Communications Stores and online at www.verizonwireless.com for $199.99 after a $50 mail-in rebate with a new two-year customer agreement.

Product Advertisement:

Whoa! It has no keyboard. And did it just click? You never clicked a screen before. Is that supposed to happen? Is it supposed to feel so right? It feels like a keyboard, just no keys. What kind of mad genius designed this?

In addition to supporting the marketing function with promotional efforts, public relations practitioners offer advice on the social implications of products and help counter attacks from consumer and special interest groups. For example, some years ago, tuna companies faced protests from environmental groups concerned about the number of dolphins getting trapped and killed in nets used by tuna fishermen. Protests and negative media headlines created a serious public relations problem that, in turn, had an impact on product sales. To regain public trust, tuna companies opened up dialogue with environmentalists and began making changes in their fishing practices to avoid doing harm to dolphins. After these changes were made and communicated, tuna companies began declaring their products "dolphin safe" and restoring their reputations through good public relations, while avoiding a marketing disaster.

Types of Public Relations Writing

Public relations writers are among the most versatile of writers. While a magazine journalist writes each article for a single mass audience—the people who read that magazine—the public relations writer prepares many pieces for a wide range of publics. A corporate public relations professional, for example, writes for employees, customers, media, and stockholders. Writing for each of those publics can require variations in message and style. Among the types of writing assignment handled by public relations professionals are:

- *Business correspondence*—internal memos that inform others in the organization about the status of projects and other subjects, external business correspondence and e-mail messages that confirm agreements and solicit support, and proposals to clients and internal supervisors that outline recommended public relations campaigns.
- *Corporate and internal communications*—news and feature stories for publication in newsletters, company magazines, and other employee publications; content for Web sites, intranets, and digital social media; scripts for training and corporate video programs; and annual reports directed to shareholders and the financial community.
- *Publicity writing*—news releases, background materials, and other written pieces designed to produce print and broadcast media coverage.
- *Marketing communications*—written materials that support marketing efforts, product promotion, and customer relations, such as product publicity, product brochures and catalogs, posters and fliers, sales literature, direct mail pieces, and customer newsletters.

- *Advocacy writing*—writing that establishes a position or comments on an issue, endorses a cause or rallies support, such as letters to the editor and articles sent to the opinion pages of print media; speeches written for executives that are delivered at industry conferences, media events, or business meetings; and corporate or "image" advertising that "sells the company," not a specific product (e.g., a corporate ad from a utility company publicly thanking the community for its patience during a power outage).

Communication and the Public Relations Writer

Public relations writing, regardless of what the specific piece is or who it is written for, is always purposeful. Its primary goal is to communicate information that will influence people. Mass communication literature identifies four mass communication goals that also have relevance to public relations writing:

- to *inform* people of threats and opportunities and to help them better understand their environment;
- to *teach* skills, knowledge, and appropriate behavior that help people adapt to their environment and feel accepted;
- to *persuade* people to adopt desired behaviors and see them as acceptable; and
- to *please* people by providing entertainment and enjoyment.

These goals have much in common with those of the public relations writer, especially the first three—to inform, to teach, and to persuade. Some public relations writing certainly has entertainment value. For example, many college public relations and communication programs across the country produce alumni newsletters. Graduates say they enjoy reading the newsletter and especially like knowing what former classmates are doing, if they have changed jobs, gotten engaged or married, had babies, or received an award for their work.

But, in addition to entertainment, this information has greater value. Publishing alumni updates helps graduates stay connected to one another and to the program. Over time, this builds loyalty and support and increases the perceived value of their college degree. The newsletter is more than just an interesting, entertaining read. It has a positive, long-term influence as a communication vehicle.

Like any good communicator, public relations writers must get feedback from their targeted publics to measure the true success of their efforts. The receiver of the message must respond in some way to indicate the message was received, processed, and understood. If you send a news release to a newspaper and the newspaper publishes the release, have you communicated with your public? Not necessarily. You have merely interested an editor enough in the subject to use the material. You can estimate the potential number of people who may have read the story by looking at the circulation figures for the newspaper. But you cannot assume that communication took place, or that people even saw your message, unless they tell you. If the goal of your news release is to inform and to encourage people to learn more about a subject, include a toll-free number in the release and ask them to "call for more information." This technique generates feedback you can measure and provides some assurance that communication occurred.

Public relations theorists and behavioral scientists point out that the traditional S-M-R communications model—sending a message through a specific channel to a desired receiver—is not effective if the intent of communication is to change behavior. They say this model is best used for publicity and awareness building. It is most effective when sending information to people who have little resistance to your message, such as consumers who already use and like your product and whose positive feelings are simply reinforced through the communication. But if the goal is to get people to form an opinion, or to reduce negative public opinion, building awareness alone is not enough.

According to the diffusion of innovations theory, people adopt new ideas as the result of a five-step process that begins with *awareness*. They must first learn about the idea. Next, they must develop further *interest* in the idea and gather additional information on the subject. Then come *evaluation* and *trial*, weighing the pros and cons of the idea and discussing it with others, followed by testing the idea to see how well it fits into their lives. If the trial is successful, the result is *adoption* of the idea.

Think about buying a car. You might first see a television ad or article in the "Auto" section of the newspaper about a particular model (awareness). Thinking this car has potential, you visit a Web site, collect brochures, and read *Consumer Reports* to get more details (interest). With more information in hand, you talk to associates at work, people you know who own the car, "friends" in a chat room or through your Facebook page, and maybe parents to get their opinions of the car's quality, value, and performance. You also look carefully at your budget to determine if this is a realistic purchase (evaluation). Their positive remarks may motivate you to visit a dealer, talk to a salesperson about the car, and take a test drive (trial). After negotiating an agreeable price, you buy the car (adoption). The late Patrick Jackson, one of the most widely known and respected public relations practitioners, developed a behavioral model of communication to explain this process as it relates to public relations (see Exhibit 1.3). According to this model, once people are aware of a product, service, or issue, they will begin to formulate a readiness to act; an event then triggers this readiness into actual behavior.

As the car example shows, publicity and public relations writing have the greatest impact in the awareness and interest stages. Well-placed media articles about the car, a creative Web site, and informative brochures, all produced by public relations writers, play a significant role. These written tools become less influential in the later stages, when personal communication and the opinions of family, friends, and peers have the most impact; it is important to keep this in perspective. Public relations writing plays a part in the acceptance of new ideas and behavioral change early in the process, but face-to-face communication and personal experience make the difference in the end. In addition, your written materials are competing with those of other organizations for someone's attention, so these pieces must do more than just communicate—they must communicate persuasively.

Exhibit 1.3
Jackson's Behavioral Communication Model

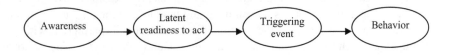

Note: Reprinted with permission of *PR Reporter*, Ragan Communications, Inc.

Persuasion and the Public Relations Writer

Persuasion is not a dirty word. "Persuade" means influence, move, motivate, convince, win over. Those aren't bad words. When you think about it, many of the things you say or do as a college student in an average day—asking your roommate if you can borrow her car, calling your parents in hopes they will send money, convincing your professor to extend an assignment deadline—are all done in an effort to influence, motivate, or persuade. Persuasion "goes bad" when you purposely mislead someone or tell a lie to get what you want. If you tell your parents you need extra cash to buy some textbooks, but they find out you used the money to buy a DVD player or new music from iTunes, those checks from home will probably stop coming.

Some people may perceive persuasion as negative because they confuse it with propaganda. While persuasion and propaganda may use similar techniques, such as symbols, stereotypes, and testimonials, the goal of *persuasion* is to provide new information or existing information in a fresh light to enable people to make up their own minds. *Propaganda*, on the other hand, seeks to manipulate the public's thinking by deliberately providing misinformation.

Public relations professionals are in the persuasion business. They are advocates for their organizations; every conversation, every proposal, every media event, and every piece of writing is intended to influence, build rapport, and win support. But winning support at any cost is never an option. There may be pressure to twist facts, omit details, or say something that just isn't true, but *do not bow to that pressure*. Once trust is lost, it is hard to regain. In a statement made at Utica College when he delivered the Harold Burson Distinguished Lecture, John Reed, an international public relations consultant and veteran practitioner, defined public relations as "ethical persuasion." Keep that definition in mind as a writer, communicator, and protector of an organization's reputation—and your own.

There are honest and reasonable techniques to make communication more persuasive. Messages that genuinely appeal to a public's self-interests, that come from trusted sources, and that suggest a beneficial course of action can be highly persuasive. These principles are illustrated in The Air Bag Safety Campaign launched by the National Safety Council. In response to an increasing number of automobile air-bag-related fatalities, the campaign stressed the importance of properly restraining children under 12 when riding in a car.

Public opinion research showed that many parents did not know the risks air bags posed to their children, and that the majority of parents did not take the necessary steps to buckle up their children. In addition, national crash test data confirmed that the greatest risk was not the air bags themselves, but the potential for injury should an air bag deploy when someone is riding without a seat belt. The campaign appealed to the most fundamental of interests: parents' desires to protect the lives of their children.

The campaign, "Air Bag Safety Means: Buckle Everyone! Children in the Back," or the ABCs of air bag safety, communicated a simple and clear call to action. The key message was, if you and your children use seat belts, you can avoid injury and a possible air-bag-related fatality. Information provided to adult drivers also clearly explained how air bags work and what can happen if someone is unrestrained and too close to the air bag when it deploys. To strengthen message impact, the National Safety Council partnered with professional organizations such as The American Academy of Family Physicians, The National Highway Traffic Safety Administration, and respected safety groups to help educate drivers about air bag safety. The campaign led to a significant increase in the number of adult drivers properly restraining children before transporting them in cars and thus to a reduced number of air bag fatalities. Follow-up surveys indicated greater awareness of the risks of air bags. Here are other tips for persuasive communication that are supported by behavioral research:

- Use a blend of rational and emotional messages. The National Safety Council's campaign shared facts, statistics, and results of air bag safety public opinion research, but it also used the media to publish stories about individual tragedies. This made the problem real: it added a human face to the problem to which other families could relate. Generally, messages directed to high-involvement audiences—those already connected to or inclined to support your organization or cause—might call for a more rational or factual approach. Low-involvement groups may need to be targeted with more emotional messages.
- Select the most appropriate media based on message content and the preferences of your target publics. Print media are best when attempting to explain complex subjects, but visual messages usually have greater influence on attitude change. Know your public and how it prefers to receive information. The fire department of a northeast city, concerned about the growing number of inner-city fires, provided information to local newspapers in hopes of educating residents about fire safety, but with minimal effect. Upon closer inspection, the department discovered a high rate of illiteracy among residents in those areas of the city where fires broke out most often. This prompted a change in strategy that involved using more face-to-face communication and broadcast media.
- Begin and end your writing with the most important messages. Studies indicate that people have higher recall of information that appears in the opening and closing of a message.

At the start of this chapter, we described public relations writing as a fine art, one requiring special skill—a skill that can be learned. To hone that skill, public relations writers must know all aspects of their organizations; have in-depth understanding of their publics and the media that reach those publics; possess finely tuned research skills and expertise in communication and persuasion theory; and be creative, strategic thinkers who can take complex, detailed material and make it simple and easy to understand.

Note

1.   Malloy, 1995, pp. 148–149.

References and Suggested Reading

Bernays, E. L. (1986). *The later years: Public relations insights 1956–1986*. Rhinebeck, NY: H & M.
BlackBerry Storm (2008). Available in US, November 21, exclusively from Verizon Wireless. Retrieved November 16, 2008 from http://news.vzw.com/news/2008/11/pr2008–11–13.html.

BlackBerry Storm commercial (2008). Retrieved November 16, 2008 from http://www.youtube.com/watch?v=GmyVzoyY9Jo.

Broom, G. (2008). *Effective public relations* (10th ed.). Upper Saddle River, NJ: Prentice Hall.

Caywood, C. L. (1997). *The handbook of strategic public relations and integrated communications.* New York: McGraw Hill.

Cutlip, S., Center, A., & Broom, G. (1994). *Effective public relations* (7th ed.). Englewood Cliffs, NJ: Prentice-Hall, Inc.

Gordon, J. C. (1997). Interpreting definitions of public relations: Self assessment and a symbolic interactionism-based alternative. *Public Relations Review, 23 (1)*, 57–66.

Grunig, J. E. (Ed.) (1992). *Excellence in public relations and communication management.* Hillsdale, NJ: Lawrence Erlbaum Associates.

Grunig, J. E., & Hunt, T. (1984). *Managing public relations.* Fort Worth, TX: Holt, Rinehart, & Winston.

Harlow, R. (1976). Building a public relations definition. *Public Relations Review, 2 (4)*, 34–42.

Jackson, P. (1990). *PR Reporter, 33 (30)*, 1–2.

Kitchen, P. J. (1997). *Public relations: Principles & practice.* Stamford, CT: International Thomson Business Press.

Lesly, P. (1998). *Lesly's handbook of public relations and communications* (5th ed.). St. Louis, MO: McGraw Hill/Contemporary Books.

Malloy, M. (Ed.) (1995). *The great rock 'n' roll quote book.* New York: St. Martin's Griffin.

Newsom, D., Scott, A., & Turk, J. V. (1989). *This is PR: The realities of public relations* (4th ed.). Belmont, CA: Wadsworth.

Newsom, D., Turk, J. V., & Kruckeberg, D. (2006). *This is PR: The realities of public relations* (9th ed.). Belmont, CA: Wadsworth.

PRSA Official statement on public relations (n.d.). Retrieved January 24, 2009 from http://www.prsa.org/aboutUs/officialStatement.html.

Public relations (2006). *Merriam-Webster's collegiate dictionary* (11th ed.). Springfiled, MA: Merriam-Webster, Inc.

Public relations (n.d.). Retrieved January 24, 2009 from http://en.wikipedia.org/wiki/Public_relations.

Seitel, F. P. (2006). *Practice of public relations* (10th ed.). Upper Saddle River, NJ: Prentice Hall.

Simon, R. (1984). *Public relations concepts and practices.* Englewood Cliffs, NJ: Prentice Hall.

Smith, R. (2004). *Strategic planning for public relations* (6th ed.). Mahwah, NJ: Lawrence Erlbaum Associates.

Wilcox, D., Ault, P. H., & Agee, W. K. (1989). *Public relations: Strategies and tactics* (2nd ed.). New York: Harper & Row.

Wilcox, D., Ault, P. H., Agee, W. K., & Cameron, G. T. (2001). *Essentials of public relations.* New York: Longman.

Wilson, L. (2000). *Strategic program planning for effective public relations campaigns* (3rd ed.). Dubuque, IA: Kendall/Hunt Publishing Company.

2

Basics of Public Relations Writing

In the classic motion picture *All About Eve*, considered one of the greatest films of all time by the American Film Institute, Academy-Award-winning screen actress Bette Davis delivers one of the most memorable lines in movie history: "Fasten your seat belts, it's going to be a bumpy night." Davis also has something to say about public relations in the film *Hush, Hush, Sweet Charlotte*. When responding to an on-screen character who works in the public relations field, Davis says: "Public relations? That sounds like something dirty."

Public relations writers have to master the fundamentals or they, too, will be in for a "bumpy" career. Another reality is that some media professionals and others in the business world still view public relations as a "dirty" business, although the public relations field has made progress improving its reputation. Even so, every piece of writing you create says something about your professionalism and gives you an opportunity to change negative perceptions of the field. The first news release you write and send as a public relations professional, and every piece of writing thereafter, will help define your competence. If that release contains inaccurate information, misspelled words, or typographical errors, your credibility will be damaged. Your writing, then, has to be correct—legally and ethically correct, as well as grammatically correct. You should choose language and content that are sensitive to the diverse audiences with whom you communicate. Certain rules of style must be followed.

This chapter focuses on some of the fundamentals important to the public relations writer. It is not possible to provide an exhaustive review of this subject in just a few pages; you might also take a look at the suggested reading list for more information. What follows are highlights— key principles relating to public relations writing, including the rules of grammar, style guidelines, cultural sensitivity, and legal and ethical considerations. The chapter concludes with a short section on the importance of rewriting and proofreading.

Grammar

Public relations writing must be grammatically correct and easy to read. Although it was produced quite a few years ago, "20 Secrets of Good Writing" (Exhibit 2.1) still provides a good blueprint for the basics of writing.

Exhibit 2.1

Twenty Secrets of Good Writing

Among the compendia of good writing principles one of the best and most useful is this list compiled by Ken Roman and Joel Raphaelson of the advertising agency Ogilvy & Mather Worldwide. "20 Secrets of Good Writing" sets forth sound, easy-to-follow suggestions for improving one's writing.

When you are speaking for Ogilvy & Mather, your writing must meet our standards. These allow ample room for individuality and freshness of expression. But "personal style" is not an excuse for sloppy, unprofessional writing.

Here are some suggestions on how to improve your writing—20 principles that all good writers follow.

1. Keep in mind that the reader doesn't have much time.
What you write must be clear on first reading. If you want your paper to be read by senior people, remember that they have punishing schedules, evening engagements, and bulging briefcases.

The shorter your paper, the better the chance it will be read at high levels. During World War II, no document of more than one page was allowed to reach Churchill's desk.

2. Know where you are going—and tell the reader.
Start with an outline to organize your argument.
Begin important paragraphs with topic sentences that tell what follows. Conclude with a summary paragraph.

An outline not only helps the reader; it keeps you from getting lost en route. Compile a list of all your points before you start.

3. Make what you write easy to read.
For extra emphasis, underline entire sentences. Number your points, as we do in this section.

Put main points into
indented paragraphs
like this.

4. Short sentences and short paragraphs are easier to read than long ones. Send telegrams, not essays.

5. Make your writing vigorous and direct.
Wherever possible use active verbs, and avoid the passive voice.

Passive	Active
We are concerned that	We believe you must
if this recommendation	act on this recommendation
is turned down, the brand's	to hold the brand's share.
market share may be	
negatively affected.	

6. Avoid clichés.
Find your own words.

Cliché	Direct
Turn over every rock for a solution	Try hard
Put it to the acid test	Test thoroughly
Few and far between	Few
Last but not least	Last
Iron out	Remove

7. Avoid vague modifiers such as "very" and "slightly." Search for the word or phrase that *precisely* states your meaning.

Vague	Precise
Very overspent	Overspent by $1,000
Slightly behind schedule	One day late

continued . . .

Exhibit 2.1

Twenty Secrets of Good Writing . . . *continued*

8. Use specific concrete language.

Avoid technical jargon, what E. B. White calls "the language of mutilation."

There is always a simple, down-to-earth word that says the same thing as the show-off fad word or the abstraction.

Jargon	Plain English
Parameters	Limits, boundaries
Implement	Carry out
Viable	Practical, workable
Interface	To talk with
Optimum	Best
Meaningful	Real, actual
To impact	To affect
Resultful	Effective, to have results
Finalize	Complete
Judgmentally	I think
Input	Facts, information
Output	Results
It is believed that with the parameters that have been imposed by your management, a viable solution may be hard to find. If we are to impact the consumer to the optimum, further interface with your management may be the most meaningful step to take.	We believe that the limits your management gave us may rule out a practical solution. If we want our consumer program to succeed, maybe we ought to talk with your management again.

9. Find the right word. Know its precise meaning. Use your dictionary, and your thesaurus. Don't confuse words like these:

To "affect" something is to have an influence on it. (The new campaign affects few attitudes.)

"Effect" can mean to bring about (verb) or a result (noun). (It effected no change in attitudes, and had no effect.)

"It's" is the contraction of "it is." (It's the advertising of P&G.)

"Its" is the possessive form of "it" and does *not* take an apostrophe. (Check P&G and its advertising.)

"Principal" is the first in rank or performance. (The principal competition is P&G.)

"Principle" is a fundamental truth or rule. (The principle behind competing with P&G is to have a good product.)

"Imply" means to suggest indirectly. (The writer implies it won't work.)

"Infer" means to draw meaning out of something. (The reader infers it won't work.)

"i.e." means "that is."

"e.g." means "for example."

When you confuse words like these, your reader is justified in concluding that you don't know better. Illiteracy does not breed respect.

10. Don't make spelling mistakes.

When in doubt, check the dictionary. If you are congenitally a bad speller, make sure your final draft gets checked by someone who isn't thus crippled.

If your writing is careless, the reader may reasonably doubt the thoroughness of your thinking.

11. Don't overwrite or overstate.

Use no more words than necessary. Take the time to boil down your points.

continued . . .

Exhibit 2.1

Twenty Secrets of Good Writing ... *continued*

Remember the story of the man who apologized for writing such a long letter, explaining that he just didn't have the time to write a short one.

The Gettysburg Address used only 266 words.

12. Come to the point.

Churchill could have said, "The position in regard to France is very serious." What he did say was, "The news from France is bad."

Don't beat around the bush. Say what you think—in simple, declarative sentences. Write confidently.

13. State things as simply as you can.

Use familiar words and uncomplicated sentences.

14. Handle numbers consistently.

Newspapers generally spell out numbers for ten and under, and use numerals for 11 and up.

Don't write M when you mean a thousand, or MM when you mean a million. The reader may not know this code. Write $5,000—not $5M. Write $7,000,000 (or $7 million)—not $7MM.

15. Avoid needless words.

The songwriter wrote, "Softly as in a morning sunrise"—and Ring Lardner explained that this was as opposed to a late afternoon or evening sunrise. Poetic license may be granted for a song, but not for phrases like these:

Don't write	Write
Advance plan	Plan
Take action	Act
Have a discussion	Discuss
Hold a meeting	Meet
Study in depth	Study
New innovations	Innovations
Consensus of opinion	Consensus
At the present time	Now
Until such time as	Until
In the majority of instances	Most
On a local basis	Locally
Basically unaware of	Did not know
In the area of	Approximately
At management level	By management
With regard to	About, concerning
In connection with	Of, in, on
In view of	Because
In the event of	If
For the purpose of	For
On the basis of	By, from
Despite the fact that	Although
In the majority of instances	Usually

Always go through your first draft once with the sole purpose of deleting all unnecessary words, phrases, and sentences. David Ogilvy has improved many pieces of writing by deleting entire paragraphs, and sometimes even whole pages.

16. Be concise, but readable.

Terseness is a virtue, if not carried to extremes. Don't leave out words. Write full sentences, and make them count.

continued ...

Exhibit 2.1

Twenty Secrets of Good Writing ... *continued*

17. Be brief, simple and natural.

Don't write, "The reasons are fourfold." Write, "There are four reasons."

Don't start sentences with "importantly." Write, "The important point is ..."

Don't write "hopefully" when you mean "I hope that." "Hopefully" means "in a hopeful manner." Its common misuse annoys a great many literate people.

Never use the word "basically." It can always be deleted. It is a basically useless word.

Avoid the hostile term "against," as in "This campaign goes against teenagers." You are not against teenagers. On the contrary, you want them to buy your product. Write, "This campaign addresses teenagers," or "This campaign is aimed at teenagers."

18. Don't write like a lawyer or a bureaucrat.

"Re" is legalese meaning "in the matter of," and is never necessary.

The slash—as in and/or—is bureaucratese. Don't write, "We'll hold the meeting on Monday and/or Tuesday." Write, "We'll hold the meeting on Monday or Tuesday—or both days, if necessary."

19. Never be content with your first draft.

Rewrite, with an eye toward simplifying and clarifying. Rearrange. Revise. Above all, cut.

Mark Twain said that writers should strike out every third word on principle: "You have no idea what vigor it adds to your style."

For every major document, let time elapse between your first and second drafts—at least overnight. Then come at it with a questioning eye and a ruthless attitude.

The five examples that follow were taken from a single presentation. They show how editing shortened, sharpened, and clarified what the writer was trying to say.

First Draft	Second Draft
Consumer perception of the brand changed very positively.	Consumer perception of the brand improved.
Generate promotion interest through high levels of advertising spending.	Use heavy advertising to stimulate interest in promotions.
Move from product advertising to an educational campaign, one that would instruct viewers on such things as ...	Move from product advertising to an educational campaign on such subjects as ...
Using the resources of Ogilvy & Mather in Europe, in addition to our Chicago office, we have been able to provide the company with media alternatives they had previously been unaware of.	Ogilvy & Mather offices in Europe and Chicago showed the company media alternatives it hadn't known about.
Based on their small budget, we have developed a media plan which is based on efficiency in reaching the target audience.	We developed a media plan that increases the efficiency of the small budget by focusing on prospects.

20. Have somebody else look over your draft.

All O&M advertising copy is reviewed many times, even though it is written by professional writers. Before David Ogilvy makes a speech, he submits a draft to his partners for editing and comment.

What you write represents the agency as much as an advertisement by a creative director or a speech by a chairman. They solicit advice. Why not you?

Note: Reprinted from Ogilvy and Mather Worldwide

Public relations educators would attest that they have seen students year after year make many of the same mistakes in spelling, punctuation, and sentence structure. The following is an additional checklist highlighting some of the more common mistakes to help improve your writing:

Spelling

- We learned it in grade school and it still applies most of the time: "i" before "e" (retrieve) except after "c" (receive). When adding a prefix that creates a double consonant (e.g., unnatural, misspell), do not drop a letter.
- If you add a prefix to a word that creates a double vowel, then you generally include a hyphen between the two vowels (e.g., re-establish).
- When you add a suffix to words ending in "e," you usually drop the "e" (e.g., true/truly). There are some exceptions (e.g., knowledgeable).

Punctuation

- Use a comma to separate a dependent clause (not as important as the main idea) from a main clause (the main idea); also include a comma before a conjunction (and, but, or) that separates two main clauses:
    - After she graduated from *college, Sue* accepted a job with a public relations firm.
    - Sue graduated from college in *May, and* she accepted a job with a public relations firm.
- Commas are used to separate descriptive phrases and supplemental or "add-on" thoughts that could be deleted without changing the meaning of the sentence:
    - Sue, who served as senior class president, graduated from college in May.
- Semicolons are used to connect two complete thoughts that form a single compound sentence, but without the use of "and" or some other conjunction:
    - Sue graduated with a public relations degree in May; she plans to move to New York City and work for a public relations firm.
- If words such as "however" or "therefore" are used to connect thoughts, use a semicolon before the word and a comma after:
    - Sue graduated with a public relations degree in May; however, she will leave the area and begin her career in New York City.
- For a single full-sentence quote, use a comma and place the attribution before or after the quote:
    - Sue said, "I'm excited about starting my job at the public relations firm."
    - "I'm excited about starting my job at the public relations firm," said Sue.

- If the quote is more than one sentence, place the attribution before the quote and use a colon, or place the attribution in between sentences:

  - Sue said: "I'm excited about starting my job at the public relations firm. The people there were impressed with my writing and editing skills so I'm glad I paid attention and worked hard in the public relations writing class."
  - "The people at the public relations firm were impressed with my writing and editing skills," said Sue. "I'm glad I paid attention and worked hard in the public relations writing class."

- Always place the attribution in front of a partial quote:

  - Sue said she was glad she "paid attention and worked hard in the public relations writing class."

- Use a hyphen to connect two words that describe something or someone; do not hyphenate if the first descriptive word ends in "y" (e.g., well-respected professional, highly respected writer). Know that certain words (e.g., firsthand, groundbreaking, marketplace) are not hyphenated.

Sentence Structure

- Subjects and verbs must agree; identify the subject as singular or plural, and make sure the corresponding verb matches:

  - *None* (singular subject) of the media *is* coming (singular verb) to the event.
  - The *media* (plural subject) *are* not coming (plural verb) to the event.

- Nouns and pronouns must correspond; singular subjects/nouns require singular matching pronouns:

  - The *company* (singular) changed *its* policy after employees expressed concerns.
  - The *board* (singular) of directors made *its* decision at the annual meeting.
  - The board *members* (plural) voiced *their* opinions about the issue.

- Related thoughts or phrases included in a single sentence should have like form— ask yourself if you are using the same verb tenses:

  - Incorrect: Sue *enjoys attending* the PRSA conference and *likes to meet* other professionals.
  - Correct: Sue *enjoys attending* the PRSA conference and *likes meeting* other professionals.

- Use active rather than passive voice in your writing to make ideas direct and crisp; try keeping the "to be" tense to a minimum to make your writing more active:

  - Passive: *It was suggested by the client* that the firm do some research.
  - Active: *The client asked* the firm to do some research.
  - Passive: *The issue is being discussed* by staff members at the meeting.
  - Active: *Staff members are discussing* the issue at the meeting.

Word Usage

- Use "that" and "which" carefully. "That" is used to identify a specific, individual item and is not preceded by a comma; "which" introduces an extra fact about the item and is preceded by a comma. Use "who" when referring to a person, not "that" or "which." (Note: Using "that" makes writing smoother and more active; you can often avoid using "which.")

  - The Web site *that* Sue created is interactive and easy to read.
  - The Web site, *which* was created by Sue, is interactive and easy to read.
  - People *who* visit the Web site say it is interactive and easy to read.

- Make sure you are using the proper word form:

  - They're hoping to raise $10,000 at the event. ("They're" is short for "they are.")
  - Their goal is to raise $10,000 at the event. ("Their" shows possession; the goal belongs to them.)

Simplicity

In addition to using correct grammar, the public relations writer must write simply. To maintain simplicity in your writing:

- Keep sentences short. Experts recommend sentences that average 17 words or so, give or take a few words. That doesn't mean you should count the words in each sentence to see if you exceed the 17-word limit. If a sentence seems too long and thoughts get hard to follow, write two sentences instead of one. When writing more lengthy articles, you will want to use some longer sentences to avoid choppiness and monotony for the reader. Short introductory sentences will ease readers into the piece and encourage them to read further.

- Use words that the average person would know. You are not writing to impress people with your mastery of vocabulary. Always choose the more familiar word with the fewest letters and syllables. There are times when you will write for people who work in the medical field, the financial community, or some other specialized area. In those instances, it is acceptable to use a few technical words common to that industry. Most people in the insurance field know what a "deductible" is, for example. Overall, however, keep the complex words and jargon to a minimum.

- Avoid redundancy. Delete extra words that have the same meaning, or that present the same idea in a different way. For example, don't write "bad crisis" (have you ever heard of a good crisis?) or "positive asset" (assets are benefits so how can they be negative?). When describing something, don't overstate. Consider this sentence: "Smith is well educated and has a doctorate in political science and a master's in history." Smith's degrees indicate that he is well educated so that phrase should be removed from the sentence.

- Don't write more than you need to. Writing concisely takes more skill than being longwinded. Be brief. This is especially true for online communications. If you are sending an e-mail message, try to keep the message as brief as you can and get to the point right away, in the first sentence or two. Articles for an electronic newsletter should be a few sentences to a few short paragraphs for optimum readability. In public relations writing, "less is more."

In addition, every writer should own a copy of *The Elements of Style* by William Strunk and keep it close to the computer. Strunk says it is good writing style to avoid "qualifier" words such as "very" and "rather," and to use the simpler versus the "fancy" word: "Do not be tempted by a twenty-dollar word when there is a ten-center handy, ready and able."

Style

Effective writing also has style. How is style defined? In the fashion industry, some believe that fashion designers and celebrities dictate style trends. Others see style as more personal—clothes that make the individual feel and look good and that help the person establish a unique identity, regardless of what the "cool people" are wearing. For public relations writers, writing style is influenced by several factors, including generally accepted rules for good writing, the writing policies of an organization and its public relations department, and the type of public relations piece you are writing. You also develop your own personal style, one that comes across in the words you choose and the way you present them.

Style is also defined by the media and your employer. When writing for the media, public relations practitioners should follow *The Associated Press (AP) Stylebook and Briefing on Media Law*, which is also used by journalists. However, you may choose to use separate style guidelines for organizational publications such as newsletters and other promotional materials. For example, *The AP Stylebook* states that job titles should not be capitalized when used after a person's name, so you wouldn't write a news release and capitalize job titles throughout. For internal publications, however, your organization may adopt its own style, one in which it is preferred to capitalize job titles whenever they are used. The key is consistency—make sure each piece you write for the media follows AP style, and each article for an internal publication follows your organization's style. Examples of the some of the most frequently used guidelines from *The AP Stylebook* appear in Exhibit 2.2.

Exhibit 2.2

Tips from *The Associated Press Stylebook*

Numbers and Money

- Numbers less than 10 are spelled out.
- Use numerals for 10 and greater.
- Spell out ordinal numbers less than 10, unless the number is part of a formal name (e.g., 1st Ward vs. first base).
- Numbers used at the beginning of a sentence should be spelled out, even if that number is 10 or above. Exception: calendar years (e.g., 2008 was a good year). References to numbers as part of a casual expression should be spelled out (e.g., Thanks a million).
- When writing about money, always use a dollar sign and numerals, even if the monetary value is less than 10 (e.g., She gave me $1).
- Monetary values less than $1 should be expressed in numerals and the word "cents" (e.g., It cost 50 cents).
- Use numerals, even if the monetary value is less than 10, and spell out the word "percent" (e.g., a pay increase of 3 percent).

continued . . .

Exhibit 2.2

Tips from *The Associated Press Stylebook* . . . *continued*

Ages and Dimensions

- Use numerals and spell out "inches," "feet," etc. (e.g., He is 5 feet 6 inches tall). Use hyphens if the dimension is being used as an adjective (e.g., The 5-foot-6-inch man).
- Ages also are expressed in numerals, even if the age is less than 10 (e.g., She is 8 years old). Use hyphens if the age is being used as an adjective (e.g. The 8-year-old girl).

Directions and Addresses

- In general, lowercase north, south, east, west, etc. Capitalize compass directions when referring to a region only. (e.g., A storm system developed in the Midwest.)
- St., Ave., Blvd. vs. Road, Drive, Circle: When referring to addresses, abbreviate "street," "avenue," and "boulevard." All other names should be written out.
- 50 North St. *vs.* North Street. The above rule applies only when numbers are used as part of the address. If no numbers are used, do not use the abbreviations for "street," "avenue," and "boulevard."

States, Cities and Abbreviations

- Martinsburg, W.Va. *vs.* Denver: Most cities should appear with their state; however, larger cities may stand alone. These exempted cities are listed under "Datelines" in the stylebook.
- NY vs. N.Y. *vs.* New York: State abbreviations according to AP style are not the same as postal codes. One difference is that AP style abbreviations always include periods. State abbreviations should always be used when accompanying a city; state names should be spelled out if standing alone.
- Alaska, Hawaii, Idaho, Iowa, Maine, Ohio, Texas, Utah: There are seven states that are never abbreviated regardless of the circumstance—the states with five or less letters and the last two admitted to the United States.
- U.S. Department of Treasury *vs.* the United States: Abbreviate "United States" when it is being used as an adjective; spell it out if it is being used as a proper noun.
- NASA *vs.* C.R.A.P.: Periods are not necessary when abbreviating organizational names, unless the letters spell out a word that would misrepresent the organization.

Titles

- Formal *vs.* functional: Formal titles, which indicate an authoritative position, are capitalized when used before a person's name (Attorney General Professor Jane Smith). They are not capitalized if used after the person's name. A functional title, which indicates a person's occupation, is not capitalized. (e.g., The attorney general presented her research).
- President George Bush *vs.* president of the United States: Follow the rule for formal titles. "President" is capitalized when used with a name, but not capitalized when the title stands alone.
- Dr. *vs.* Ph.D.: Use "Dr." as a formal title when used before a name of someone who holds a medical degree. "Dr." also may be used as a formal title before a name of someone who holds a doctorate in a nonmedical field; however, the person's academic specialization should be referenced to avoid confusion.
- Movies, TV programs, and books *vs.* reference materials: The titles of creative works should be enclosed in quotation marks; reference books, such as encyclopedias, almanacs and dictionaries, should not.

Dates and Times

- Months are abbreviated when they accompany a day (e.g., Jan. 31, 2009); spell them out when they are standing alone. Do not use a comma between the month and the year (e.g., January 2009).

continued . . .

Exhibit 2.2

Tips from *The Associated Press Stylebook* . . . *continued*

- The preferred style for expressing the time of day is to use a numeral with "a.m." and "p.m." (e.g., 11 a.m.); "noon" and "midnight" are spelt out. *Caution*: If using this format, be careful not to be redundant by using "this morning" or "this evening." If you want to use these phrases, indicate the time of day followed by "o'clock," although a.m. or p.m. is preferred. Never express the top of the hour with ":00."

Capitalization

- Academic and organizational departments should not be capitalized (e.g., the department of history) unless there is a proper noun or adjective within the title (e.g., the English department). Departments should be capitalized as part of a formal name (e.g., the U.S. Department of Energy).

Another factor that defines style is the type of piece written. A news release announcing a company merger should be written in *news* or *inverted pyramid* style. This means that the release begins with the most important information in the first few paragraphs and concludes with background material that isn't as crucial to the story (more on this in chapter 6). An article for a hospital publication that focuses on the special contributions of a volunteer is written in *feature style*, with quotes and interesting details that create a vivid picture of the volunteer's personality and humanity.

How the reader is addressed differs between news and feature-style writing. For the most part, materials sent to the media are written in third person and avoid personal terms; however, when writing for a specific public, such as readers of employee newsletters or customer brochures, it is good style to keep messages personal and "you-focused." Let your writing talk directly to the reader. For example, "this product will help you and your family live longer, healthier lives." The use of "I" and "you" also is common in memos and e-mail communication to keep messages direct and personal.

There is a broader sense of style that applies to writing, as well. It relates to the language and techniques a writer uses—those qualities that identify a piece of writing with the person who wrote it. Think about your favorite musical artists or groups. There's probably something that characterizes them—the special sound of the electric guitars, the beat of the drums, the pitch of the singer's voice and how that singer holds a note, how a group's songs often begin and end a certain way, or common themes that run through an artist's music. Look at the work of newspaper columnists, and you'll see how each has a characteristic style.

Your public relations writing style may not be quite as obvious as the vocal style of your favorite singer, or as evident as your favorite painter's style of using shape and colors. Your style will come through in the way your feature articles set a scene, describe people, and use quotes; in the headlines and subheads you write for brochures and promotional pieces; and in the leads you develop for news releases. It's not something you will try hard to create; it will come about naturally and feel comfortable to you. People who read your writing will say, "I could almost hear you saying those words." Your writing style will be an expression of who you are, as a writer and a person.

Diversity, Bias, and Cultural Sensitivity

According to the U.S. Census Bureau's 2008 population projections, minorities, collectively, will become the majority in 2042. The survey also projects that, by 2030, nearly one in five U.S. residents will be at least 65 years old and that, by 2050, the U.S. population will be made up of: Hispanics (30%); Blacks (15%); Whites (46%); and, Asians (9%).

Today's public relations practitioner is faced with a diverse population that is not just characterized by racial and ethnic backgrounds. Organizations must also design internal and external communications for audiences and people with varied lifestyles—male and female, single parents and married persons, gay and straight, part-time and full-time workers. Marketers are also recognizing the value of targeting diverse groups. Some companies develop specific marketing communications programs to target the lifestyle and interests of the gay and lesbian community. Others reach out to the Hispanic population, which, as evidenced in the U.S. Census projections, is one of the fastest-growing ethnic groups in the United States.

Public relations professionals must reflect this diversity in their writing, both in the language they use and the creative approaches they take. It is more gender-sensitive to use "chairperson" rather than "chairman." Women are not referred to as "girls," "gals," or "ladies." Instead of writing, "A public relations professional should know his audience," it is better to make the statement more inclusive:

A public relations professional should know his or her audience.

OR

Public relations professionals should know their audiences.

Writers can use "his" or "him"—they do not have to delete these pronouns from their vocabulary entirely. If the subject is male, then using words such as "chairman" or "spokesman" is fine. When a subject could be a man or a woman (e.g., public relations professional), using the plural form of the subject makes good sense. When using singular pronouns, make sure you write "her" in some instances and "his" in others to achieve balance.

Some additional sensitive language: refer to senior citizens as "seniors" or "elderly," not as "old folks." "Gay" is the preferred term for a homosexual male, and "lesbian" is preferred for a homosexual woman; homosexual can be used for both. Persons with disabilities and serious illnesses should not be described as "victims," "crippled," or "suffering from a disease," to avoid characterizing them as helpless. Feature writers should take care when describing skin color and other physical attributes that might stereotype or offend racial and ethnic groups such as Native Americans, African Americans, and Italian Americans, among others. As a guideline, always ask yourself whether the information is necessary for the piece you are writing.

On a broader level, public relations writers must understand the culture of diverse groups. For example, AIDS public information campaigns directed to teens and minority groups have to take into account distinct aspects of those cultures, including long-held perceptions of the immoral nature of homosexuality and beliefs that AIDS is a "White gay man's disease."

Knowing your target audience also affects your method of delivery. A 2008 tracking survey conducted by the Pew Internet & American Life Project showed that 75% of Americans use the Internet—an important means of public relations communication. According to the survey,

English-speaking Hispanics lead the way in Internet usage, with 79%, compared with Whites (75%) and Blacks (70%). Eighty percent of suburban residents use the Internet, compared with those who live in urban areas (75%) and rural areas (64%). Internet usage increases with the level of household income and education. Though one study alone does not necessarily provide the whole picture, these statistics suggest which demographics would be more effective to target by Internet.

These examples demonstrate the significance of culture and lifestyle to effective writing and communication. Public relations writers cannot just assume which messages and media will produce the best results, especially when communicating with a population whose traditions and mindset may be unfamiliar. Research, including interviews, focus groups, and surveys, can help increase cultural awareness and strengthen the impact of written materials and their messages. Practitioners should also take advantage of professional development programs, such as those offered by PRSA (Public Relations Society of America), that focus on multiculturalism and diversity. PRSA has actively pursued a diversity initiative that, among other objectives, aims to expand programs featuring diverse speakers and topics.

Legal Issues

Perhaps the most unflattering comment a person could make about something you've written is, "It sounds like a lawyer wrote this." Now, this is not an attack on lawyers. The fact is, however, many legal documents are complex and hard to understand. While public relations professionals should avoid writing like lawyers, they do need to think like lawyers when preparing publicity and other written materials. For example, consider the following situations:

- A news release announces that a new drug is the most effective for reducing high cholesterol.
- A not-for-profit organization creates a series of public service announcements featuring the songs of pop music stars.
- A corporate public relations professional places the full text of a positive product review published in a trade journal on the company's Web site.
- A school system kicks off a campaign titled "Just Do It," aimed at increasing academic achievement.
- A story on a new company vice president is published in the employee newsletter accompanied by a photograph of the vice president and her family.

Now, which, if any, of these scenarios pose legal problems? If you guessed "none," you could be right. But if you guessed "all of them," you could be right, too.

Puffing

The product news release may be okay, if there are substantial scientific data and many reputable sources to support the "most effective" claim. If not, you may be in trouble with the Federal Trade Commission (FTC), a government agency that regulates fair trade practices and monitors advertising and corporate communications for false and misleading information.

Any communication that includes *"puffing"*—nonobjective and exaggerated claims that are hard to verify (e.g., "the one and only product of its kind")—is subject to investigation by the FTC. The FTC takes a special interest in prescription drugs and products that position themselves as safer than others, as well as messages directed to children and the elderly. You should also familiarize yourself with FTC guidelines for labeling something "environmentally friendly" and the evidence needed to support that claim. A not-so-obvious problem involves use of the word "new." The FTC says any product more than six months old cannot be described as new, unless the product is being test marketed. In that case, you can promote it as new up to six months after the product is introduced in its final form. In general, it's best to stay away from glittering generalities.

Corporate vs. Commercial Speech

It is important for public relations practitioners to understand the difference between corporate and commercial speech. Corporations "speak" through various public relations tactics, such as news releases, letters to the editor, and position statements. These tools allow the corporation to inform its publics about news going on within the organization, as well as to share formal opinions and positions. Commercial speech involves communication aimed at making a profit, such as advertising. While commercial speech is regulated by truth in advertising laws, corporate speech is not. That almost changed in 2002, however, when a lawsuit nearly labeled traditional public relations practices as commercial speech.

The case involved Nike, which was being accused of poor working conditions in its foreign plants and was using public relations techniques to respond to the allegations. Marc Kasky, a consumer activist from California, sued Nike, claiming the company's responses were not corporate speech, but instead were false advertising and, thus, subject to commercial speech regulations. The first court to hear Kasky v. Nike sided with Nike; however, that ruling was overturned by the California Supreme Court. The case eventually ended up before the U.S. Supreme Court, which reviewed it but did not issue a ruling, instead returning it to the lower court. PRSA, other professional associations, and the media were among approximately 150 organizations that filed "friend of the court" briefs urging the Supreme Court to rule that corporate speech is protected under the Constitution. Before the case could be reheard, it was settled out of court, leaving the issue unresolved.

Copyrights

The second and third situations listed at the beginning of this section bring up the issue of *copyright* infringement. Copyright protects the unauthorized duplication of original, published work. Most printed materials, as well as photographs, videos, music, and choreography, are covered by copyrights. Copyrights protect the "fixed form" in which this material appears, not the ideas and facts themselves. Original work that is written, designed, or performed is automatically protected by copyright; it does not have to be registered with the U.S. Copyright Office, although registration will help protect you if you try to prove infringement in court. Copyrights are identified by the copyright symbol, (c), along with the year the material was created and the owner of the copyright.

Ownership of the copyright varies. In most cases, the person who created the work owns the copyright. However, there are exceptions. Work you create while employed by a company is owned by the company; this is referred to as "works made for hire." If you work for a public relations firm or are a freelance practitioner, the work you create typically belongs to the client for whom it was created.

Generally, you have to get the copyright owner's permission, and sometimes pay a fee, to reproduce copyright-protected work. Popular songs and published media articles are among the items protected by copyright law. So, you can't produce that public service announcement, with even a few seconds of a song, until you've secured permission from the record company, the artist, or whoever the copyright holder is. An article published in a newspaper or magazine is owned by that publication and is therefore subject to copyright law, so if you want to publish a media article in its entirety on your Web site, you must contact the publisher for approval first. *Reprints*—copies of the article, made for you by the publication for a fee—can be obtained for mass distribution as well. Services such as Dow Jones Reprints (www.djreprints.com) allow you to order and distribute reprints by e-mail or display them on your Web site the same day an article is published. And if you're thinking about using an illustration of Bugs Bunny, Mickey Mouse, or some other cute cartoon character on promotional materials, don't do it until you've cleared it with the copyright owner.

With the vast amount of information available on the Internet, it may be tempting to download articles, pictures, and videos for your own use, or copy and paste them to your own Web site. Any original work published on the Internet is protected by copyright, as well. For example, comments made by someone in an online discussion group technically become the property of that person once they appear on the screen and are protected by copyright. So, if you reproduce an article from an electronic publication or download and distribute copy from someone's Web site without permission, you are probably violating copyright. Most Web sites include copyright information at the bottom of the page. The Digital Millennium Copyright Act of 1998, among other things, gives copyright holders the right to ask service providers to remove material that has been used illegally. Access the Electronic Frontier Foundation (www.eff.org) to learn more about online electronic rights and copyright.

A word about *fair use*, an aspect of copyright law important to public relations writers: the fair use rule permits you to use short passages from copyrighted works, without the author's permission—if the purpose of your writing is educational—to report news or to comment on an issue. For example, if a noted consumer group endorses your product in a national magazine article, you could use a brief quote from that magazine piece in an employee newsletter article, as long as you cite the source (the name of the magazine, the publication date, and the name of the author of the piece). You cannot, however, reprint several paragraphs or an entire page of the article without permission. Using that same product quote in a sales brochure sent to prospective customers without first getting permission will most likely violate copyright, since your company stands to gain financially from the sales piece. If the quote is two short sentences, and the entire article is 2,000 words, permission may not be necessary, but you still might want to talk to your company's attorney about it. It is probably wise to get permission to use any copyright material in marketing communications pieces that support sales and profit-making.

The length a copyright lasts is determined by the date it was created. For material created after January 1, 1978, copyrights last for the life of the author, plus 70 years. Copyrights for anonymous works and works made for hire last 95 years from the first date of publication or 120 years from the year they were created.

Trademarks

Similar to copyrights are *trademarks*—symbols or words that are identified with a particular product or company. They exist to protect the relationship between a product and its parent company. Like copyrights, trademarks automatically exist by virtue of being created and used. Trademarks may be identified with the symbol ™, or the symbol ®, if they are registered with the Patent and Trademark Office. Trademark law also includes the protection of brand names. When you write names such as Kleenex®, Xerox®, or Coke®, make sure you are not treating them generically. While trademarks protect products, *service marks* protect services offered by a company. Service marks are identified by the symbol ᔆᴹ.

Privacy

What about the photo of the new vice president and her family? Any time public communication includes personal information, you risk invading someone's *privacy*. In this instance, you should obtain the vice president's permission to publish the photo because it relates to her private life. If the photograph was just a "head and shoulders" shot of the vice president only, then getting approval to use it would not be necessary, although it might be the polite thing to do (let's face it, we all want to look our best, right?). Still, obtaining written consent is a wise move when dealing with pictures of people and their personal information. This is especially important for public relations practitioners working in health care. The Health Insurance Portability and Accountability Act (HIPAA) requires that strict guidelines be followed when obtaining authorization from patients to use their photos and personal information.

You also need to be aware of *appropriation*—using photos of employees, celebrities, or others, or their likenesses, in advertisements and other materials designed to promote profit. Never do this without first getting written permission. In addition, if you write a news release focusing on an individual, it's probably wise to have the person read over, initial, and approve the release before it is sent to the media. This way, you protect yourself against sending out inaccurate, sensitive, or inappropriate information. The same holds true for subjects of a highly sensitive nature. Releases of that type should first go through the proper senior management review channels before you distribute them.

Defamation

Not only is it unethical to communicate falsehoods, but doing so may also be illegal. Traditionally, *defamation* has been referred to as either *libel*, if written, or *slander*, if spoken, although the umbrella term of "defamation" is being used more and more. Public relations practitioners should be aware of the criteria for defamation. While there are many complexities to the law, simply put, defamation is communicating a false statement about someone that does that person harm. A person claiming defamation needs to have been identified by name or in some other way, and the person must have been harmed (for example, loss of reputation or business) as a result of the alleged defamatory statement. In addition, it must be proven that the statement: (1) included false information; (2) was communicated to a third party; and (3) was made either because of negligence or, in the case of public figures, malicious intent.

Ethical Issues

All professionals—lawyers, doctors, teachers, accountants—confront ethical dilemmas on the job. This is not exclusive to public relations work, although some still define the function based solely on perceptions that public relations people deceive and "cover up." Consider this definition of public relations: "an effort to gull, diddle, and otherwise bamboozle people into thinking that something is different from what they believe it to be. The public relations man tilts reality to suit his taste."

As you can probably tell, this quote from *Playboy* magazine is a bit dated. The use of "public relations man" instead of a nongender-specific phrase is a sure tip-off. The fact is, good public relations professionals don't "diddle." They gain credibility by advising companies to always tell the truth and by being honest communicators themselves, even in times of crisis. A public relations professional puts the best interests of an organization and its publics first. Those who pursue a public relations career because they want to go to fancy parties, maybe meet celebrities, and be on TV should consider another occupation. Besides, most practitioners will tell you, it's not that glamorous; public relations is hard work.

The Member Code of Ethics of the PRSA provides some guidance for communicating with integrity (Exhibit 2.3). Much of the battle, however, often takes place before anything is written or officially communicated. Do further research to substantiate that something is "unique," rather than simply sending out that message because "the boss told you so." Convince others that communicating bad news quickly is better than saying "no comment." Public relations professionals are advocates for organizations, but they should also be advocates for "doing the right thing."

Exhibit 2.3
PRSA Member Code of Ethics

PRSA Member Statement of Professional Values

This statement presents the core values of PRSA members and, more broadly, of the public relations profession. These values provide the foundation for the Member Code of Ethics and set the industry standard for the professional practice of public relations. These values are the fundamental beliefs that guide our behaviors and decision-making process. We believe our professional values are vital to the integrity of the profession as a whole.

ADVOCACY
- We serve the public interest by acting as responsible advocates for those we represent.
- We provide a voice in the marketplace of ideas, facts, and viewpoints to aid informed public debate.

HONESTY
- We adhere to the highest standards of accuracy and truth in advancing the interests of those we represent and in communicating with the public.

continued . . .

Exhibit 2.3

PRSA Member Code of Ethics . . . *continued*

EXPERTISE

- We acquire and responsibly use specialized knowledge and experience.
- We advance the profession through continued professional development, research, and education.
- We build mutual understanding, creditibility, and relationships among a wide array of institutions and audiences.

INDEPENDENCE

- We provide objective counsel to those we represent.
- We are accountable for our actions.

LOYALTY

- We are faithful to those we represent, while honoring our obligation to serve the public interest.

FAIRNESS

- We deal fairly with clients, employees, competitors, peers, vendors, the media, and the general public.
- We respect all opinions and support the right of free expression.

PRSA Code Provisions

FREE FLOW OF INFORMATION

Core Principle

Protecting and advancing the free flow of accurate and truthful information is essential to serving the public interest and contributing to informed decision making in a democratic society.

Intent

- To maintain the integrity of relationships with the media, government officials, and the public.
- To aid informed decision making.

Guidelines

A member shall:

- Preserve the integrity of the process of communication.
- Be honest and accurate in all communications.
- Act promptly to correct erroneous communications for which the practitioner is responsible.
- Preserve the free flow of unprejudiced information when giving or receiving gifts by ensuring that gifts are nominal, legal, and infrequent.

Examples of Improper Conduct Under this Provision

- A member representing a ski manufacturer gives a pair of expensive racing skis to a sports magazine columnist to influence the columnist to write favorable articles about the product.
- A member entertains a government official beyond legal limits or in violation of government reporting requirements.

COMPETITION

Core Principle

Promoting healthy and fair competition among professionals preserves an ethical climate while fostering a robust business environment.

continued . . .

Exhibit 2.3

PRSA Member Code of Ethics . . . *continued*

Intent
- To promote respect and fair competition among public relations professionals.
- To serve the public interest by providing the widest choice of practitioner options.

Guidelines
A member shall:

- Follow ethical hiring practices designed to respect free and open competition without deliberately undermining a competitor.
- Preserve intellectual property rights in the marketplace.

Examples of Improper Conduct Under this Provision

- A member employed by a "client organization" shares helpful information with a counseling firm that is competing with others for the organization's business.
- A member spreads malicious and unfounded rumors about a competitor in order to alienate the competitor's clients and employees in a ploy to recruit people and business.

DISCLOSURE OF INFORMATION

Core Principle
Open communication fosters informed decision making in a democratic society.

Intent
- To build trust with the public by revealing all information needed for responsible decision making.

Guidelines
A member shall:

- Be honest and accurate in all communications.
- Act promptly to correct erroneous communications for which the member is responsible.
- Investigate the truthfulness and accuracy of information released on behalf of those represented.
- Reveal the sponsors for causes and interests represented.
- Disclose financial interest (such as stock ownership) in a client's organization.
- Avoid deceptive practices.

Examples of Improper Conduct Under this Provision

- Front groups: A member implements "grass roots" campaigns or letter-writing campaigns to legislators on behalf of undisclosed interest groups.
- Lying by omission: A practitioner for a corporation knowingly fails to release financial information, giving a misleading impression of the corporation's performance.
- A member discovers inaccurate information disseminated via a Web site or media kit and does not correct the information.
- A member deceives the public by employing people to pose as volunteers to speak at public hearings and participate in "grass roots" campaigns.

continued . . .

Exhibit 2.3

PRSA Member Code of Ethics . . . *continued*

SAFEGUARDING CONFIDENCES

Core Principle
Client trust requires appropriate protection of confidential and private information.

Intent
- To protect the privacy rights of clients, organizations, and individuals by safeguarding confidential information.

Guidelines
A member shall:

- Safeguard the confidences and privacy rights of present, former, and prospective clients and employees.
- Protect privileged, confidential, or insider information gained from a client or organization.
- Immediately advise an appropriate authority if a member discovers that confidential information is being divulged by an employee of a client company or organization.

Examples of Improper Conduct Under this Provision

- A member changes jobs, takes confidential information, and uses that information in the new position to the detriment of the former employer.
- A member intentionally leaks proprietary information to the detriment of some other party.

CONFLICTS OF INTEREST

Core Principle
Avoiding real, potential, or perceived conflicts of interest builds the trust of clients, employers, and the publics.

Intent
- To earn trust and mutual respect with clients or employers.
- To build trust with the public by avoiding or ending situations that put one's personal or professional interests in conflict with society's interests.

Guidelines
A member shall:

- Act in the best interests of the client or employer, even subordinating the member's personal interests.
- Avoid actions and circumstances that may appear to compromise good business judgment or create a conflict between personal and professional interests.
- Disclose promptly any existing or potential conflict or interest to affected clients or organizations.
- Encourage clients and customers to determine if a conflict exists after notifying all affected parties.

Examples of Improper Conduct Under this Provision

- The member fails to disclose that he or she has a strong financial interest in a client's chief competitor.
- The member represents a "competitor company" or a "conflicting interest" without informing a prospective client.

ENHANCING THE PROFESSION

Core Principle
Public relations professionals work constantly to strengthen the public's trust in the profession.

continued . . .

Exhibit 2.3

PRSA Member Code of Ethics . . . *continued*

Intent
- To build respect and credibility with the public for the profession of public relations.
- To improve, adapt, and expand professional practices.

Guidelines

A member shall:

- Acknowledge that there is an obligation to protect and enhance the profession.
- Keep informed and educated about practices in the profession to ensure ethical conduct.
- Actively pursue personal professional development.
- Decline representation of clients or organizations that urge or require actions contrary to this Code.
- Accurately define what public relations activities can accomplish.
- Counsel subordinates in proper ethical decision making.
- Require that subordinates adhere to the ethical requirements of the Code.
- Report ethical violations, whether committed by PRSA members or not, to the appropriate authority.

Examples of Improper Conduct Under this Provision

- A PRSA member declares publicly that a product the client sells is safe, without disclosing evidence to the contrary.
- A member initially assigns some questionable client work to a non-member practitioner to avoid the ethical obligation of PRSA membership.

Note: Reprinted with permission from the Public Relations Society of America (PRC Search/PRSA.org)

As a public relations writer, you will find yourself in some interesting situations, especially when dealing with the media. Take a look at the situations that follow:

- A news release on a company expansion includes a quote from the CEO that you created, since the CEO was not available for an interview.
- A story idea is presented as an "exclusive" to a trade publication and a business newspaper.
- Your company invites reporters to its corporate headquarters to preview a new product line, and agrees to cover the reporters' travel expenses.

See any ethical problems? You're probably thinking, "I would never make up a quote and put it in a news release. That's wrong." But counseling someone on how to best frame a message and then working with the person to write that message is acceptable in public relations practice. The president of the United States, for example, has communication staff members who help write the words we hear in presidential speeches. Following a plane crash, airline public relations staff will work closely with top management to write an initial state-ment for the CEO, conveying the right sympathetic tone while also sticking to the facts to avoid legal repercussions. You will find that senior executives sometimes have difficulty articulating their thoughts. They rely on the expertise of public relations staff to find just the right words to convey points succinctly and sensitively. The challenge for public relations writers is to prepare simple, hard-hitting quotes and statements that reflect the personality of the source, that sound like real words that person would actually say, and that reinforce import-ant public relations and organizational messages. Before any such quotes become public communication, make sure the source has the chance to review, revise, and approve what you've written.

The second example requires that you know what an exclusive is. The definition of *exclusive* is "select" or "unshared." When you promise an exclusive to a publication, that means no one else is getting that story at that time. You are giving that publication something special. From an ethical standpoint, you cannot tell one publication that it has exclusive rights to a story, and then offer that same exclusive to a second publication, in hopes that at least one of them will publish it. If, based on the example above, the trade journal rejects the idea, then you can suggest it to the business newspaper. Used occasionally, but never for hard breaking news, an exclusive can strengthen a relationship with an editor who sees you considering her individual editorial needs. But once that editor finds out she's been deceived (and she will find out), your credibility will be damaged, and you'll have a hard time placing publicity items in that publication in the future.

In the third situation, an organization has a major news announcement and wants the media to travel to some location to cover it. The sponsoring organization agrees to pay expenses, which can be attractive to smaller publications and freelancers who lack the funds to make the trip. But is it ethical to offer all-expense-paid trips and other "freebies" to the media? Does this amount to buying media coverage, and how does it affect media relations? Nowadays, of course, technology and the Internet make it possible for the media to have this kind of experience without leaving their desks. But when sponsoring this kind of media event, known as a *junket*, don't ever tell reporters that you expect a positive story in return for paying their way. You should rarely demand that the media cover your news, anyway; this could look like an attempt to buy coverage and would clearly be unethical. Don't offer travel monies without first knowing the policy of news operations. You can assume that most major newspapers and broadcast media have strict rules about paying their reporters' travel expenses. There's no need to force money on anyone, either. Simply let people know you can help them cover their travel and hotel expenses if necessary.

Bottom line—make sure the news that you are asking the media to cover is truly newsworthy and avoid even the perception that you are seeking positive coverage in return for "freebies." To do otherwise could result in the loss of respect and credibility for both the organization and the public relations practitioner.

Rewriting and Proofreading

Good writers rewrite and proofread, and they know the first draft is seldom a final draft. In agency work, when you write a news release, it often has to be reviewed by your internal supervisor and the account executive for quality before it goes to the client. The copy may then come back to you and require some revision. Then, it is sent to the client, who usually sends it back with additional revisions. Finally, depending on the subject, a corporate attorney may need to read it to weed out any legally sensitive wording and to provide counsel on potential legal risks. One piece of advice in regard to rewrites—always consider the approval process when setting up a time line for writing copy. Build in an extra week or two, when you can, to allow for approvals and rewrites. Establish an absolute deadline for final copy, and attempt to complete and get approval of the final draft several days before that deadline.

After the final rewrite comes the critical task of proofreading. You must become skilled at proofreading your own copy. There won't always be someone around to look over your work, so it's up to you to make sure your writing is clear and error-free. Imagine if a critical letter is dropped from the word "heroine," and the copy goes out to the media that way. Or, "tutoring" somehow becomes "torturing" in the literacy article you're writing. These are both true examples of errors that occurred on college application essays. Whoops! Here are some tips for better proofreading:

- Don't rely on spell check. It will not correct sound-alike words (your copy has the word "grate," but it should be "great"). If a word looks like it might be misspelled, or if you're not sure of the spelling, look it up in the dictionary. Get a copy of Webster's Speller or a similar reference book. You can also "Google" a word and check spelling through other resources on the Web.
- Leave your work for a while and come back to it later. After you've scanned a piece of writing again and again, it's easy to overlook obvious errors. Set it aside for a while. When you begin reviewing it again, you'll not only catch mistakes you missed earlier, but you also may find a better, smoother way to write that sentence.
- Have someone else who knows nothing about the subject read it. He or she may find errors that you didn't spot and pinpoint phrases or ideas that are hard to understand.
- Be on the lookout for typographical errors and spacing problems. Carefully review the communication for letters that are dropped out of words, reversed letters within words, reversed or transposed words, missing or misplaced periods and punctuation, extra space between the letters of a word, and extra or no space between two words in a sentence.

ASSIGNMENTS

Assignment 2.1—The Writing Test (Part A)

 You have applied for a position at a public relations firm. During the first interview, you are asked to take a writing test. The first phase tests your knowledge of spelling and word usage. Your interviewer hands you the test that follows, and says you have 10 minutes to complete it.

Part One of Writing Exam: Spelling and Word Usage

I.   In the space next to each word below, please provide the correct spelling of that word. If the word is correctly spelled, simply rewrite it as shown:

definately	liaison
ocassion	inovative
stratagy	concensus
tomorrow	tenative
comittee	knowledgable
superviser	pharmacutical

II.   Circle the correct word in parentheses in the sentences below:

(a)   Corporate executives are concerned about the (affect/effect) the product recall will have on future sales.

(b)   The vice president (complimented/complemented) her for doing excellent work on the publicity campaign.

(c)   Melissa accepted the position as the governor's press (aid/aide).

(d)   Cory said he was not (averse/adverse) to working in New York City.

(e)   He is one of the company's (principle/principal) stockholders.

(f)   The client said she would go no (further/farther) with the discussion until she had more information.

(g)   The editor said the magazine would not publish the news release because he was (disinterested/uninterested) in the subject.

(h)   She told the interviewer that she (all ready, already) knew something about the company.

(i)   The spokesperson (alluded/eluded) to a change in management.

(j)   Jim ordered more (stationary/stationery) from the printer.

(k)   The CEO sought the (advice/advise) of public relations (council/counsel) about handling the upcoming layoffs.

(l)   Public relations professionals must be skilled writers who can quickly (compose/comprise) copy at the computer as well as alert advisors who keep management (appraised/apprised) of changing public sentiment.

III.   Select a simpler, more familiar word for:

equitable
stringent
endeavor

proficient
segregate
deficiency
acknowledge
predominant
disseminate
immense
foster
surpass

IV. Revise the following sentences to eliminate bias or insensitive language:

(a) Humphrey Bogart, Cary Grant, and Ms. Hepburn are some of the greatest motion picture stars of all time.

(b) AIDS patients often have difficulty paying for medical care.

(c) Each employee will be asked for his opinion about the need for an on-site day care program.

(d) She was amazed at how easily he moved through the crowd, especially since he was confined to a wheelchair.

(e) In nominating the secretaries for the award, he said: "These girls do a great job for me. I don't know how I could do my job without them."

(f) The student needs extra help because he is a slow learner.

(g) He is one of the most successful businessmen in the city.

(h) His research focused on the work ethic of the Oriental community. ∎

Assignment 2.2—The Writing Test (Part B)

For the next phase of the writing test (see Assignment 2.1), you are asked to edit the following news release for distribution to the national business and financial media. You are instructed to correct grammatical and Associated Press style errors, simplify phrasing, and reduce wordiness to improve readability. You have 10 minutes to edit the release.

LEADING U.S. FINANCIAL FIRM NAMES NEW PRESIDENT

The Board of Directors of Connors-Walsh, Incorporated, one of the world's premiere financial planning companies, voted to elect a new president and chief operating officer today.

Frances A. Kennedy was chosen to replace Allan Edwards, who has announced his retirement and will leave his current post after having served as president for a total of twenty years. Kennedy will assume her many responsibilities as president in a few weeks, on March 1.

Kennedy brings a vast amount of business and financial planning knowledge to her new post due to the fact that she has worked in the field for a number of years. Prior to joining Connors-Walsh, she was the Executive Vice President of Equity, Inc., a major life insurance company, for eight years, and she also served as a Top Executive for many other notable firms including Nathan-Thomas Inc., an investment firm that has offices across the nation and throughout the U.S.

With a Bachelor's of Arts degree in history from Syracuse University and a Master's in Business Administration from Cornell U., Kennedy belongs to a great number of professional groups and organizations whose members work in the financial planning arena. These groups are the National Financial Planners Association, of which she is a former president and is still a member, the Boston Business Executives, The New England Insurance Association, a group she also served on the board for and the International Association of Investment Bankers.

Connors-Walsh is one of the top financial firms in the country, with more than thirty million dollars in assets, and they are a leading provider of life insurance and business pension plans in the United States. The firm's services encompas a wide range of areas including mutual fund management, real estate investment, and financial brokerage services.

Assignment 2.3—An Editing Exercise

 As a senior intern in your college's public relations office, you are responsible for coordinating the production of a program for the upcoming inauguration of the college's new president. You are now gathering all the copy for the program. The first page of the program—an historical overview of the college—is submitted for your review by another intern in the office. Below is the copy you received. Edit the copy for errors in spelling, punctuation, and grammar:

Upton Colleges (UC) origins can be traced back to the 1930s, when Collier University (CU) first offered extension courses in the Upton, NY area. Seeing a need for a college in the Upton area business and community leaders urged Collier University to open such a college. As a result, CU established Upton College of Collier University in 1945 as a private two year undergraduate institution.

Upton Colleges opening convocation was held on September 30, 1945 at the original downtown Upton campus. In spring 1946, the College added upper level courses to their two year academic structure.

In 1952 the Upton College Foundation was established as a separate entity to support the College, and four years later they began their first official fundraising drive to finance the development of a new campus. The College moved from their downtown location to the current campus on Ballantine Road in 1961.

Upton College and Collier University maintain an academic relationship, however, Upton became financially and legally independant from CU in 1994. At this time, UC established their own board of trustees and began using Upton College as their corporate name. UC also uses the name Upton College of Collier University which reflects their CU ties.

The newly-established UC board of trustees, insted of Collier Univerity then became responsible for selecting the president of the College. This happened for the first time in the 1996–97 academic year and this is Upton Colleges first presidential inauguration.

Regardless of there undergraduate major, students who graduate from Upton Colleges bachelors degree programs receive the Collier University bacalaureate degree, as they have since the Colleges first convocation in 1945. In January 1998, the College began it's first graduate program. Graduates of Upton Colleges master's degree programs receive the Upton College degree.

References and Suggested Reading

An older and more diverse nation by midcentury (2008). Retrieved December 9, 2008 from http://www.census.gov/Press-Release/www/releases/archives/population/012496.html.

Carden, A. (2002, August). A new era of patient confidentiality. In *Public Relations Tactics*. New York: Public Relations Society of America.

Demographics of Internet users (2008). Retrieved December 9, 2008 from http://www.pewinternet.org/trends/User_Demo_10%2020%2008.htm.

Frequently asked questions about copyright (n.d.). Retrieved December 9, 2008 from http://www.copyright.gov/help/faq/.

Goldstein, N. (Ed.). (2007). *The Associated Press stylebook and briefing on media law* (Rev. and up.). Cambridge, MA: Perseus Publishing.

Moore, R. L., Farrar, R. T., & Collins, E. L. (1997). *Advertising and public relations law*. Mahwah, NJ: Lawrence Erlbaum Associates.

Newsom, D., & Carrell, B. (2007). *Public relations writing form and style* (8th ed.). Belmont, CA: Wadsworth.

PRSA member code of ethics 2000 (2000). Retrieved December 9, 2008 from http://www.prsa.org/aboutUs/ethics/preamble_en.html.

Smith, E. L., & Bernhardt, S. A. (1997). *Writing at work: Professional writing skills for people on the job*. New York: McGraw Hill/Contemporary Books.

Smith, R. F. (1999). *Groping for ethics in journalism* (4th ed.). Ames, IA: Iowa State University Press.

Smith, R. D. (2007). *Becoming a public relations writer* (3rd ed.). Mahwah, NJ: Lawrence Erlbaum Associates.

Strunk, W. (2008). *The elements of style*. Boston: Allyn & Bacon.

3

The Public Relations Process

Before they step onto the playing field, football players and other athletes must carefully consider who and what they will be up against, and then come up with a plan of attack for reaching a predetermined goal—to win the game. Joe Paterno, the legendary head coach of the Penn State college football team, explains it by saying, "The will to win is important, but the will to prepare is vital" (Boone, 1999, p. 31).

Public relations professionals should heed coach Paterno's advice and prepare before they "take the field." Winning public relations programs, publicity efforts, and written materials always start with an effective game plan. This chapter introduces the four-step public relations process.

The Four Phases

Every public relations piece you write is usually part of a larger program. That product news release you prepare fits into a broader plan for creating consumer interest and advancing sales goals. Employee newsletters support an ongoing internal communications program aimed at keeping employees informed and building trust and morale. Good program development involves these key elements: *Research* (conducting a *situation analysis*); *Planning* (identifying the *target publics*, setting *goals* and *objectives*, determining *strategies* and *tactics*, and establishing a *budget* and *timetable*); *Execution* (implementing the plan); and *Evaluation* (measuring its success).

Research

The goal of this start-up phase is to try to gain a thorough understanding of a problem or some other situation your organization is facing. The introductory section of a written program plan that summarizes research results is called the *situation analysis*. The following is an edited version of a situation analysis included in a winning entry submitted to the 2008 PRSA Silver Anvil Awards competition:

St. Rose Dominican Hospitals has served southern Nevada for over 60 years. In that time, the three campuses that make up the organization have focused on creating an environment of service that centers on quality, compassionate care. The hospitals have achieved a great deal of success in that effort and have been continually recognized for having the highest levels of overall patient satisfaction in the community. St. Rose's Siena Campus emergency department continually sees extremely high patient volumes due to treating everything from trauma cases to the common cold. Patients with higher severity afflictions are seen first, which sometimes means long waits for those with minor ailments. In late 2006, key patient satisfaction scores in the emergency department averaged near 65 percent while the hospital as a whole averaged near 90 percent and some departments were near 100 percent. The challenge became increasing satisfaction in a very hectic and varied environment. Secondary research showed that one of the primary ways to increase patient satisfaction in an emergency department setting was to provide greater and more frequent information about wait times. It was clear that a patient satisfaction campaign would have to address not only volume issues, but also communication factors.

This summary gives you an idea of the kind of information a situation analysis produces: relevant background information on the organization and its mission; a statement of the public relations problem in relation to that mission; and research findings that clarify public perceptions and provide a greater understanding of the problem and its effects. The situation analysis also points out special planning challenges (e.g., increasing satisfaction in a hectic and varied environment). The situation analysis is critical to your planning success because it justifies the need for your program and lays the foundation for the ideas that follow. The research phase is detailed in chapter 4.

Planning

Target Publics

Target publics are chosen for a public relations program based on the issue of the campaign and the publics' interest in that issue. They are the groups of people that must be reached and influenced in order for the program to be successful. In the St. Rose example, the primary publics were "patients visiting the emergency room with a focus on women 25–50 years old." The campaign also identified secondary publics who could be influencers and support St. Rose's program messages: "healthcare workers including physicians, nurses, technicians, etc."

Goals and Objectives

Goals establish the program's direction and purpose. Goals may be *awareness-based*, focused on informing and educating; *acceptance-based*, aimed at changing the target public's interest level or attitude; or, *action-based*, which are concerned with changing opinion or behavior, or motivating people to do something. The St. Rose campaign had one primary goal: increasing patient satisfaction in the emergency room, which is an action-based goal.

The terms "goals" and "objective" are often used interchangeably. Both are awareness-, acceptance-, or action-based; however, objectives are much more specific than goals. Goals set the general course; objectives spell out the returns more exactly. Objectives commonly state specific expectations for change within a given time frame (e.g., increase donations by 10% this year); they become yardsticks by which the success of a program is measured. For example, one of the objectives for the St. Rose campaign was:

- "Increase overall patient satisfaction in the emergency room by a mean score of greater than 3% for the campaign period (therefore exceeding the identified national average)."

Strategies and Tactics

Goals and objectives state what you want to accomplish. Strategies and tactics outline how you will accomplish them. Strategies are the general approaches you devise to reach goals and objectives. Tactics are the tools used or a series of activities carried out to execute the strategy. Public relations program strategies often fall into three categories:

- *relationship-building strategies*, which involve cultivating support through one-on-one discussions and establishing partnerships with credible individuals and influencer groups who support, endorse, and promote your program;
- *communication strategies*, which involve providing information to publics through face-to-face tactics (i.e., meetings, seminars, presentations), mass media/publicity tactics (i.e., news and feature stories in magazines and newspapers, radio public service announcements, television and satellite interviews), and directed media tactics (i.e., brochures, e-mail, newsletters, videos, online forums, Web sites, blogs, and social networking vehicles), which are personalized to a specific audience;
- *event-oriented strategies*, which use organized activities to influence groups of people and create publicity.
    The St. Rose campaign focused on three strategic approaches:
- Reorganize the flow of patients through the emergency room.
- Use communication to create a feeling of respect and mutual understanding between patients and caregivers.
- Target patients with collateral materials that will encourage them to take a more active role in communicating their needs.

By now, your campaign is starting to take shape; the next step, and most detailed, is identifying the most appropriate tactics to use. Tactics are the means by which you will carry your message; they are an extension of your strategies. For example, if you have a communication strategy, your tactics may include brochures or news releases. Tactics used in the St. Rose campaign included a script for employees to follow, posters, and thank you cards

Budget

Before implementing program strategies and tactics, people will want to know their cost. Actually, it is helpful to know budget limitations at the start of the planning process. That way, you can decide on research, strategic direction, and tactics that are realistic based on available monies. Can you do original surveys and focus groups, or will you have to rely on less costly, informal research methods? Will it be possible to sponsor an elaborate event, or is a simpler and more cost-effective activity all you can afford? Don't miss the point here, though. Always plan programs to include activities that will best target your publics and get results. Remember that a simple and inexpensive idea can be just as effective as a big one costing "megabucks." The budget for the St. Rose campaign was $5,000.

Budget procedures vary depending on the type of organization for which you work. Corporations, businesses, and many organizations allocate annual operating budgets to public relations departments. These cover staff salaries and costs incurred for publications, and special events and other public relations projects coordinated by the department during the year. Not-for-profit groups often supplement their public relations program budgets with monies from corporate sponsors and foundation grants. Public relations firms establish budgets, to a large degree, based on time. They may charge fees based on individual projects or charge monthly fees or *retainers* to cover the number of hours agency staff spends counseling, writing, planning, and coordinating projects. In addition to retainers, they bill clients for "out-of-pocket" expenses such as printing costs and travel.

Timetable

Besides establishing a budget that specifies all program costs, you must also create a time-table to guide you in executing the program. This document includes a listing of weekly tasks to be completed, deadlines for each task, and the individual(s) responsible for completing each task.

It identifies dates when significant events will occur, such as major meetings and campaign launch events; it indicates when any written materials should be drafted, approved, printed, distributed, and followed up; and it designates when other critical planning and promotional activities should occur. Organize separate timetables for major events since they involve numerous and detailed planning steps, such as securing a site, confirming speakers, and making media contacts. More information on the planning phase can be found in chapter 5.

Execution

The execution phase is the most visible of the four phases in a public relations plan. That's why it's tempting to jump ahead and start here. But, as you have hopefully seen by now, there is a lot of "behind-the-scenes" work that needs to take place first to ensure the success of the overall plan. Chapters 6–13 explain in-depth how to create and implement the most popular tactics.

Evaluation

Your public relations program is not over once your tactics have been implemented in the execution phase; you will need to demonstrate its success. You must think about how you will measure success during the initial stages of campaign planning, not as an afterthought once the campaign has ended. Setting goals and objectives is closely linked with evaluation, since the most basic measure of program success is to ask yourself, "Did we reach our goals?"

Evaluation cannot be underestimated in the public relations process. Public relations professionals must provide hard evidence of their accomplishments, and how the work they did helped further the organization's business plan. Success has to be measured based on legitimate criteria, not personal feelings ("We think this was a good program.") or superficial judgments ("That story about us in the newspaper looked great, didn't it?"). The CEO expects marketing, sales, finance, and other key departments to show tangible results, and public relations must do the same to earn respect and justify the value of the function to the organization.

The public relations practitioners behind the St. Rose campaign were able to prove the success of the program because they conducted a survey, which revealed, with hard data, that patient satisfaction scores in many key measures increased by as much as 12 points.

Chapter 14 discusses the various ways you can measure your campaign.

Exhibit 3.1 shows how all these parts come together as a public relations plan.

Exhibit 3.1

2008 PRSA Silver Anvil Award Winner, Reputation/Brand Management: Siena Campus Emergency Department

2008 PRSA Silver Anvil Award Winner: Reputation/Brand Management

Siena Campus Emergency Department: The Patient Satisfaction Turnaround

St. Rose Dominican Hospitals with Team AMC

SUMMARY

St. Rose Dominican Hospitals—Siena Campus emergency department continually sees extremely high patient volumes due to treating everything from trauma cases to the common cold. Patients with higher severity afflictions are seen first, which sometimes means long waits for those with minor ailments. This situation caused key patient satisfaction scores in the emergency department to run nearly 25% below the hospital average. The challenge became increasing satisfaction in a hectic and varied environment. Despite this challenge, the campaign exceeded expectations through an innovative mix of procedural changes, staff scripting and improved collateral materials which facilitated patient communication and understanding.

SITUATION ANALYSIS

St. Rose Dominican Hospitals, a nonprofit organization, has served southern Nevada for over 60 years. In that time, the three campuses that make up the organization have focused on creating an environment of service that centers on quality, compassionate care. The hospitals have achieved a great deal of success in that effort and have been continually recognized for having the highest levels of overall patient satisfaction in the community.

St. Rose's Siena Campus emergency department continually sees extremely high patient volumes due to treating everything from trauma cases to the common cold. Patients with higher severity afflictions are seen first, which sometimes means long waits for those with minor ailments. In late 2006, key patient satisfaction scores in the emergency department averaged near 65% while the hospital as a whole averaged near 90% and some departments were near 100%. The challenge became increasing satisfaction in a very hectic and varied environment.

Secondary research showed that one of the primary ways to increase patient satisfaction in an emergency department setting was to provide greater and more frequent information about wait times. It was clear that a patient satisfaction campaign would have to address not only volume issues but also communication factors.

continued . . .

Exhibit 3.1

2008 PRSA Silver Anvil Award Winner, Reputation/Brand Management: Siena Campus Emergency Department *. . . continued*

Despite these challenges, the Siena Campus emergency department patient satisfaction campaign exceeded expectations by raising scores in many key measures by as much as 12 points (118%+ increase) over the baseline measures. This was accomplished by an innovative mix of procedural changes in patient flow, staff scripting, and improved collateral materials which facilitated patient communication and understanding.

RESEARCH

St. Rose used primary and secondary research to gain an understanding of the issues involved, reviewed related best practices and established baseline metrics. Key findings showed that messaging should focus on timeliness, patient care excellence and compassion. In addition, strategies and tactics should help to humanize clinical staff and empower patients to openly communicate questions, concerns and issues.

Reviewed secondary research from a large variety of case studies and reports. Findings revealed:

- Happy physicians and staff had a greater influence on patient satisfaction than the environment or conditions of care.
- Hospital staff members are often too clinical in their approach and fall short in the little things such as treating a person as a fellow human being rather than simply a patient.
- Satisfaction with emergency services increases dramatically by simply providing patients with more information at frequent intervals.
- Emergency departments across the country are full, and ambulances are regularly diverted to other facilities. Those patients that remain face long wait times, a factor that significantly impacts satisfaction.
- Nationally, hospitals with the greatest commitment to improvement averaged a 2.7% mean score increase in patient satisfaction over the previous year. An analysis showed that most St. Rose scores were already very high, with month to month variability, but yearly increases in the mean average were less than 1%.
- Utilized an existing contract with Avatar (no new cost for the campaign was incurred) to survey patients and formulate baseline measures of patient satisfaction. Four core measures of patient satisfaction were selected.
- Based on the secondary research, the four survey questions that were singled out included measures for overall department improvement, a patient's likelihood of returning to the Siena ED if needed, a patient's likelihood of recommending the Siena ED to others and how well the patient was kept informed.

It was anticipated that the initial thrust of the campaign would last 5–6 months and, since research and planning began in November 2006, baseline data for the four core measures were collected for the period from December 2005 to April 2006 and used to compare with the same time period in 2007.

PLANNING

Objectives

- Increase overall patient satisfaction in the ED by a mean score of greater than 3% for the campaign period (therefore exceeding the identified national average).
- Encourage employees to comply with the new scripting procedures and achieve a 3% mean score increase in the "kept informed" metric over the initial campaign time period.
- Promote usage of both the scripting and collateral materials to achieve a 3% mean score increase in the "likely to return" and "likely to recommend" metrics over the initial campaign time period.

continued . . .

Exhibit 3.1

2008 PRSA Silver Anvil Award Winner, Reputation/Brand Management: Siena Campus Emergency Department . . . *continued*

Target Audiences

Primary

- Patients visiting the emergency room with a focus on women 25–50 years old.

Secondary

- Healthcare workers including physicians, nurses, technicians, etc.

Strategy

- Decrease patient wait times through the reorganization of patient flow through the system.
- Encourage specific employee actions and words designed to correspond with language found in the surveys as well as create a feeling of mutual understanding, communication and respect between caregivers and patients.
- Motivate patients to take a more active role in communicating needs through targeted collateral materials.

Budget

There was no additional cost for the patient surveys, employee scripting or placing a patient flow restructuring. The total budget for the project was $5,000 and was primarily spent on collateral production and framing.

EXECUTION

Decrease Wait Times:

Key to decreasing wait times was a reorganization in flow so that the patient would spend less time waiting and more time seeking answers with caregivers. This reorganization included the placement of a physician in the triage area. Low acuity patients met with the doctor in triage and in many cases were diagnosed, treated and released without ever waiting for an emergency room bed. This process significantly expedited the care for patients with less severe ailments and freed up space for those with more severe conditions.

Encourage Targeted Employee Actions and Words:

A script was created for employees that highlighted key language in the surveys and helped to humanize the interaction and promote patient communication. At first, the nurses felt awkward in purposefully smiling or telling the patient he would receive excellent care. However, after continual practices employees became more at ease and positive responses became more of a norm than a rarity.

Motivate Patients to Communicate Needs:

Large team posters were placed in the waiting room, and smaller employee posters were placed in individual patient bays. In addition, 15,000 thank you cards were produced for caregivers to hand out. All materials featured manager contact information, key words from survey questions, and real staff photos and interests to help humanize the caregivers. The materials were introduced in January of 2007, and the employees were very happy with the results. They began to show a great deal of pride in the campaign and that feeling quickly spread to the patients. In February all key measure scores began a significant upward trend.

EVALUATION

In the weeks following each patient visit a survey was sent out by the Avatar group and included questions pertaining to the four core measures. On average, 70 patients responded per month.

continued . . .

Exhibit 3.1

2008 PRSA Silver Anvil Award Winner, Reputation/Brand Management: Siena Campus Emergency Department . . . *continued*

Following are the results:

- Increased overall patient satisfaction in the ED by a mean score of greater than 3% for the campaign period.
- Achieved a 10.92% mean score increase compared to the base period, exceeding the target by 364%.
- Encouraged employees to comply with the new scripting procedures and achieved a 3% mean score increase in the "kept informed" metric over the initial campaign time period.
- Achieved a 7.29% mean score increase compared to the base period, exceeding the target by 243%.
- Promote usage of both the scripting and collateral materials to achieve a 3% mean score increase in the "likely to return" and "likely to recommend" metrics over the initial campaign time period.
- Achieved an 11.09% mean score increase compared to the base period for "likely to recommend," exceeding the target by 370%.
- Achieved a 12.40% mean score increase compared to the base period for "likely to return," exceeding the target by 413%.
- Following the evaluation period, similar campaigns were implemented in departments at all three campuses.

Note: Reprinted with permission from the Public Relations Society of America (PRC Search.PRSA.org)

ASSIGNMENTS

Assignment 3.1—Alcohol Awareness Month (Part A)

As public information specialist for the Council on Alcohol and Drug Dependence, your job involves using a variety of communication methods to help better educate area residents of all ages about the use, misuse, and abuse of alcohol and other drugs. The council is a nonprofit health agency and receives funding primarily from the United Way, the state health department, foundation grants, and corporate and private donations. It provides the community with a variety of free services such as short-term counseling for individuals affected by alcohol and drug abuse, education and prevention programs directed to schools, and referrals to other substance treatment programs, to name a few. These services are administered by paid staff, most of whom are trained social workers, counselors, and educators.

You report to LaToya Glover, the council's executive director, who oversees all agency operations—this includes managing the budget, handling fundraising and development, and working with the board of directors on policy matters. Before you joined the staff just a few weeks ago, the executive director also handled marketing and public relations in conjunction with a board sub-committee. The public information position was recently added to relieve the executive director of day-to-day marketing and public relations tasks and to make it possible for one individual to put all of his or her focus on these important activities.

It is now early December and, at a Monday staff meeting, a discussion begins about plans for Alcohol Awareness Month in April. Typically, the council sponsors special events and attempts to gain more extensive media coverage during that month; it often does this by focusing on a current alcohol- or drug-related issue that has been receiving much attention both in the community and in the local and national press. By emphasizing a newsworthy issue, one that has generated much social concern, the council positions itself and its staff as experts on the issue, leading to greater visibility for the agency and its services.

After some deliberation, it is decided that the focus of next year's Alcohol Awareness Month campaign should be binge drinking, generally defined as the heavy consumption of alcohol over a short period of time. Because there are several colleges and universities in your community, there is a great deal of local interest in this subject. Area educators and education administrators have been trying to tackle this dangerous problem, which has been the cause of an increasing number of accidental deaths due to alcohol overdose on college campuses nationwide.

At the staff meeting, the executive director asks you to take a major role in planning and coordinating Alcohol Awareness Month activities, to include the preparation of various publicity and written materials. As binge drinking is a subject you have heard about, but are not overly familiar with, you take the logical first step—asking more questions and conducting additional research.

Exercises

1. What additional steps would you recommend taking to help you learn more about binge drinking and design a public relations program for Alcohol Awareness Month?

2. Develop a public relations program for Alcohol Awareness Month, following the outline in this chapter.

Assignment 3.2—Theater Company's 25th Anniversary

Established more than two decades ago, The Star Theater is a professional theater company. It has gained a reputation as one of the top 20 regional theater companies in the country. Star's season runs from September to May and features six productions, mainly dramas and comedies, although it often features a musical during the Christmas season.

The company's producing director is Richard West, a former New York City-based actor and director with many stage credits, including some Broadway hits. He oversees the company's operations and $3 million annual budget, and works closely with the artistic director on the selection of the seasons' shows. He also serves as liaison to the board of directors; the board is made up of corporate and community leaders who provide counsel on business and operational issues and play a major role in fundraising and development. Under West's direction, Star's ticket sales in the last three years have increased 10%, but there are indications that sales are slowing. Season subscription sales so far this year are about 25% behind where they were in the previous year.

The company offers an interesting variety of plays, from classics written by well-known playwrights such as Tennessee Williams, Neil Simon, and Noel Coward, to newer productions that had recent runs on- and off-Broadway. It will occasionally stage a lesser-known work by an up-and-coming playwright, and often likes to feature works of great social significance. Most of the actors are professionals from across the United States who belong to the Actors' Equity Association; local talent is used on occasion to fill smaller roles. The company has a tradition of using area children in its Christmas show, for example. All actors are paid for their work.

You have recently been hired as a public relations and marketing assistant for Star. You report to Emily Bonaventura, the director of public relations and marketing, who, in turn, reports directly to West. One morning, Bonaventura visits your office to talk about a meeting she had that morning with West.

"You know that next year is our 25th anniversary, and Richard and I were talking about that this morning. He really wants to make a 'big splash' with this anniversary, not just with the media, but in the community as well. As we were talking, he suggested that we might want to think about some programming next year that really helps us reach out into the community in some new ways. Maybe start building some new relationships with groups that don't fit the basic Star theatergoer mold."

"From what I can gather," you say, "people who buy season subscriptions fit a certain profile, don't they? They're usually 50+, professional, tend to be higher income, right?"

"That's pretty much the type, yes. We do bring in the occasional school groups, and get some younger professionals, but we haven't really tapped into those audiences as well as we could. The last survey we did showed those groups weren't too aware of what we do here—some even mentioned that they viewed theater as 'boring entertainment'—but those students and 20- and 30-somethings who had come to a show or two really enjoyed the experience."

"I thought you said that we do some programs in the local schools? Aren't they having much of an impact?"

"We do, but usually that involves Richard or actors from some of the shows speaking to a class here and there about theater and acting careers. We do have an excellent relationship with the local colleges and universities and their theater programs, and we offer internships and other special programs for those students. It's really the junior and senior high school students—even the elementary school kids—that we want to focus on. Richard sees a real opportunity to get more young people excited about and interested in theater—'the patrons of tomorrow,' as he puts it."

"So, how did you leave it with him? It sounds like we're starting to develop a focus for this anniversary campaign."

"He wants to see a plan from us, and I'd like your help putting it together. You've already given some thought to media activities, so I really don't want to bring that into this plan. Let's focus on public relations and community outreach efforts that can help us start building relationships with younger people. If we could generate media interest in some of these programs, that's great, but it shouldn't be the primary concern."

Bonaventura continues: "Of course, we don't want to forget our loyal patron base in all this, either. We'll want to look at ways for this 25th anniversary campaign to impact them in some way, too. Don't worry about budget too much at this point. Just keep in mind, we don't have a fortune to spend. Why don't you start giving this some thought, maybe even jot down some ideas that we could talk more about next week?"

Exercises

Working alone or in teams of two, prepare a preliminary public relations program plan (not to exceed three pages) for the 25th anniversary of the Star Theater that includes the following elements:

- introduction/situation analysis;
- goals and objectives;
- publics (be specific, and briefly explain your reasons for targeting each group);
- strategies (for each strategy, include two or three key tactics that support that strategy;

emphasize any special timing considerations as they relate to specific strategies/tactics);

- evaluation methods.

Assignment 3.3—A Hospital's Public Relations Challenge (A)

You are a communications professional working for Mercy Hospital, one of the largest hospitals and health-care facilities in a major city in your state. It is located in an area of the city undergoing a transformation that includes recently built luxury condos and trendy restaurants and shops. Previously, that area had been somewhat run-down and experiencing crime at a higher rate than other neighborhoods in the city. In the past year, the crime rate has dropped significantly. Mercy has gained a national reputation for its cardiac care unit, which draws patients from throughout your state and the country. The hospital recently completed a physical expansion to provide state-of-the-art facilities for its fast-growing family practice and maternity services.

Recently, the hospital's communications and marketing department conducted survey research with a representative sample of current and former patients who used a hospital service in the past two years. In the last 12 months, there has been some drop-off in the number of area residents seeking care at Mercy Hospital. Charles Kepner, the hospital's vice president of marketing and communications, along with other senior leadership, thought this would be a good time to do a local study to examine communication issues and find out what might be contributing to the declining number of patients.

Overall, respondents gave the hospital high marks for quality of care and medical staff. The survey results revealed the following about important audience segments:

- Among those 50+ in the community and region, use of hospital services, especially repeat visits, continues to be high. This group, in general, says they come back to Mercy Hospital because of the outstanding doctors and the emphasis on "personal attention and follow up."
- Young parents 25–40 do not seem to be fully aware of the hospital's services. Almost 50% of that group said they were not aware of the recent expansion and the hospital's high-quality maternity services. Also, two thirds of that group said they might have considered coming to the hospital for family medical care and other services, but their fear of crime in that neighborhood prevented them from doing so.

With this information in hand, Kepner meets with you to discuss next steps. "There's clearly a disconnect with the 25–40 group. The hospital has to be able to show our board and others that all the money we've invested in the expansion has been worth it. But if we don't get more of these people in the door, especially the young parents, that's going to be hard to do."

You say, "Why don't I give this some more thought and come back to you in a week or so with some ideas on how we can do a better job reaching the young-parent audience."

Exercise

Design a public relations program for Mercy Hospital targeting young parents 25–40 and following the process outlined in this chapter—research (situation analysis), planning (goals, messages, strategies), execution (public relations methods and communications channels you would employ), and evaluation.

References and Suggested Reading

Boone, L. E. (1999). *Quotable business* (2nd ed.). New York: Random House.

Broom, G. (2008). *Effective public relations* (10th ed.). Upper Saddle River, NJ: Prentice Hall.

Cameron, G., & Wilcox, D. (2006). *Public relations strategies and tactics* (8th ed.). Boston: Allyn & Bacon.

Lattimore, D. L., Baskin, O., Heiman, S., & Toth, E. (2006). *Public relations: The profession and the practice* (2nd ed.). New York: McGraw Hill.

Siena Campus Emergency Department: The patient satisfaction turnaround (2008). Program nomination submitted to PRSA Silver Anvil Awards. New York.

Wilson, L. (2000). *Strategic program planning for effective public relations campaigns* (3rd ed.). Dubuque, IA: Kendall/Hunt.

Part Two

RESEARCH

4

Research

Tycoon Donald Trump has probably become best known for "You're fired," the statement made at the end of every episode of "The Apprentice," a popular television show featuring a diverse group of entrepreneurs and professionals vying for a coveted position in the Trump organization. But Trump is also known in the business world for doing his homework. "When I started out in business," Trump says, "I spent a great deal of time researching every detail that might be pertinent to the deal I was interested in making. I still do the same today. People often comment on how quickly I operate, but the reason I can move quickly is that I've done the background work first."

To be most effective, public relations professionals also have to do "the background work" and shape their programs around research. Public relations research has two general purposes: (1) to build understanding of a situation that an organization is facing or of public perceptions prior to engaging in a public relations program, which can help practitioners craft the most effective messages and strategies; and, (2) to identify opportunities or matters of concern to the organization. The latter is referred to as issues management. It is important for public relations practitioners to keep "their finger on the pulse" of their publics, the organization itself, and the environment in which the organization operates. Identifying and acting on problems identified during issues management can prevent those problems from becoming crises.

Regardless of why you are conducting research, the research methods are the same. This chapter focuses on how to conduct the most common research methods.

Secondary Research

When facing a research problem, first consider *secondary sources*, those created by someone else but still useful to you. Secondary sources provide background information that increases your general understanding of a problem or subject. They also can offer some initial insight into public concerns or opinions about the subject. The Internet has made access to secondary sources much easier and more efficient. What used to take a day or two at the public library can now be done in an hour or two at your desktop. However, don't rule out the resources available through public and university libraries. Libraries contain numerous reference books, major newspaper indexes, statistical abstracts, and census reports valuable to the public relations writer. To save time, contact a reference librarian and enlist his or her support in identifying the best sources for your search. Some other background research sources useful to public relations writers include:

- *Files and archives*. Letters, proposals, and other business documents stored in personal and company files can provide a good research starting point. Maintain a "clippings file" of media articles published about your organization and on issues that impact your organization. For example, if you are a public relations director for a pharmaceutical company, you should be clipping articles regularly from mass media and trade publications relating to the industry, competitor news and product stories, and consumer health trends. Such articles may provide excellent points of reference when you begin campaigns, prepare proposals, or update written materials. Many organizations also have in-house archives where they maintain historical data and copies of previously published brochures, annual reports, newsletters, and other useful background pieces.
- *Existing survey data*. Universities, professional associations, government agencies, polling organizations, and some consulting firms regularly conduct regional and national public opinion studies. It is likely that someone has conducted a survey and gathered data on a subject you want to investigate (see Exhibit 4.1).

Exhibit 4.1
Online Research Sources for Public Relations Writers

Dow Jones Interactive (www.dowjones.com)
This site is a great source for current news and business stories.

Gallup (www.gallup.com)
This well-known polling organization's site makes it possible to monitor current national public opinion on business, economic, lifestyle, and political issues.

Institute for Public Relations (www.instituteforpr.com)
This nonprofit organization serves as a clearinghouse for research on public relations topics.

LEXIS-NEXIS (www.lexis-nexis.com)
This excellent online resource contains news and business stories, legal articles and court cases, government documents, public records, tax, and regulatory information.

National Opinion Research Center (NORC) at the University of Chicago
(www.norc.uchicago.edu)
This site maintains an extensive library of public attitude surveys conducted on health, education, and social issues.

Online Public Relations (www.online-pr.com)
This easy-to-use, extensive catalog of public relations, media, and marketing resources features links to hundreds of online media sites, product and industry information, reference books, statistics, and e-mail directories.

continued . . .

Exhibit 4.1

Online Research Sources for Public Relations Writers . . . *continued*

PR Newswire (www.prnewswire.com)
This is one of the leading wire services specializing in the electronic distribution of news to the media and financial community.

ProfNet (www.profnet.com)
This Internet service links public relations professionals with journalists looking for expert sources.

PR Place (www.prplace.com)
This site features addresses and links to public relations organizations and publications, news sources and services on the Web, and online and other commercial databases.

PR Web (www.prweb.com)
A good general source of free information for public relations professionals, this site features news, articles written by public relations counselors, and lots of news releases.

Roper Center for Public Opinion Research at the University of Connecticut (www.ropercenter.uconn.edu)
This site houses a large archive of current research including survey data from Gallup and many other polling organizations.

U.S. Census Bureau (www.census.gov)
This site provides demographic data based on the most recent census, including detailed information about the U.S. population, income and education levels, housing, occupations, ancestry, and many other subjects.

The Pew Research Center for the People and the Press (www.people-press.org)
This public opinion research group studies attitudes toward the press, politics and public policy issues.

- *Case histories*. Professional associations, such as PRSA, and many public relations books and textbooks available in college and public libraries detail public relations campaigns undertaken by various organizations. Often, these case studies outline research techniques and findings, strategic planning, communications efforts, and evaluation methods from successful campaigns and can give you ideas for your public relations programming.
- *Media directories*. Researching the media and creating and updating media lists are routine in public relations work. Media generally fall into one of two categories: mass media (i.e., daily newspapers, television) that reach a wide consumer audience, and specialized media that focus on the interests of more narrowly defined consumer and industry groups. Directories published by Bacon's and other companies offer comprehensive, state-by-state listings of newspapers, magazines, broadcast media, and business publications. Local chapters of the PRSA and other professional communications groups may produce a media directory for a specific city or area, as well. Some of the most popular media directories are listed in Exhibit 4.2.

Exhibit 4.2

Helpful Media Directories and Web Sites

Burrelle's (http://www.burrellesluce.com)

Editor and Publisher (http://www.editorandpublisher.com/eandp/index.jsp)

Gebbie Press (www.gebbiepress.com)

MarketWire (www.marketwire.com)

MediaFinder (www.mediafinder.com)

Newslink (www.newslink.org)

PR Newswire MediAtlas™ (www.prnewswire.com)

PR Place (www.prplace.com)

Vocus (www.vocus.com/content/index.asp)

- *Online databases and networks.* Databases and online retrieval services such as Lexis-Nexis make it possible for you to access thousands of publications and millions of news articles and other documents. Commercial online services such as Yahoo! not only offer their own exclusive databases, but also features such as e-mail, Internet access, and chat rooms for interactive discussions of various topics in "real-time," meaning people respond to your comments instantly, as if you were having a face-to-face conversation.
- *Listervs.* A listserv is an electronic mailing list distribution system. When you join a specific listserv group, you receive e-mail communication from others who subscribe to that mailing list, and you can send e-mail messages to them as well. Listserv messages are sent to the e-mail addresses of everyone within that listserv group. Some mailing lists, however, are designed to deliver e-mail only.
- *World Wide Web.* Many organizations now have their own Web sites, and many publications have online versions for the Web. If you're looking for news stories, or for facts about a competitor, a prospective client, or a major issue, it's likely you'll be able to find it. Blogs, short for Web logs, also are increasingly being used as sources of information. Individuals and companies use blogs to express their viewpoints on a variety of issues. Online forums and social networking sites, such as Facebook, are another good way to track trends and find out what people are talking about. A word of caution about gathering information through the Web, however—consider the credibility of the source. It doesn't take a lot of time, effort, or money to construct a Web site, which may contain false or misleading information, or to post a blog that, by its nature, is based on opinion.

Primary Research

Secondary sources are a great place to start when conducting research and, sometimes, they can produce much of the background information you need. It is usually necessary, however, to do some ***primary research***, gathering firsthand information from people who are know-ledgeable about the subject to get additional facts. If you are asked to write publicity materials for a new consumer product, you might ask the company's marketing manager some questions to learn more about the product's development, what distinguishes it from other products on the market, and how it has been designed to meet a specific and timely consumer need.

Once this kind of background research is completed, you need to assess if more feedback is required from the public being targeted. Maybe you are launching an employee publication or creating a program to educate people about sexual harassment in the workplace. Making assumptions about employee reading habits or about their knowledge of what constitutes sexual harassment is not enough. If you don't know with certainty what their attitudes are, then you risk producing a publication employees won't read, or designing informational materials that overlook important and misunderstood messages about harassment in the workplace.

For example, when Carpet One, a national floor covering retail group, identified children and schools as the most important issues in the communities where its stores were located, members of the American Library Association were interviewed to find what kinds of program would be beneficial to schools. It turned out that donating books or permanent floor covering directly to local schools posed problems because of varying institutional requirements; however, the school librarians said an in-school reading program could be valuable. Specialists in children's theatre and elementary reading were then interviewed to create a program that would have educational value and hold children's interest. The result was a highly successful, creative after-school reading program, with great public relations value for Carpet One in leading this effort.

As illustrated in the Carpet One case, ***interviews*** can help public relations professionals uncover what people think and design programs that most closely address the problem or meet the public relations need. ***Focus groups***, ***surveys*** and ***content analysis*** are other research methods that are beneficial to public relations and the writing process.

Interviews

Interviews are a type of qualitative research. Through the use of qualitative techniques, you can collect in-depth information on the reasons behind attitudes, opinions, and behavior. What an interviewer does is comparable to the labors of a painter and a psychologist. A talented interviewer, like a painter, can create a mood and, like a psychologist, can get people to open up in ways they never thought possible. Some interviewing tips:

Before the Interview

- Make an appointment and let the person know how long you expect the interview to run. Prior to the interview, send an e-mail message to confirm the time, place, and expected length of the interview. Remind the person of your goal and include some of the questions you plan to ask to help him prepare.
- Find out what you can about the person being interviewed—is this a talkative person, or someone who shares less freely? Talk to others who have interviewed or met this person, and get some suggestions from them on establishing rapport with the individual.

- If you plan to use a tape recorder, ask the person in advance if he or she is comfortable with that. Check the recorder's batteries and make sure you have enough tape. Bring a notepad and an extra pen or two in case the first pen you use runs dry.

Conducting the Interview

- Start by finding some general topic to talk about that is unrelated to the interview. A relevant item from the day's news is a safe choice. This can increase comfort levels and indicate how the person will interact with you as the interview progresses. Don't drag this out, though, and be alert to signals that say, "I don't want to make small talk; let's get down to business."
- Begin the interview by restating the goal. Tell the person what you are writing, why you are writing it, and how it will be used. Even though this ground may have been covered in a previous conversation or e-mail message, the people you interview are often busy and juggle multiple responsibilities, and they may need reminding.
- Come prepared with a written list of questions. Ask general, easy-to-answer questions first. Have the individual discuss his current job description or talk about his education and professional background to ease into the interview. Questions should be phrased to prevent "yes" or "no" answers. Don't ask, "Are you happy to be working as an executive for this company?" Do ask, "What do you think will be the most rewarding aspects of this job?" Follow up on short, non-revealing answers to get more descriptive, detailed responses. If the person says, "I took this job because the company has a good reputation," follow up by asking, "What specific aspects of the company's reputation appealed to you?"
- Listen. Try not to interrupt people when they are talking. And don't feel like someone always has to be saying something. Brief pauses here and there are okay. Acknowledge the person's responses with genuine interest, good eye contact, a nod of the head and a smile, but don't overdo.
- Don't think you have to stick to the script. When you ask people to share their knowledge or talk about themselves, they can easily get sidetracked. If what's being said has merit, go with the flow, but make sure the interview doesn't lose focus. Offer a smooth transition to get things back on track: "That must have been quite an experience for you. I can tell you're proud of that accomplishment. I don't want to take up too much more of your time, however, I would like to ask you a few more questions before we finish, if that's all right."
- Look over the questions you came in with before wrapping up the interview. Make sure you've asked all the important questions. Ask a final question that will produce a strong concluding thought or quote for your article. This could be a follow-up question that reinforces a main point or theme discussed during the interview: "You said earlier that you are going to help the company explore new ways to be more competitive in the global marketplace. Maybe you could offer a final thought on why this is so important at this point in the company's history." Say "thank you" and, as a courtesy, let the person know your time frame for completing the piece.

After the Interview

- Review your interview notes right away. Find a chair in a hallway or do it in your car (you shouldn't be driving, of course) before you get back to the office. When writing fast, it sometimes is difficult to read your own handwriting. Reviewing your notes immediately after the interview, while the conversation is fresh in your mind, will make deciphering your notes a bit easier when you return to look at them later.
- Send a copy of the published article with a brief thank you note. Some organizations may require that you clear all quotes with the source before public relations materials are published or distributed, so make sure you're following policy.

E-mail Interviews

E-mail can be used effectively to conduct interviews; however, it's important to understand its limitations as well as its advantages:

Advantages

- If someone is on the other side of the country, or the other side of the world, you can correspond easily and quickly by e-mail. This will save on travel and phone costs, and you can complete the interview rather quickly.
- Having the interviewee respond via e-mail ensures accuracy of quotes and other information.

Disadvantages

- E-mail interviews are static. You send the questions and wait for a response, without the opportunity to observe gestures or nonverbal reactions that add color to feature articles and other pieces. Personal interviews are more fluid: you ask a question, and the person responds at that moment. There's more give-and-take between interviewer and interviewee.
- If someone receives your e-mail questions and finds a few of the questions vague, that person will have to send an e-mail back to you asking for clarification. In personal or phone interviews, that clarification occurs within seconds after the question is asked. E-mail clarification could take a while, depending on how soon the receiver accesses and reads messages that day.
- E-mail does not allow you to follow up the moment the question is asked (unless you're in a chat room) and to ask someone to elaborate on a response. You have to wait until the answers to questions are e-mailed back, and then follow up if more detail is needed. At that point, another e-mail or a phone call may be necessary to flesh out responses.

Another new technology useful for interviews is *Skype*, downloaded software that enables users to make long-distance audio and video calls over the Internet. Using Skype can be much less costly than video conferencing (more on Skype at www.skype.com).

Focus Groups

Focus groups, another type of qualitative research, are small group interviews that allow public relations and marketing professionals to probe the attitudes of an audience. Each focus group consists of 8 to 12 participants who share some common characteristic. A moderator asks open-ended questions, and participants have the chance to discuss in depth their reactions to a situation, product, or program. Focus groups attempt to find out why people feel or think the way they do. Often, focus group findings are used to identify key concerns that shape the questions for a larger-scale survey.

Focus groups are economical and can be relatively easy to organize. They help you to get a quick reading of public opinion on an issue, or to receive helpful feedback on the quality of communication tools. However, the opinions shared in focus groups do not represent the majority view, and you should not present findings in that way. On their own, focus groups can help public relations writers shape messages with greater impact. They can also provide insight into a public's views on how to best deliver a message so people will read it, understand it, and believe it.

Fleishman-Hillard public relations firm conducted focus groups with women in California's Hispanic community in response to increasing illnesses and deaths caused by consumption of homemade, or "bathtub," cheese made by unlicensed Hispanic vendors. The focus groups showed that, while Hispanic consumers were aware of the risks of eating unlicensed cheese, they felt that the benefits of better taste and lower cost outweighed those risks. They also indicated that they could tell by tasting the cheese if it was safe to eat; however, salmonella and other bacteria in the unlicensed cheese cannot be detected by taste, sight, or smell.

Based on the focus group research, the California Milk Advisory Board, with Fleishman-Hillard, launched a campaign to educate Hispanic consumers about the health risks of unlicensed cheese and to correct some of the misconceptions they had about detecting unsafe cheese. Focus groups showed that Hispanics had a long-held cultural practice of purchasing unlicensed cheese, so participants stressed that a campaign to impact those buying habits and change behavior had to feature strong messages about the potential for serious illness or death.

Focus group members indicated that Edward James Olmos, a well-known Hispanic actor, would have credibility as a media spokesperson on this issue; the campaign eventually featured Olmos in a series of Spanish-language public service announcements. Brochures had a soap opera format and presented the problem as a "real-life drama," an approach that focus group members said would encourage readership by Hispanic consumers. Materials also stressed that it is not possible to simply taste cheese and know whether it is tainted. They also presented tips for storing and handling homemade cheese to prevent contamination. The campaign generated extensive media exposure and favorable response in the Hispanic community. Focus group findings served as the foundation for this successful campaign.

In addition, focus groups can help ensure that organizations sponsor publicity activities that target audiences will support. Reynolds Metals Company, to celebrate the 50th anniversary of Reynolds Wrap aluminum foil, considered sponsoring a publicity event to draw attention to the product. One idea was to unfurl a huge roll of Reynolds Wrap over San Francisco's Golden Gate Bridge. Focus group participants, however, reacted negatively to this idea and stated they would be more receptive to purchasing products from companies that help worthy causes.

As a result, Reynolds teamed up with the National Association of Meal Programs to lead a major volunteer recruitment drive for the "Meals on Wheels" program. This partnership made sense since Reynolds Wrap is a staple of the program, which delivers hot and cold meals to homebound people. The recruitment became the key message of the anniversary campaign, appearing on Reynolds Wrap cartons, grocery bags, the Reynolds Web site, and all other promotional materials. The goal was to recruit 50,000 volunteers during the 50th anniversary year. The campaign recruited more than 70,000 volunteers, far surpassing the 50,000 goal, and helped Reynolds gain much attention and respect for its charitable efforts. Focus groups made the difference.

Surveys

If you want to assess public opinion of a large or geographically widespread group of people, then a survey may be the best research tool. Surveys fall under the category of quantitative research, a more scientific and systematic gathering of information that reduces data to percentages and other mathematical expressions. Different methods can be used in survey research. Telephone polls are used to survey community members about election issues and voting preferences. Mail surveys are sent by automobile manufacturers, immediately after a new car purchase, to find out how the new car owner rates the quality of service provided by the dealer and the salesperson. Registration cards are included with new products to analyze buyers' demographics and preferences. E-mail surveys are sent by product manufacturers to people who have visited a Web site to gauge reactions to the site and to the products. Web-based surveys are gaining in popularity, along with "do it yourself" survey research sites such as SurveyMonkey.com and Zoomerang.com.

Whatever the method, results are most exact when the individuals surveyed have been chosen in such a way that each person in a group has an equal chance of being selected. So, you might begin with a list of 1,000 names and select every 20th name; that will produce a random sample of 200 people. This scientific method ensures that the findings will better represent how everyone in that group feels about an issue. Whenever possible, it's best to survey all members of a group. Accurate results also depend on the way the survey questionnaire has been constructed (see Exhibit 4.3 for tips on how to develop good questions for a survey).

Surveys can help public relations professionals clearly see what large numbers of people know or don't know about a subject. Messages can then be formed and sent that reinforce what people know and, more importantly, explain what they don't know and how this lack of knowledge affects them.

When public health battles escalated regarding the dangers of trans fat, Dow AgroSciences saw an opportunity to promote Omega-9 Oils, made from its Nexera™ canola and sunflower seeds, to restaurant owners and foodservice directors. The company knew, however, that the target publics were sometimes resistant to change, concerned that the healthier alternative might come at the expense of better taste and less cost. According to the company's winning entry submitted to the 2008 PRSA Silver Anvil Awards competition, primary research was conducted to "understand the details of restaurant owner oil purchasing habits, familiarity with oil alternatives, and what would influence them to convert to healthier oil in their kitchens."

Exhibit 4.3

Constructing Questionnaires

Data gathered through survey methodology are only as good as the survey itself. The accuracy of the answers you receive will depend on how well you construct your questions. Be sure you are developing questions to effectively obtain the information you are seeking. For example, when conducting focus group research, questions that can be answered by "yes" and "no" really won't give you much information. Here are some additional guidelines:

Questions

- Determine the type of question you want to ask. ***Close-ended questions*** are paired with a choice of answers from which the respondents can select; ***open-ended questions*** allow the respondents to answer using their own words.
- List questions in a logical order and keep similar topics together.
- Avoid leading questions. Questions should be neutral. You don't want respondents to answer a certain way because you have "signaled" to them there is a preferred answer. For example, "Most students say the curriculum needs to be revised; do you agree with them?" may imply that, if a respondent doesn't answer "yes," he or she will be in the minority.
- Likewise, you should avoid biased questions, such as "How high would you rate the tastiness of food?" or "How accommodating would you rate our customer service?" The questions are phrased in a way that indicates the food is tasty and the customer service is accommodating.
- Avoid double-barreled questions (asking two questions at the same time). "Do you like turkey and stuffing at Thanksgiving?" really asks two questions. If a respondent likes one but not the other, you will get an inaccurate response.
- Be specific with the words that you use. Make sure they can't be interpreted in multiple ways. For example, when you use the phrase "quality care," what are you really trying to obtain information on? Promptness? Bedside manner? Cleanliness? "Quality" means different things to different people.
- Keep your questions focused on the information you really want to find out. It's easy to go astray.

Answers

If you are asking close-ended questions, you will need to provide answer choices. As mentioned earlier, "yes" and "no" answers really don't provide much information. The Likert scale is one of the most popular rating scales used for answering questions. This scale offers two opposites, such as "strongly agree" and "strongly disagree," with a number of choices, such as "agree" and "disagree" in between. You might also have respondents choose along a scale of "poor" to "excellent," using terms such as "fair" and "great" in between, but these terms may have multiple interpretations. One way to lessen ambiguity is to have respondents rate the questions on a scale of 1 to 5, with 1 being "poor" and 5 being "excellent." Numerical scales can also be used with other polar opposites, such as "boring" and "exciting," to gauge perceptions.

In addition to rating scales, checklists are a popular response mechanism. These are predetermined answers that the respondent can select. You may have respondents check as many as apply (e.g., "How did you hear about this program?"), or limit the answer to the one that best mirrors their opinion. When providing predetermined answers, be sure there is no overlap. For example, if asking the question "How many hours do you spend on the Internet every day?" the answers should be exclusive of one another: "Less than 1 hour," "1 or 2 hours," "3 or 4 hours."

The survey found that:

- Eighty-seven percent of decision makers said they would "consider changing frying oils if they knew it could decrease trans and saturated fats without compromising taste or cost."
- Eighty-three percent said they would likely try a new oil if it would "perform well at high temperatures and have a 50% longer fry life, allowing food-service decision makers to lower oil costs."
- Seventy-eight percent said they would be likely to try a new oil if it offered a "superior nutritional profile, with zero trans fats and low saturated fats."

The findings made it clear—the target publics were most likely to be influenced by taste, health, and cost-effectiveness, a three-pronged approach that would be integral in developing the subsequent campaign to "differentiate Dow's healthier oils from others on the market."

Sometimes, it's what people know and like that becomes the focus of public relations efforts. Nabisco Foods wanted to do something special to mark the 85th anniversary of Oreo® cookies. Nabisco used an 800 number to survey 100,000 consumers about their views of the Oreo®. The company learned that most everyone, regardless of how they preferred to eat an Oreo®, liked to "play" with the cookie and had "fun" eating it. Adults said eating Oreos brought back fond childhood memories. In response to consumer feedback, the anniversary campaign focused its key messages on the nostalgia and fun associated with eating Oreos. This included an "Only Oreo® Moments" contest that asked people of all ages to share special Oreo® moments through photographs, essays, or tapes. The winner received $10,000, and the winner's story became an Oreo® commercial. In the end, Nabisco scored a "slam dunk" (you can't talk about Oreos without using the word "dunk"), with sales up 40% and consumer excitement about the cookie greater than ever—proof that success can be sweet for public relations professionals who make survey research integral to their efforts.

Content Analysis

Public relations practitioners commonly use content analysis to track trends in media coverage. Content analysis, another type of quantitative research, can help reveal how prominently your organization is being mentioned in the media, whether the coverage is positive or negative, what kind of coverage your competition is getting, the status of the political or economic environment in which your company operates, or the issues confronting your industry or community. In addition to media coverage, content analysis can be useful in tracking customer attitudes, advertising trends, and corporate reputation.

When Frito-Lay, a leader in making healthier snack foods, was developing a campaign to change the perception of people who still thought of the snacks as "junk food," it conducted a content analysis. Through an analysis of print, broadcast, and online media coverage, the company discovered that its SunChips® brand received positive coverage, while its Cheetos® and Doritos® brands received negative coverage. This led the company to highlight the heart-healthy oils in its brands other than SunChips® and focus on its overall health and wellness innovations.

In its most basic form, you could conduct a content analysis with a pencil and piece of paper by making a table of what you want to measure and recording data. But first you must:

- determine what you want to measure, for example, the name of your organization, the names of your competition, key words or phrases. Carefully define these terms so they are as objective and denotative as possible;
- determine the source of communication you want to monitor, such as news articles, letters to the editor, customer comments, or blogs. You must also determine the breadth of those sources (e.g., local, regional, or national media);
- develop a coding sheet. This may resemble a table, with the far left column representing the data you want to measure, and the top row representing the data source. From these raw data, you can figure overall percentages;
- train the coders. The results of your content analysis are more valid if more than one person is involved in the coding. To ensure that coders understand what they are looking for and, thus, respond more consistently, you should conduct training prior to the research. Even though you will do your best to objectively phrase the terms to be measured, many times they will still be open to interpretation. Training will help to decrease the chances of multiple meanings.

Additional Primary Research

- *Mail and telephone analysis.* Analyzing an organization's incoming mail and telephone calls is a simple, yet often overlooked, method of tracking public opinion. In this type of research, mail and telephone calls are tracked for positive and negative comments on a daily basis. The tracking sheets are then periodically analyzed to detect emerging issues.
- *Call-in lines.* Another way to track public opinion is through toll-free telephone numbers for customer service, information, or complaints. Such "call-in" lines provide immediate feedback to an organization so it can keep on top of emerging issues. It also offers two-way interpersonal communication and the positive image of a concerned organization that goes with it.
- *Field reports.* Employees working on the "front line" are some of the best resources an organization has. Whether an employee works at a reception desk or as a sales-person, he or she has direct access to the customer and can provide important feedback and observations. Some organizations offer these employees special training so they can provide even more insight from their dealings with customers.
- *Audits.* Audits come in many shapes and sizes, but all take an in-depth look at an organization's target publics and communication efforts. An organization might want to audit its publics occasionally to make sure they haven't changed. A publications audit reviews an organization's collateral materials to make sure they support the corporate identity and deliver a consistent message. A communication audit focuses on messages the organization sends, the media used, and the impact of the messages, to help identify missing linkages or blockages in the communication process. Communication audits can be time consuming, but are essential if an organization wants to make sure it is communicating successfully with both internal and external publics.

Exhibit 4.4 lists specific research methods that can be used when planning specific public relations projects. Additional evaluation techniques can be found in chapter 14.

Exhibit 4.4

Which Research is Best for Your Project?

Strategic Planning

If you need to ...	**then try these methods to collect data:**
Identify and/or segment your target publics	Field reports, communication audits, content analysis, phone/mail analysis, call-in lines
Measure your target publics' perceptions	Focus groups, phone/mail analysis, content analysis, surveys
Obtain demographics of your target publics	Online databases/networks, reference books, Web sites, library references
Identify lifestyle trends of your target publics	Surveys, focus groups, online databases/networks, library references, Web sites
Identify media preferences of your target publics	Surveys, focus groups, online databases/networks, media directories, Web sites, library references
Identify purchasing patterns of your target publics	Surveys, focus groups, online databases/networks, library references, Web sites
Identify readership preferences of your target publics	Surveys, online databases/networks, media directories, Web sites
Identify readership habits of your target publics	Focus groups, interviews, online databases/networks, Web sites
Identify motivators for your target publics	Focus groups, surveys, online databases/networks
Monitor issues important to your publics and/or organization	Focus groups, surveys, content analysis, Web sites
Monitor trends within your publics and/or organization	Focus groups, surveys, content analysis, Web sites, organizational files/archives
Monitor trends within your industry	Web sites, online databases/networks, content analysis, organizational files/archives
Measure public opinion on a large scale	Surveys, online databases/networks, listservs, Web sites, library references
Measure public opinion on a smaller, in-depth scale	Focus groups, online databases/networks
Identify potential problems	Communication audits, content analysis, phone/mail analysis, call-in lines, Web sites, online databases/ networks, listservs
Identify strengths and weaknesses of the organization	Communication audit

continued . . .

Exhibit 4.4

Which Research is Best for Your Project? *. . . continued*

Determine the effectiveness of current communication strategies and tactics	Communication audit
Formulate strategy	Surveys, case studies, organizational files/archives, Web sites
Get ideas for a campaign or special event	Case studies, organizational files/archives, Web sites
Get ideas for news articles	Online databases/networks, Web sites
Generate publicity	Surveys
Shape questions for a survey	Focus groups
Test new messages	Focus groups
Test a new logo and/or slogan	Focus groups, organizational files/archives, Web sites
Obtain facts and figures to support a proposal	Databases/networks, library references, Web sites
Identify and/or monitor your competition	Web sites, content analysis, organizational files/archives, surveys, online databases/networks, field reports
Identify prospective clients	Web sites, content analysis, online databases/networks
Prevent a crisis	Communication audits, content analysis, phone/mail analysis, call-in lines, Web sites, online databases/networks, listservs
Get a reality check	Field reports, communication audits, content analysis, phone/mail analysis, call-in lines, Web sites, listservs

Tactics

Create a brochure	Organizational files/archives, Web sites, focus groups
Develop a backgrounder	Interviews, organizational files/archives, Web sites
Write a news release, media alert, or pitch letter	Interviews, organizational files/archives, online databases/networks, media directories
Write and/or test a fundraising letter	Organizational files/archives, focus groups
Write a speech	Interviews, organizational files/archives, online databases/networks, Web sites
Write a "how to" article	Interviews, organizational files/archives, Web sites
Write an organizational history	Interviews, organizational files/archives
Write a letter to the editor or op-ed	Organizational files/archives, content analysis, online databases/archives, Web sites, media directories
Write newsletter articles	Interviews, online databases/networks, Web sites

continued . . .

Exhibit 4.4

Which Research is Best for Your Project? . . . *continued*

Evaluation

Measure change in awareness	Benchmark surveys, content analysis, distribution numbers, media impressions, Web site hits
Measure change in attitude and/or interest	Benchmark surveys, phone/mail analysis
Measure change in behavior	Benchmark surveys, attendance numbers, money raised
Measure change in public opinion	Benchmark surveys, focus groups
Measure publicity	Content analysis, media impressions, advertising equivalency

ASSIGNMENTS

Assignment 4.1—Going Organic

Organic food is one of the fastest growing sectors of the American food marketplace. Since the early 1990s, the world organic food market has grown 20% a year, and it's estimated that this growth could be as high as 50% in the future, depending on the country. "Organic" generally describes food that is grown free of synthetic fertilizers, herbicides, pesticides, and other chemicals. Organic farmers enrich the soil for their crops using natural substances such as manure and compost, rather than chemicals.

You are an assistant account executive working for a marketing communications firm. One of your clients is Dairy Fresh, a manufacturer of milk, cheese, and other dairy products. The company's products are primarily sold in the United States, with the largest sales on the East Coast. The company sees potential to grow its product line and be even more competitive, expanding to capture a larger share of the market in other parts of the United States and moving north into Canada.

Your supervisor, Margaret Bogan, the Dairy Fresh account manager for the firm, stops by your office to tell you about her recent meeting with Dairy Fresh executives.

"It looks like our client has a big interest in getting into the organic market. They've been seeing their competitors jump on the band wagon and boosting their profits, not only because people seem to be demanding more organic food but because organic products are generally more costly, too."

"That sounds like a pretty smart idea," you say. "I just read an article about organic food. I remember seeing statistics that said something like two thirds of organic milk and half of organic cheese and yogurts produced are sold through supermarkets."

Bogan adds, "It sounds like the Dairy Fresh people want to go in this direction, and obviously, it would be great for us if we had a new organic product line to market and promote. They need our help to get started, so that's why I stopped by."

"What can I do?"

"There's a lot more we need to know about the organic market, what the market potential is like, what our competitors are doing, and the benefits to consumers, those kinds of things.

I'd like you to help us pull together more information on the organic foods market that we could share with our client, but that also helps us to get up to speed on the subject. I think we can use this, too, to make our own recommendation about whether Dairy Fresh should 'go organic.'"

You add, "We might also want to think about getting some feedback from our customer base, or potential customers, to see if this is something they would respond to. Organic is definitely hot, but it would probably make sense to do that. I'll start doing some research and get a report together for you in a week or so."

Exercises

1. Conduct secondary research and prepare a report (no more than three pages), in memorandum form, that includes information on organic foods that would be relevant to your client and inform a recommendation to Dairy Fresh about entering the organic foods market. Include a recommendation to your client and justify your decision.

2. Your firm agrees to work with Dairy Fresh to conduct consumer research to further inform a decision to develop and market an organic dairy product line. In a memorandum, outline for your client the qualitative and/or quantitative methods you would suggest using, keeping in mind that your client wants to be sensitive to cost and is interested in a few high-impact research methods that will generate the most beneficial results. Be as specific as you can about the audiences to be targeted, the methods to be used, and the execution of those methods. Justify those choices versus other approaches that could be used.

Assignment 4.2—The Web Site Research Project

Shortly after graduation, you begin your first job at a small public relations firm. One of your firm's primary specialty areas is public relations and marketing communications work for the high-technology industry. One of your major projects is to help revamp the firm's Web site.

You are now preparing for a meeting with Eva Newhart, one of the firm's account managers, who is supervising the Web site project. She plans to discuss in more detail the site's history and to share her ideas for reworking the site. Before the meeting, you talk to a few employees to get some background on the site, fully review the agency's client roster, and do some reading on Web site development and online writing.

At the meeting, Newhart says the firm has been trying to update the Web site somewhat regularly, but mostly by doing "little things," such as adding information on new staff and clients. She believes the site provides the necessary information about the firm, its staff, and its services, but the overall content could "have more spark" and be more interesting.

"Plus," she adds," we serve many high-tech businesses, so our Web site should have more of a high-tech look and feel."

Newhart continues: "The site needs to be informative and tell people who we are, but it also needs to say something about what we do for clients and how we do it. What I mean is, we stress to clients and prospective clients that we are creative problem solvers and copywriters, but our Web site doesn't reflect that claim all that well. Frankly, it's a bit dull, and the copy is dry. It's a functional site, but we'd like it to be more than that. If the site does a great job of creatively and persuasively positioning us, then it would say something to prospective clients about how we could do the same for them."

Newhart suggests that at this point it might be useful to conduct an analysis of other Web sites, not only to get some tips for rewriting your firm's site, but also to get some ideas on how to distinguish your site's content from the others.

Exercise

Review two Web sites produced by public relations firms. Examine each site, its content, and its presentation. Then prepare a written analysis to include the following:

- Two-paragraph overview of each site. State the name of the firm and give a brief description of the firm, its major clients, and services. Summarize what you believe are the key goals and audiences of the site.

- Content and Web site presentation. Summarize content areas, multimedia and other features, and design elements used in each site. Note and describe what you think are distinguishing features of each site, as well as copy you think is creatively presented and well written. Cite an example of good writing from each site, and briefly explain why you think this is good writing.

- Conclusions. Discuss the implications of this analysis as they relate to content and presentation for your firm's updated Web site. Make specific recommendations for content, features, and design, based on your analysis, that could help make your firm's site stand out and be more effective. ■

Assignment 4.3—*Educating Men on Weight Loss*

BeechamClark, Inc. is one of the leading consumer health-care companies in the world. Two years ago, the company introduced goodLife, a Food and Drug Administration (FDA)-approved weight-loss product that can be purchased without a prescription. Like its primary competitor in this product category, goodLife helps people lose significantly more weight than they could through diet and exercise alone by blocking the absorption of some of the fat in foods they eat. In its first two years on the market, goodLife has performed well and is now being used by several million consumers to help them lose weight safely and effectively.

As a member of the marketing communications team, you take part in a meeting to talk about building on the product's success, particularly with men. An analysis of product sales shows that women tend to be the primary purchaser and consumer of the product at this time, although information shared during your meeting, based on consumer research, provides some food for thought relating to men and weight loss:

- Four decades ago, the National Health and Nutrition Examination Survey estimated that 49% of men age 20 and over were overweight. Estimates today put that percentage at close to two thirds of men who are overweight.

- According to the National Center for Health Statistics, obesity rates have increased significantly in the last 25 years, and, in men, there has been a notable increase in obesity prevalence.

- The Harvard Health Professionals Study has tracked more than 50,000 men since 1986 and shown that three lifestyle factors predict weight gain for men: less time exercising, more time watching television, and eating between meals. Similar studies conducted by BeechamClark using an independent research firm reinforce these findings.

- Men who are even moderately overweight face serious health risks. Men tend to gain excess fat in their trunk and abdomen; excess abdominal fat increases the risk for diabetes and heart disease.

- Recent articles in medical publications written by reputable physicians and nutritionists point to the idea that men tend not to seek advice and support from others about weight loss. Unlike women, men tend to be less process-oriented—they don't want to talk about losing weight, they just want to do it.

You also learn that a primary marketing communications strategy will involve educating male consumers about weight loss issues relevant to them, while simultaneously building awareness of goodLife as a solution to those issues, thus helping to drive product sales.

Before going further with this project, the team agrees that additional research is needed to better understand male perspectives on weight loss and weight loss products, and to provide critical information to shape the most effective messages and strategies.

Exercises

1. Identify and execute secondary research activities on the subject of men and weight loss, and compile additional facts and statistics that would be useful for your public relations efforts and the messages and communications materials you would create.

2. Assume that you have decided to conduct primary research, which includes focus groups. In a memorandum, outline a plan for conducting these focus groups. Be specific about goals, audience, and logistics (how, where, and when will these be conducted; how many groups should be planned; length and format, etc.) Prepare five to six general questions that you would use to guide the focus group discussions, and offer a brief justification for the importance of each question.

References and Suggested Reading

Brody, E. W., & Stone, G. C. (1989). *Public relations research.* Westport, CT: Praeger Publishers.

Broom, G. M., & Dozier, D. M. (1996). *Using research in public relations: Applications to program management* (2nd ed.). Upper Saddle River, NJ: Prentice Hall.

Broom, G. (2008). *Effective public relations* (10th ed.). Upper Saddle River, NJ: Prentice Hall.

Cameron, G., & Wilcox, D. (2005). *Public relations strategies and tactics* (8th ed.). Boston: Allyn & Bacon.

From junk food to good food: Building advocates to change the perception of Frito-Lay snacks (2008). Program nomination submitted to PRSA Silver Anvil Awards. New York.

Lattimore, D. L., Baskin, O., Heiman, S., & Toth, E. (2006). *Public relations: The profession and the practice* (2nd ed.). New York: McGraw Hill.

Removing trans fat from America's menus (2008). Program nomination submitted to PRSA Silver Anvil Awards. New York.

The Carpet One magic carpet time tour (2002). Program nomination submitted to PRSA Silver Anvil Awards. New York.

Wilson, L. (2000). *Strategic program planning for effective public relations campaigns* (3rd ed.). Dubuque, IA: Kendall/Hunt.

Part Three

PLANNING

5

Planning and Message Design

Actor Brad Pitt doesn't look forward to dealing with the media. He once said:

> You shouldn't speak until you know what you're talking about. That's why I get uncomfortable
> with interviews. Reporters ask me what I feel China should do about Tibet. Who cares what I
> think China should do? They hand me a script. I'm a grown man who puts on makeup.

Pitt's statement is relevant to public relations professionals. As he points out, you
must understand a subject before you can effectively speak or write about it. As explained in
chapters 3 and 4, you gain knowledge and understanding of issues and perceptions by
conducting appropriate secondary and primary research. Based on research findings, you
then create a public relations program plan; this involves identifying the publics that your
program must reach and influence, setting goals and objectives, developing strategies and tactics,
and establishing a budget and timetable. This "roadmap" will lead you to a critical stage of
planning—creating appropriate public relations messages.

Developing the Message

The planning process is not just used for public relations programs; it also is applied to each
piece of writing you create—starting with research. Just as research is used to help identify
the problem or situation an organization is facing, it also is used to identify the best way to
write your message. A writing project might begin with some scribbled notes left on your desk
by a supervisor who asks you to "look into this and write something up by tomorrow." Most
of the time, you have to figure out on your own how to get started. The people you need to
talk to are out of town for a week or don't return your e-mails or phone calls. You'd like to
survey public perception about an issue as the basis for a campaign, but the client doesn't want
to spend much money on that kind of research. So, you gather information in the most efficient,
economical, and creative manner possible, often with little time to spare. Whatever the project,
there are key questions you should always ask to guide the research effort:

1. Why am I writing this piece?
2. Who is my audience, and what do they know or think?
3. How will the piece be distributed and what form should it take?
4. What facts do I have, and what additional information do I need?

Why am I writing this piece? Always begin by asking the question, "Is there a good reason for writing this?" If you are writing a news release, first make sure that you have legitimate information to share and that you're not doing this simply to make your organization look good or to satisfy the personal whim of a staff member. A company news release about a planned expansion is newsworthy; a release announcing that the company softball team won its game over the weekend is not.

You must be clear about the purpose of the piece and its value to the organization. News provided by public relations professionals about major staff changes is published regularly in local newspapers' business sections, in business publications, and in trade journals. Staff releases create goodwill by publicly recognizing employees and making them feel like they are officially "on board." They also help organizations to stay continually visible to important audiences. Potential customers or clients who know and respect someone your company has hired might take notice, which could lead to new business opportunities. On the other hand, the media will simply not care about the company softball team's record and will view such a release as a blatant attempt to get exposure. If, however, that softball game took place as part of a community fund raiser and the team raised significant money for a local charitable cause, then an editor might see news value in the story.

You need to know about deadlines up front, as well. Find out if a deadline has already been established by someone, whether that be an editor who's expecting the material or a graphic designer who needs the copy to prepare a brochure lay-out for the printer. If no deadline is in place, then look realistically at the project and set a deadline that all involved parties think is reasonable. Establishing deadlines at the start helps you determine how much time can be devoted to research and how extensive that research can be.

Who is the target public, and what do its members know or think? Everything you write is written for somebody and to influence people in some way. Before you start collecting facts, make sure you understand who the intended public is. Is a fundraising piece directed to long-time donors in hopes they will donate again, or is it targeted to potential first-time donors? If the latter, your writing will need to provide more background information, since these people may not know much about the organization and its goals. In addition, it should be more persuasive in its approach than a letter sent to those who already support the cause.

Research is especially critical when you are writing for unfamiliar publics. Before you write, find out what the public knows about you and if it is even interested in what you have to say. For example, suppose you are preparing to write that letter to first-time donors. Research might show that potential donors question how much of the money raised is really used to help the neediest people in their area. In that case, a fundraising letter can be more persuasive if it indicates details such as the percentage of dollars allocated to help those in need, explains how funds are distributed and to whom, and includes personal stories to show how donations have benefited specific local individuals.

How will the piece be distributed and what form should it take? Once you know who you want to reach and what you want to tell them, it's time to focus on how to deliver the message. The way a message is distributed and the format it takes depend on the target public and the message itself. If the message requires sharing detailed information, a written communication or a meeting is more appropriate than a quick phone call. If the goal of a message is to draw attention to an upcoming event, a print or e-postcard followed by e-mail reminders could work best. Chapters 6 to 13 outline the many different writing formats and activities from which to choose when selecting the best way to reach your target public.

If you are delivering your message through mass media, consider the many options available and the media preferences of your target public (see Exhibit 5.1). In addition to daily and weekly newspapers, TV, and radio, trade publications and cable channels offer opportunities to deliver messages to publics that have become much more segmented. Print and online publications today reach narrowly defined publics with a wide range of interests, from animal lovers and auto racing enthusiasts to working women and young professionals.

Exhibit 5.1
Types of Media

Daily Newspapers
Dailies can serve small- to medium-sized cities and are primarily circulated in one local area; major metropolitan areas (e.g., The *New York Times*) that serve a local market, but also have regional editions and national distribution; or the nation, like *USA Today*. Dailies publish Sunday editions, columns, event calendar listings, and weekly feature sections on business/money, food, health, technology, and other subjects that can be good publicity outlets.

Weekly Newspapers
Weeklies are community and hometown newspapers read by residents in specific towns, villages, or suburban areas. In addition to hard news of interest to people in that community, content typically focuses on community events; news about local residents and businesses; and articles/columns on health, family, home, and quality of life. Business, arts and entertainment, and other special interest newspapers are published in many cities and regions.

Magazines
National magazines include general interest (e.g., *TV Guide*, *People*), news and business (e.g., *Time*, *Business Week*), and special interest (e.g., *Good Housekeeping*, *Vogue*, *Men's Health*). Some regional and local magazines are published for readers in a certain city or geographic region (*Rochester Business Journal*, *Colorado Parent*, *Arizona Senior World*). Special interest magazines are good outlets for personality profiles and feature articles on lifestyle, consumer, and business trends. Magazines plan and prepare editorial content several weeks to several months before publishing an issue.

Trade and Business-to-Business Publications
Trade newspapers and magazines are designed for people who work in a specific industry and who want to stay current with happenings in their industry (e.g., *Real Estate Executive*, *Modern Healthcare*, *Florida Farmer*). Trade media also target business professionals whose companies use products and services produced by a specific

continued . . .

Exhibit 5.1

Types of Media . . . *continued*

industry and are affected by changes in that industry (e.g., *Electronic Buyers' News*, *Pollution Equipment News*). Content includes articles on industry trends, information on new products and services, and employee and business news relating to specific companies serving that industry. These publications generally circulate on a weekly, biweekly, and monthly basis.

Radio

Radio stations may be in local markets that broadcast local newscasts and talk/public service programming, as well as national networks, such as CBS and National Public Radio. Radio reaches people at all times of the day and in more places than most other media. Targeting radio is a good way to get your messages to specific groups of people, especially in local markets. Top 40 stations' primary listeners are teens and young adults, while an all-news-and-talk station will appeal more to older adults and professionals.

Television

Television stations also are in local markets, as well as national networks, such as FOX, ABC, and ESPN. Television, while it can and does target specific audiences, has the main benefit of reaching large numbers of people. According to The Nielsen Company, the average American home has 2.5 people and 2.8 televisions sets, and the average American watches TV for 127 hours and 15 minutes per month. Television presents opportunities for national and local news exposure. National and network television exposure is difficult to secure; unless your story is of major significance to a national audience, or highly unusual or controversial, it probably won't make it onto a network news broadcast.

Cable

Hundreds of cable television channels are now available. According to Nielsen, the average American home receives nearly 119 channels. Creative public relations practitioners target cable TV networks that focus on a defined public with an interest in travel, cooking, golf, or any number of specialized subjects. In addition to the wide array of national cable networks, local cable networks feature news, public affairs, and other interview-type programs on issues affecting a particular community and look to area organizations for sources and guests.

Online Publications

A growing number of Americans are turning to the Web for news and other information. According to The Pew Research Center for the People and the Press, the number of Americans who say they get news online at least three days a week has increased 6% since 2006, from 31% to 37%. Many daily newspapers, magazines, and other publications have online versions. E-commerce businesses, consumer product companies, health and trade associations, and other organizations produce online newsletters targeting a variety of special interests. Online newsletters are included as a link within Web sites and are e-mailed directly to interested consumers upon request.

Blogs

In addition to online publications, blogs are rapidly increasing in popularity. Technorati, a search engine for blogs, reports it has indexed 133 million blog records since 2002. While the number of blogs is increasing as this chapter is being written, the actual number of influential blogs is relatively low. Identifying bloggers who cover your industry and starting a conversation with them can be a highly effective way to get out your organization's message.

What information do I have, and what facts do I need? Jot down anything you already know about the subject. Include any details provided by the person who assigned the writing project. The, draw up a list of questions that will produce additional information you need, keeping in mind the purpose of your written piece and the public(s) for which you are writing.

Let's say you are an intern in a corporate communications department. You are asked to write an article about a new vice president. Your supervisor tells you the piece will be published in the next issue of the company newsletter. At that moment, upon receiving the assignment, there are some key questions you should ask:

- How long should the piece be, in total words or pages (e.g., 500 words or two pages double-spaced)?
- What is the preferred tone of the piece—a straightforward news approach announcing this vice president has joined the staff, or a human-interest piece focusing more on the person?
- Do you have any materials that would help me get started, such as a résumé?
- What is my deadline, and who will need to review and approve the article draft? (Note: Your copy will most often have to be reviewed by someone else, especially when writing about a specific person who wants to see the piece before it's published. Or, as a matter of professional courtesy, you might offer to let someone take a look at your draft. Rewriting could be necessary, as well. You should typically build enough time for review, approvals, and rewrites into the writing process in order to meet your deadline.)

Once you get the answers to these questions, you can begin the research process by making some preliminary notes. You know the vice president's name and title, his phone number, and e-mail address. You know he started two weeks ago and which division of the company he will head. Your boss told you that the new vice president came to your company from another Fortune 500 firm. That's about all you know.

Now, you make a list of questions to get additional facts for your story. You need more specifics about the vice president's background and experience. A résumé will provide some information, but you will need to talk directly with the vice president to get interesting quotes and more detail to fill out the article. You want to get a sense of the vice president's strengths, expertise, and business philosophies. This information will help build employee confidence in his managerial abilities. Some specific questions to ask:

- How has the managerial experience gained in previous jobs prepared you for your position with this company?
- Why did you decide to make the move to this firm? What attracted you to this company and to the division head post?
- What are your goals as division head, and how do you plan to achieve them?
- What personal and professional qualities do you bring to this position that will help you do an effective job?

You could get personal information about the vice president's family and hobbies, if this kind of material is appropriate for the "new executive" articles published in the newsletter.

There are times when much of the information you need is supplied primarily by talking with one source or maybe two, like in the previous example involving the new company vice president. But in other instances, you need to use different methods and consult a variety of sources, such as those reviewed in chapter 4, to get all the facts. The trick, many times, is to use those methods and sources that will produce the greatest results in the shortest period of time, and do so cost-effectively.

The Planning Outline

A planning outline will help you take all the information you have gathered thus far and organize it to help you develop the most effective, appropriate message.[1] It is especially helpful when constructing persuasive messages that require greater insight into your publics.

Type of Project

Identify the type of piece are you writing. Is it a news release? A letter to the editor? A brochure?

Situation

As mentioned earlier in this chapter, identifying why you are writing a piece is the first question you should ask yourself when you begin the planning process. Is the company celebrating an anniversary? Is the company launching a new product? Are you advocating a cause? Write a brief answer to that question here.

Objectives

As part of the planning process, you should have already set objectives for your public relations program. You can use those here or create objectives specifically for the writing piece; however, be sure that all objectives are aligned and lead to your campaign goal(s). For example, an overall campaign objective may be to create awareness of a new product by 30% of your target public within three months. You could use the same objective for the writing piece, or, because awareness starts with exposure, a related objective for a news release would be to garner 500,000 media impressions. Most campaigns have a mix of awareness-, acceptance-, and action-based objectives. That's because you must make people aware of something before they can express an interest in it and, ultimately, act upon it. A smart public relations practitioner ties awareness-based goals to action-based goals that contribute to the "bottom line."

The types of objective you have chosen also will identify the type of message you will need to send to your publics. While awareness-based objectives generally require only factual messages, acceptance-based and action-based objectives require persuasive content.

Target Public(s)

Your target publics should already be identified as part of the program planning process. List them here and be as specific as possible. Listing "residents of Atlanta" or "men and women between 18 and 65" is not sufficient. The more specific you can be, the better you will be able to conduct the next step—analyzing what motivates them.

WIN Analysis of Key Public(s)

WIN stands for wants, interests, and needs. What makes your target public "tick"? What prompts them to buy a product? What issues are they concerned about? This analysis often begins by looking at Abraham Maslow's hierarchy of needs. Maslow theorized that humans are motivated by certain desires that are achieved in order of the most basic to the most complex. The five stages of the hierarchy, starting with the most basic, are: (1) physiological, which involves needs such as food, water, and sleep; (2) safety, which involves financial security and health; (3) social, which includes love and belonging; (4) esteem, which includes confidence and respect; and (5) self-actualization, which includes creativity and morality.

In an age when the average person is exposed to hundreds, if not thousands, of commercial messages a day, analyzing your target publics in order to develop a highly persuasive message aimed at their self-interest will help you cut through the clutter.

Specific Appeal(s) to be Used

In *The Art of Rhetoric*, Aristotle proposed three modes of persuasion: (1) *logos*, appeals based on logic and reason, such as facts, statistics, and scientific evidence; (2) *pathos*, appeals based on emotion, such as love, patriotism, and fear; and (3) *ethos*, appeals based on the credibility of the message source.

All messages should include logos appeals; many will require pathos appeals, especially if you are trying to persuade your target public. Behavioral research has shown that communication is more persuasive when using a blend of rational and emotional messages. This research also shows that messages are more effective when they are sent by a source that is perceived by the receiver as trustworthy and credible.

When planning your message, think about the types of appeal that will persuade and motivate your public. This is why you conducted the WIN analysis in the previous step—it will help lead you in the right direction. It will also help you identify the most effective message sources—who to quote in a news release or who to have sign the letter for the fundraising drive.

Core Message

The core message is the main idea you want to communicate to your public. It will evolve from the WIN analysis, along with the logos and pathos appeals you have identified. The core message states why your message is important to the publics; in other words, what's in it for them?

Communication Channel

As mentioned previously, it is important during the planning stage to consider how your message will be distributed. The communication channel you choose will depend on what is appropriate for the specific piece you are writing. For example, media alerts go to the media, but brochures go to customer publics. The channel also depends on the preferences of your public and the best way to reach them, which can be discovered through the WIN analysis.

Evaluation Methods

As mentioned in chapter 3, evaluation is not an afterthought. You must consider how your program will be measured as part of the planning process. Chapter 14 outlines the various ways to evaluate results of a public relations plan. You can also use these tools to evaluate your writing piece.

The most important part of identifying evaluation methods is to make sure those you select are actually measuring the objectives you set. For example, if you set an acceptance-based objective aimed at changing attitudes, you will need to conduct a survey; changes in attitude can't be measured by how many hits you received on your Web site. You also need to make sure your evaluation methods are consistent with the communication channel you selected. You can't use media exposure as an evaluation tool if you aren't using the media to communicate your message.

Exhibit 5.2 shows a fictional planning sheet based on the 2008 PRSA Silver Anvil Award case "Inspired by Diabetes: How are you inspired?"; a blank planning sheet that can be copied and used for writing projects is located in Appendix A.

Exhibit 5.2
Planning Outline

Type of Project:
News release

Situation:
Eli Lilly & Company has created an art competition to allow people with diabetes to express how it impacts and inspires them on a daily basis.

Objectives:
Awareness:	Secure 75 million media impressions through national and local media coverage during campaign.
Acceptance:	Attract 7,500 unique visitors to InspiredbyDiabetes.com during year one of the campaign.
Action:	Secure 500 entries into the Creative Expression Competition.

Target Public(s):
Families with children or adults with diabetes

WIN Analysis of Target Public(s):
People, in general, want:
- to be able to express their creativity
- to be respected by others
- to gain the self-esteem that comes from achievement

People with chronic illnesses are concerned about their health

continued . . .

Exhibit 5.2

Planning Outline . . . *continued*

People with diabetes who have hands-on support and motivation between doctor visits achieve better health outcomes

People with chronic illness respond positively to creative and personal story-telling

---

Specific Appeal(s) to be Used:
Logos: Global and U.S. statistics on diabetes, contest criteria
Pathos: Self-expression, health, meaning
Ethos: American Idol finalist Elliott Yamin, who has type 1 diabetes

---

Core Message:
Inspired by Diabetes is a global campaign asking people moved by the triumphs and challenges of those with diabetes and those who care for them to express their inspiration and share it with others around the world.

Communication Channel:
Traditional/new media (national and global)

Evaluation Methods:
Awareness: Measure media impressions
Acceptance: Check Web site data
Action: Count number of submissions

ASSIGNMENTS

Assignment 5.1—A Controversial Media Interview

It's late on a Saturday afternoon, and you're checking e-mail on your iPhone. You see that you've been copied on a message from your boss, the dean of a major college that has a worldwide reputation for its academic programs and research focused on workplace issues. Among the college's specializations are labor–management relations, unions and collective bargaining, and human resources. You recently joined the college as public relations director.

The message relates to a request for an expert from your college to appear on *The Other Evening News*, a major cable television talk program hosted by a well-known comedian known for his satirical look at news, politics, and the world. The show has heavy viewership by males 18–40.

The show's producers have invited a senior faculty member from your college to appear on the show and talk about the recent writers' strike that has affected the entertainment and television industry, including the show in question. Writers are currently in the process of negotiating a new contract, but the discussions have been moving slowly. The show in question has made the decision to resume production without its writing team. On the first show to air since the strike began, the host wants to interview an expert about the strike, talk generally about how strike negotiations work, and get opinions about possible outcomes of the talks.

In the message, Gary Holloway, the senior faculty member invited to appear on the show, has let the dean know about it and asked for the dean's opinion as to whether he should accept the offer to be on the show. He says in his e-mail message that, while he understands the issues this may raise with college labor faculty and even some alumni who work in the labor relations field—especially since he would have to cross a picket line to enter the studio where the interview will be taped—he believes that their primary role as academics is to share information and help the public understand situations like this one, and not really to take sides on the issue. The dean agrees and gives his blessing to appear on the show.

As public relations director, you have some concerns about this interview. Since you are just learning about it and have few other details about the media opportunity based on the information shared in the e-mail message, you decide to call Holloway.

"Hi Gary, I just saw your e-mail exchange about the media interview you're considering about the writers' strike. I thought it might be helpful to talk through some of the issues before we agree to anything."

Holloway says, "Well, the fact is, I've already committed to do the interview. It tapes Tuesday at 6 p.m. As I told the dean, I think it's okay for us to do this. It's not our job to be pro-union or pro-management, but to be educators and help provide insight that informs the discussion more broadly. There is an element of academic freedom at play here. The college today takes a broad look at work and problems like this that affect workplace relationships, so it seems fitting that we talk about this subject.

"Okay, I understand that, but I think there might be some push-back from some of our faculty and some of our alumni. I'm thinking about someone like Robert Infanger. Not only is he a high-ranking labor leader, but he's one of our alumni board members. I suspect that people like Bob, and some of our other alums who are pretty high-profile, will probably not share your point of view, especially since you have to cross a picket line to do the interview."

"I thought about that and I decided to reach out to Bob," Holloway says. "We talked by phone about an hour ago. While he wasn't thrilled about the decision, and can't feel comfortable supporting it, he did understand my point about the role we should be playing as educators, and how it relates in this case. I assured him that I'm not planning to go on the air and take sides, or to make a joke out of this situation, since the host, being a comedian, might try to get me to do that. The dean and I talked this through, and we both agree on the approach. This is really a chance for us to help people understand how these bargaining situations work, and where both sides—labor and management—fit in, and to get some national exposure for the college at the same time."

You add, "It might be a good idea for us to map out some strategy and to think a bit more carefully about all of this. I'm all for getting great media coverage—this is a major placement on a top talk show—but I want to be sure we're covering all the bases and helping our major stakeholders understand what we're doing and why."

Exercises

1. Would you recommend that this interview proceed as planned, or should you call the show and tell them you can't participate? Justify your decision.

2. Assume that the interview will take place. You decide that a plan is needed to communicate this decision to key publics. Draft a plan to include: (1) a brief summary of

the situation and the public relations issues that need to be addressed; (2) goals, publics you need to reach, and the key messages to be communicated to those publics; (4) communications methods to be used; and (5) timing (when should specific actions take place).

3. Use the planning outline in Exhibit 5.2 to map out a plan for an internal e-mail message for faculty and staff (this should be listed as the "Type of Project"). The e-mail will be sent by the dean announcing this decision and that the interview will take place.

Assignment 5.2—Recruiting PRSSA Members

Founded in 1968, the Public Relations Student Society of America (PRSSA) is the pre-professional, student counterpart of the PRSA; PRSA is the world's largest association for public relations professionals. PRSSA helps prepare students for membership in the professional society and, more generally, for successful public relations careers by providing career development activities as well as networking opportunities with practicing public relations professionals. PRSSA members pay annual dues that entitle them to receive PRSA and PRSSA publications, reduced conference rates, and a reduced PRSA associate member rate upon graduation.

Your college's PRSSA chapter has been active for many years. The chapter sponsors several guest speakers and panel discussions on public relations and career topics throughout the year, and operates a public relations firm that provides services to various campus groups. For example, the firm handles publicity of concerts, films, and other student entertainment sponsored by the college's Student Activities Office and programming board. On occasion, the chapter assists nonprofit groups in the community with the planning of fundraising events and public service campaigns.

Like many other PRSSA chapters, your chapter has been struggling to recruit new members. As a member of the chapter's board, you meet with your faculty advisor, Kendra Williams, to talk more about the situation.

"This just seems to be an ongoing problem," you say. "Every year, we get a pretty good turn-out at the first organizational meeting of the semester, but as the year goes on, attendance at the meetings drops off. A small group of members are very active and do most of the work."

"That's usually the case, even with some of the professional chapters," Williams says. "It's hard to get people involved, especially when they have such busy schedules. I know, in the past, I've heard students say they don't have time to be involved, when they're juggling full course loads and one, or even two, part-time jobs."

"We hear that a lot, and that people don't want to pay the dues," you say. They don't really see how the money they pay leads to any direct benefits. I know that I've met a lot of people through PRSSA, and my involvement helped me get that internship last summer at the PR firm in New York City. Somehow, we need to get the message across that being in PRSSA is a good investment for people, but I'm not sure we've figured out yet how to do that."

Williams says, "Why don't we reach out to members and prospective members and find out exactly what they're thinking and what might be holding people back from joining the chapter. It might be that some students don't even know what PRSSA is, or that we have a chapter here. We just assume that the right people would know that, but it's not always the case."

Exercises

1. Identify current members and nonmembers of the PRSSA chapter at your college or university. Conduct interviews with current members to better determine why they joined PRSSA and the benefits they get from membership. Interview nonmembers to find out what they know, or don't know, about PRSSA and to gauge their interests and perceptions. (Note: Your instructor might want to organize this research effort and make specific assignments to student teams in the class, to avoid duplication.) Once the interviews are completed, summarize the key findings in a written report and share those with the other students in the class.

2. Based on the collective research findings, create a public relations campaign for PRSSA. Your plan should include: (1) goals and objectives; (2) publics to be targeted and the messages you will want to communicate to those publics; (3) proposed strategies and tactics (include any timing considerations, such as when you might want to kick off your campaign or execute specific activities); (4) budget (your instructor might want to give you a budget total to work with and that should not be exceeded); and (5) evaluation methods.

Assignment 5.3 — *The Virtual Volunteering Campaign*

More and more not-for-profit agencies, schools, and other organizations that rely on volunteer support are getting involved in virtual volunteering, also known as online volunteering or cyber service. Virtual volunteers use the Internet, or a home or work computer, to complete a wide range of volunteer assignments. This is a convenient alternative to traditional volunteering since it allows people who have time constraints to volunteer and make a difference without having to leave their homes or offices.

Virtual volunteering projects generally fall into one of two categories: technical assistance or direct contact. Technical assistance includes projects such as doing Internet research to help an agency gather information for a newsletter or a grant proposal, using desktop publishing to design a publication, or providing online consulting. Direct contact might involve establishing an e-mail relationship with a homebound individual, offering online instruction to help high school students with their homework questions, or staffing a chat room that gives advice and support to people with problems or questions (similar to a telephone hot line). Virtual volunteers often combine these online activities with onsite or face-to-face contact.

The Volunteer Center in your community wants to draw more attention to virtual volunteering. Funded primarily by individuals, businesses, and private foundations, The Volunteer Center is a nonprofit agency whose primary mission is to promote increased volunteerism and help local agencies fill their volunteer needs. Agencies with virtual or other volunteer assignments can list those positions with the Volunteer Center, which then does outreach to recruit community-wide volunteers. In essence, the center helps agencies extend their individual volunteer recruitment efforts.

You have begun a public relations internship with The Volunteer Center, and the center's director has asked you to help execute a campaign to better inform people in the area about virtual volunteering and its benefits, with an ultimate goal of recruiting more virtual volunteers. Your first assignment is to prepare public relations tools that target two specific audiences.

"Obviously, there are lots of different people using computers today, but we've identified two primary target groups," the director tells you. "One is busy executives and professionals in the 30-to-50 age range. Across the community, this is an age group where the number of volunteers is somewhat low; our research shows that virtual volunteering might be a way to get more of them to volunteer. We're also looking at the college and higher education community, not just students but faculty and staff, too. A majority of this audience is using computers and the Internet almost every day, and has become comfortable with the technology. This has the potential to be an excellent pool of virtual volunteers."

Exercise

Conduct additional research and gather facts and information to help you shape messages for a public relations campaign aimed at building awareness of virtual volunteering and recruiting more virtual volunteers. In a written report, summarize your research findings. Based on those findings, and using techniques described in this chapter, craft messages that you think should be directed to the target publics identified in this assignment. Also, recommend for each target public no more than two or three communications/public relations activities or tools that you think would be most effective for delivering your messages, and justify your choices. ∎

Note

1. Ronald Smith proposes a multi-part planning sheet in his book, *Becoming a Public Relations Writer*, upon which this outline is loosely based.

References and Suggested Reading

Aristotle (1992). *The art of rhetoric* (H. Lawson-Tancred, trans.). New York: Penguin Group.

Inspired by diabetes: How are you inspired? (2008). Program nomination submitted to PRSA Silver Anvil Awards. New York.

Inspired by diabetes Web site (2008). Retrieved November 19, 2008, from http://www.inspiredbydiabetes. com.

Key news audiences now blend online and traditional sources (2008). Retrieved November 19, 2008, from http://people-press.org/report/444/news-media.

Maslow, A. H. (1943). A theory of human motivation. *Pyschological Review, 50*: 370–96.

Nielsen's three screen report (2008). Retrieved November 18, 2008, from http://www.nielsen.com/pdf/ 3_Screen_Report_May08_FINAL.pdf.

Rea, P. J., & Kerzner, H. (1997). *Strategic planning: A practical guide*. Hoboken, NJ: John Wiley & Sons.

Smith, R. (2002). *Strategic planning for public relations*. Mahwah, NJ: Lawrence Erlbaum Associates.

Smith, R. (2007). *Becoming a public relations writer* (3rd ed.). Mahwah, NJ: Lawrence Erlbaum Associates.

State of the blogosphere (2008). Retrieved November 19, 2008, from http://technorati.com/blogging/state-of-the-blogosphere/.

Wilson, L. (2002). *Strategic program planning for effective public relations campaigns* (3rd ed.). Dubuque, IA: Kendall/Hunt Publishing Company.

Part Four

EXECUTION

6

News Releases

When author Mark Twain was 74, newspapers published rumors that he had died. Advising the Associated Press that the stories of his death were false, Twain said, "The report of my death was an exaggeration . . . I would not do such a thing at my time of life." The news release hasn't died either, even though you might occasionally hear or read about how this tool has outlived its usefulness.

It is true that some news releases deserve a swift burial because they fail to report legitimate news, they don't get to the news until the fifth paragraph on a second page, or they are loaded with grand statements that hype an organization. You have to think like a journalist when identifying news subjects and preparing news releases, but that thinking has to be balanced with your responsibilities as a public relations professional to position your organization in the most positive way and to support business objectives.

In *PR Week*'s 2008 Media Survey, journalists said they get nearly 73% of their information about a company from news releases. Public relations professionals succeed at placing news releases when they write about newsworthy subjects, create headlines and leads that get the media's attention and content that meets journalistic standards, consider timing issues and emphasize local angles, and select the best means of distribution.

Types of News Release

Take a look at the following headlines:

- Coors Elects Two New Board Members, Announces Quarterly Dividend
- Mattel Announces Disaster Relief Support for China and Myanmar
- Papa John's Receives Highest Customer Satisfaction Rating among National Pizza Chains for Ninth Consecutive Year
- Kellogg Acquires Specialty Cereals Pty Limited, a Leading Natural Cereal Manufacturer in Australia
- JCPenney Recalls Arizona® Newborn and Infant Pants Due to Choking Hazard

These headlines are taken from actual news releases sent out by each of the companies identified. They illustrate the variety of news announcements that organizations make through news releases. These announcements can be grouped into three main categories:

- *Routine news events*, such as staff hirings and promotions, staff appointments to boards of community and professional organizations, meetings and seminars held by clubs and organizations, and reports of quarterly company earnings.
- *Significant, one-time news events*, such as the launch of new products or services, expansions or mergers, company and employee awards and distinctions, and charitable activities such as community fundraising events and monetary donations to the arts, education, or other worthy causes.
- *"Bad news" events* such as product recalls, work force reductions and plant closings, environmental spills and other accidents, and responses to activists.

Components

The physical format of your news releases may vary depending on how they will be distributed. News releases for print, broadcast, and the Internet are laid out differently (this will be discussed later in this chapter). Regardless of their final destination, however, the components and writing style are basically the same.

News releases are straightforward and should be printed on company letterhead. Stay away from decorative paper and fancy typefaces. Indent paragraphs, use 1½- to double-line spacing, and make margins at least 1 inch to allow editors to make notes on the release.

News releases have an identifiable format. They include the name, organization, and phone number of a contact person, usually the public relations person, who can be reached for more information. *Contact information* is often included at the top of the release, although e-mail news releases and releases posted on Web sites usually include contacts at the bottom so that the reader can get to the news right away.

Releases should also include *release information* to let the media know when the material may be published. Many releases carry the line "For Immediate Release" near the top of the page and above the headline. In addition to the release date, include the date that the release is being distributed to the media.

As the previous examples show, always begin your news release with a concise and informative *headline* that summarizes the story in a way that will get an editor's attention. Understand that many of the headlines you write will not appear in print as you've written them. Their primary purpose is to help media quickly determine the news value of your story. The Papa John's headline—Papa John's Receives Highest Customer Satisfaction Rating among National Pizza Chains for Ninth Consecutive Year—effectively conveys the main news point. In addition, the headline gives extra weight to the story by noting that this is a national story. (For more on good headline writing, see Exhibit 6.1.)

A point-of-origin *dateline* appears at the start of the first sentence of releases sent out regionally and nationally. The dateline notes the city, and in most cases the state, from which the news originates. The *AP Stylebook* includes a detailed list of how datelines should appear. The date that the release is being distributed may appear beside the dateline or above the headline.

Exhibit 6.1

Tips for Writing News Release Headlines

- Keep your headline crisp and clear, about 8–12 words. It's okay to be creative, but don't sacrifice clarity for cleverness. The headline should get the point across quickly. You can use bold type or underscore the headline to make it stand out.

- Always include an active verb (e.g., "announces," "launches," "introduces," "names," "awards," "presents").

- If something is "first," "new," or unusual in another way (and you can prove it), say so in the headline. Be careful with the word "unique." It is difficult to back up such a claim, and the word itself can be a turn-off.

- Emphasize the local angle. Stories about a "local businessperson," a "community" event, or "area residents" should use words and phrases like those in the headline. Remember to be specific about the area you are talking about, however. "Local" means different things to different people.

- Appeal to the special interests of editors and your target audience. A news release headline for a new weight loss product sent to health/fitness publications could include words and phrases such as "dieters," "healthy lifestyle," and "fat burning."

- Consider using a subhead that expands on the main headline by singling out a key aspect of the story. This can help the receiver size up the news value even more quickly and further entice her to keep reading.

If your release is two pages, make sure the word "more" appears at the bottom of the first page (do try, however, to keep news releases as short as possible). In the top left corner of the second page, include a *slug*—a few words that summarize the story, along with the page number. End the release with "30" or "###" so editors know there are no additional pages.

Body of the Release

The body of the news release should be structured using the ***inverted pyramid style***, with the most important facts presented in the first few paragraphs (the news summary) and supporting details in later paragraphs. Write the release so the first two or three paragraphs can stand alone and tell the story. The first paragraph, known as the ***news lead***, describes the news focus of the release and why the information is important. The next one or two paragraphs include details—who, what, where, how, and when. Subsequent information is then included to complement and expand on the facts already provided. Conclude the release by describing the organization. Statements at the end of the release that attempt to wrap up the story come off looking like the writer's opinions. Instead, include a summary paragraph or "***boilerplate***" that provides further background on the organization's history, mission, product line, and standing in the industry. Boilerplates should be used consistently and should not change too much from release to release.

Here are some additional pointers for writing body copy:

- Write short paragraphs, especially the first few paragraphs, and simple sentences. Limit paragraphs to a few sentences; three is okay for paragraphs that come later in the release, but keep the sentences short. Sentences should convey one thought at a time. Use commas sparingly.

- Avoid using adjectives (e.g., exciting, great, groundbreaking). News releases should be written objectively; if the product or event is newsworthy, it will sell itself. If the focus of the news release truly is "groundbreaking," write such subjective information as a quote.
- Don't use personal language. Avoid words such as "we," our," and "you."
- If your organization uses an acronym, spell it out on the first reference. For example, use Public Relations Society of America the first time and PRSA in subsequent references. There are exceptions to this rule, however, that are listed in the *AP Stylebook*.
- When mentioning people in the release, give their first and last names on the first reference, but only their last name thereafter. The last name can stand alone; you don't need to include courtesy titles such as "Mr." and "Ms." Also, don't forget to identify who the people are by including their titles.
- Use strong quotes. In addition to being good vehicles for including subjective information and opinions in an otherwise objective news release, quotes can increase the release's value. Many reporters like to get firsthand quotes from your sources; a quote within your release can let reporters know a credible source is available for comment. Take care in selecting the best person to deliver your message in the quote. This may be the CEO of your company, a customer, or a third party.

Quotes should neither rephrase facts that have already been presented, nor should they state the obvious. For example, don't use a quote to state "The festival will begin at 2 p.m." Instead, explain why people should attend the festival and what benefits they will receive by doing so. Strong quotes expand on facts by offering something new and by advancing the story. If a news release states that a company expansion will add 100 new jobs and help the area's economy, follow that statement with a quote from a company official that talks about the kinds of job being added and the company's opinions on what this growth means for the community and its future. Don't waste valuable space by quoting the company official as being "excited," "pleased," or "happy" about the company expansion. Think about it—if you weren't pleased and excited, would you be writing the release in the first place?

Leads

The lead, more than any other element of the release, is the key to the success of your news release. Editors and news directors at major media receive hundreds of news releases each day, so there isn't always time to read the complete release before deciding to keep it or dump it (another reason why releases are written in inverted pyramid style with the most important information at the top). A scan of the lead tells an editor right away if your news is relevant and worth publishing. In the Bennett & Company annual media survey, one journalist responded, "Write crisp leads that describe what you're writing about. If I want flowery, I'll go to a florist." It is essential, then, that the main news point is stated clearly in the lead paragraph.

The public relations writer's lead has subtle differences from that of the journalist's lead. Journalists are trained to write news leads that give the reader a sense of "who, what, when, where, why, and how." While that information should be included in the top half of a news release, such details seldom appear in the public relations writer's lead. Instead, the lead focuses on the most significant aspects of the story and carefully brings in a detail or two that has public relations value:

> Barnes & Noble, Inc. (NYSE: BKS), the world's largest bookstore, announced today the launch of the annual Barnes & Noble Holiday Book Drive taking place in stores across the country from November 1 to January 1. The Barnes & Noble Holiday Book Drive invites customers to share the joy of reading with children in need and donate books through locally designated nonprofit organizations. Many recipients are schools, libraries, literacy organizations, family social service agencies and homeless centers.

In this lead, Barnes & Noble notes its status in the industry, which is a common technique used by publicity writers. The journalist might leave out such a description in a first paragraph and choose to stress the charitable project over the company (e.g., "A new literacy campaign will share the joy of reading with children in need"). In addition, the campaign name might not be mentioned in the journalist's lead. Still, the public relations techniques used in this lead never overpower the key news point.

Other tips for writing good leads are:

- Keep it to one or two sentences, maybe a bit longer, if sentences are short and copy is lively and interesting to read. Leads that are too long risk burying the news in unnecessary detail.
- Use active voice. Writing "XYZ Company named a new chief financial officer this afternoon" sounds more current than writing "A new chief financial officer was named today by XYZ Company." You can't always avoid the less-active verb form, especially if your release announces something that happened a few days ago. In those cases, use the present perfect tense and avoid mentioning the "day" the event took place: "The XYZ Company announces that Kim Behrens has been named chief financial officer." Or, even more active, "Kim Behrens is the new chief financial officer for The XYZ Company, a leading U.S. manufacturer of . . ."
- Tailor the style of your lead to the story subject. A *straight* or *hard lead* works best for announcements of staff appointments and other hard news:

> Mattel announced today it will provide more than $125,000 in immediate and long-term disaster relief to support victims of the devastating earthquake in Sichuan province of China and the aftermath of Cyclone Nargis in southwest Myanmar.

For other subjects, write *interest* or *feature leads* that are softer, less straightforward, and more creative in their approach. An example:

> Summer is around the corner and with warm weather comes all kinds of tough stains. From dirt and grass stains on baseball uniforms to greasy food stains like barbeque, hamburgers and hot

dogs that have a way of ending up on clothes in the kitchen or during picnics, don't let stains spoil the fun. Tide introduces Tide® with Dawn® StainScrubbers™, a new detergent that helps remove tough stains—including greasy food stains—better than the next leading competitive detergent plus pre-treater combined.

Instead of starting the release with "Tide is introducing a new detergent to help remove tough stains," a rather dry lead approach, the writer brings in a timely hook and focuses first on using familiar references that may encourage the editor to read on and help to build interest in the story.

The following feature lead demonstrates how a company can design a news release around consumer research and a major holiday to gain publicity:

Still searching for that perfect Father's Day gift? Don't make Dad suffer through another year of misfit Father's Day gifts like bad ties and craft projects gone wrong; a fun, reasonably priced gift is at hand. In a recent survey conducted by eRewards on behalf of Blockbuster Inc., 85% of dads said they would be excited about receiving a favorite movie as a Father's Day gift, and 92% said watching movies is a good way to spend time with family.

- Avoid starting with a preposition or a quote. Prepositional phrases such as "At a ceremony held at city hall" or "After a meeting to discuss board policy" delay the news. Instead of beginning your release with a direct quote, paraphrase for better style. Consider the following:

  > "Present market conditions are continuing to erode prices and it is not likely that OPEC will be able to change the current trend. There is, therefore, a good chance that the price of gasoline and heating oil may drop by 5 to 10 cents a gallon by the end of the year." This statement was made by Mr. John G. Buckley, vice president, Northeast Petroleum Corporation, during a speech today at the spring convention of the Empire State Petroleum Association in Ellenville, N.Y.

This lead has some good qualities. It shares a main idea from the speech rather than stating, "John G. Buckley gave a speech today . . .", and it summarizes the key facts of the story in a few sentences. It is long, however, and the most newsworthy element is mentioned in the second sentence of the quote. A stronger lead is:

A New York state petroleum executive said today that gasoline and heating oil prices may drop 5 to 10 cents a gallon by next year. John G. Buckley, vice president of Northeast Petroleum Corporation, made this prediction at the spring convention of . . .

The revised lead deletes details that are better mentioned in a second and third paragraph. Notice how moving the speaker's name and title to the second sentence simplifies the lead without reducing its news value, and that the lead is now active, not passive. Exhibit 6.2 offers additional lead-writing guidelines.

Exhibit 6.2

Lead with Your Best Stuff: Adding Value to News Release Leads

The lead of a news release should do more than simply summarize the story. Before writing the lead, you need to begin by sizing up the **news value** of the story. Ask yourself, why is this newsworthy?

For example, a grocery store chain in a northeastern city decides to launch a unique program with local police in an effort to get handguns off the street. Each person who turns in a handgun during a designated two-week period will get $50 worth of free groceries from the store. This story has news value for several reasons: it involves two major **local** organizations; it is **unusual** in that the chain has never taken part in a program like this and because it is not a typical community outreach program for a grocery store; it is **significant** because it has the potential to greatly **impact** the community by reducing crime; and it is **timely** because the program responds to a sharp increase in drive-by shootings in that city in recent months.

Once news value has been determined, decide on the best **news angle**. What will the focus or slant of the story be? What information needs to be played up to hook the media and convince them that the story has value? Consider the "local" and "unusual" aspects of the story:

Two local organizations—starting an innovative new crime prevention program—that involves giving free groceries to area residents who turn in handguns.

The news angle then lays the groundwork for your news lead. But try to write your lead so that it gets the main news point across in an interesting and creative way:

A major supermarket chain is joining with local police to launch an unusual program aimed at taking a bite out of crime—exchanging guns for groceries.

Localizing

Each release you write should have "local" interest. An old adage among reporters and editors is that "news is only news when it's local." Simply put, newspaper editors want to know how your story affects people who live in their city or area. Trade magazines want news that is relevant to people who work in a certain industry. *Localizing* is a technique that allows you to increase the number of media placements for a single news announcement. You do this by creating multiple versions of a news release, with each version emphasizing local points of interest for media serving specific geographic areas or populations. This may entail simply rewording the lead. An illustration:

Cobb Medical Center, one of the largest health care facilities in the Midwest, today named Roberta Brown as its chief executive officer.

This is a lead for the version of this news release sent to media in the city where Cobb is located and hospital trade media. But the creative public relations writer knows that localizing this release makes it possible to extend coverage significantly. By raising a few questions about Brown's background, the writer creates several local angles. One localized version is the *hometown release* sent to the media in the town or city where Brown grew up:

Former Cleveland Resident Assumes Top Hospital Post

Roberta Brown, a native of Cleveland, has been named chief executive officer of Cobb Medical Center, one of the largest health care facilities in the Midwest.

This new version of the release, written exclusively for Cleveland media, highlights Brown's connection to that area in the headline and the lead. If Brown held previous positions in Cleveland, has parents still living in that area, or has achieved some distinction while living there, those facts can be included in the release as well. Publications produced by colleges that Brown attended and by professional associations she holds membership in are other targets for localized releases.

Keep in mind that all localized versions of news releases include much of the same information. Local information is always stated at the beginning of the release. After the lead,

Exhibit 6.3

Working with Local Media: Bigger is Not Always Better

You've been asked to publicize something in a local market. Your first instinct might be to send publicity materials to the daily newspapers or local television stations in that city or area. While the daily newspaper or television news broadcasts in a local market reach thousands of people and promise widespread message exposure, they may not provide the most effective channels for reaching specific populations in that community. Consider some of the specialized media in a local market that can help you get messages more directly to niche groups and result in publicity efforts with greater impact:

Newsletters
Professional and business organizations, churches, and other community groups typically produce newsletters or bulletins for their members, and may be receptive to publishing your publicity material if it is relevant to their readers.

Local television and radio talk shows
Some markets have locally produced talk and public affairs programs that air on cable access and local public television stations. Some local radio stations, especially those with all-news and talk formats, feature local programming or call-in shows on issues affecting the community.

Special interest newspapers
Most cities have weekly or hometown newspapers that publish news geared to residents of specific towns and suburbs. In addition to business newspapers and arts and entertainment publications, you also can find specialized newspapers targeted to parents, African Americans, and other ethnic groups. Many of these smaller publications may even reprint your news release or publish your photo "as is."

High school and college media
Many publish daily or weekly newspapers and some operate radio stations that have a loyal listener base in that community. These media provide an excellent way to reach students, teachers, administrators, and school staff, as well as other community residents.

sprinkle other local facts throughout the rest of the release, where appropriate. Any release on Brown's new position would give more details about her duties, her previous positions within the hospital and other related jobs, background on the center, and possibly a quote from her or the head of the hospital board on her appointment.

National companies get better media coverage when they localize. If a company is introducing a product nationwide, it can localize the news for media in a specific city by having a dealer in that area make the announcement. Organizations can also get local coverage by connecting themselves and their executives to national trends:

> The U.S. Center for Disease Control and Prevention says some flu medications may be forming a resistance to certain strains. The pharmacists at Riverside Neighborhood Pharmacy say they have seen an increase in calls from customers wanting to know about alternative remedies.

Exhibit 6.3 offers additional information on working with local media.

Formats

There are three basic physical formats for news releases: ***traditional print***, ***broadcast***, and ***social media***. Traditional print news releases are the most common and include all the features discussed so far (see Exhibits 6.4–6.6 for strong examples). Broadcast and social media news releases require different formats, however.

Broadcast Print Releases

Generally, the news release you write for print media is suitable for broadcast media. Television and radio news staffs, for the most part, aren't looking to use your material word for word. Your release is a starting point from which to develop and write their own story using their own reporter. There are times, however, when it is preferable to write a news release specifically for broadcast. If a major story breaks at 5 p.m., writing a shorter broadcast-version of your print news release makes it easier to get the news on the air without much copy revision.

Broadcast media contacts, like their counterparts in print, have certain expectations of public relations materials. News releases must be newsworthy, accurate, clear, and written in simple language. The newspaper editor who finds value in your news release might assign a reporter who does further interviews, adds detail, and produces a half-page article. A television news story on the same subject, however, may last only a half a minute. Broadcast news stories don't have the luxury of space or time, so they need to emphasize the key facts and leave out much of the detail seen in print articles.

Broadcast writing and print media writing differ somewhat in their style and approach. Broadcast writers have to consider how words will sound and blend with visual images. What are the characteristics of good broadcast news writing?

- Don't lead with the hard news. Instead, write what is referred to as a ***soft*** or ***throwaway lead*** (similar to a feature lead) that will attract the listener's attention, but not provide important details that can be missed during the first few seconds of an aired story.

Exhibit 6.4

Traditional News Release: UPS

UPS Pressroom

❌Close Window

The UPS Foundation Awards $1 Million to Environmental Groups

New Environmental Initiative Is Launched

ATLANTA, Oct. 14, 2008 - The UPS Foundation, the charitable arm of UPS [NYSE: UPS], today announced five grants totaling more than $1 million to support a variety of environmental programs and organizations worldwide.

The grants, which include funds for planting trees, conservation, youth education and volunteerism, reflect the establishment of environmental stewardship as a new focus area by the Foundation.

The new grant awards include:

- $300,000 to The Nature Conservancy to assist with tree-planting efforts in the Atlantic Forest of Brazil, conservation initiatives for rural residents in the Yunnan Forest in China and reforestation efforts in East Africa's Highland Forest.

- $300,000 to the Earth Day Network to support its national civic engagement project to educate youth about environmental issues and provide teachers with lesson plans and environmental impact online tools.

- $220,000 to Keep America Beautiful (KAB) to support its environmental education initiatives, including the creation of KAB affiliates on college campuses, support for a community volunteer initiative, a challenge grant for KAB affiliates and an environmental partnership grant for UPS Global Volunteer Month to encourage employee participation.

- $200,000 to the National Park Foundation to fund youth-engagement programs, including First Bloom, which provides children in urban locations (grades 4 through 6) with hands-on environmental learning.

- $50,000 to the Arbor Day Foundation to plant one tree for each of the first 50,000 UPS customers to begin using UPS electronic billing solutions, which eliminate the need for paper invoices.

At the beginning of 2008, The UPS Foundation adopted a new global philanthropic strategy to strengthen its impact and better leverage UPS's capabilities. In addition to the new environmental sustainability focus area, the Foundation's other focus areas include community safety, non-profit effectiveness, economic and global literacy and diversity.

"Protecting the environment is increasingly important to our company, to our customers, our employees and the communities in which we operate around the world, so it is a natural fit for The UPS Foundation," said Lisa Hamilton, president of The UPS Foundation. "We are proud to partner with each of these esteemed organizations and to support the important work of nurturing our planet."

Founded in 1951, The UPS Foundation has a tradition of providing support through grant programs and initiatives that help improve the quality of life in communities where UPS employees live and work. Last year, the Foundation donated nearly $46 million to charitable organizations worldwide. For more information on the Foundation, visit community.ups.com.

UPS (NYSE: UPS) is the world's largest package delivery company and a global leader in supply chain and freight services. With more than a century of experience in transportation and logistics, UPS is a leading global trade expert equipped with a broad portfolio of solutions. Headquartered in Atlanta, Ga., UPS serves more than 200 countries and territories worldwide. The company can be found on the Web at UPS.com. To get UPS news direct, visit pressroom.ups.com/RSS.

# # #

For more information, contact:

Rebecca Treacy-Lenda
404-828-8396

Note: Courtesy of UPS

Exhibit 6.5

Traditional News Release: Travelers

News Release

<< Back

Travelers Risk Control Launches Improved Web Site

Enhanced Web site features industry-specific TravSourcesSM

SAINT PAUL, Minn.--(BUSINESS WIRE)--Feb. 16, 2009-- Today, Travelers (NYSE: TRV) launches an enhanced Risk Control Web site offering customers and agents easier access to industry-specific risk management tools. New Web site features include Web-based Industry TravSources[SM] and improved search functionality, among others.

With the availability of TravSources, Risk Control's essential collection of safety and risk management resources in the Risk Control Customer Portal, customers will now be able to take advantage of helpful risk management guides, sample safety programs and training that can help reduce exposures and potential loss. TravSources are currently available for specific industries including manufacturing, construction, restaurants, auto dealerships, educational institutions, technology and the printing industry. Travelers will be adding additional industry-specific resources throughout the year.

"TravSources offer our customers industry-specific resources that can help manage unique industry risks, while providing valuable information on emerging issues, major loss drivers and exposures," said Marty Henry, vice president of Travelers Risk Control. "Our customers will benefit by having this relevant information aggregated into one area."

Each TravSources collection consists of a risk profile summarizing the industry's major loss drivers and exposures, and organizes relevant resources by category. Categories include business continuity, driver & vehicle safety, employee safety & health, general liability, post-injury management, product safety, professional liability, property/facility management and safety administration.

continued . . .

Exhibit 6.5

Traditional News Release: Travelers ... *continued*

In addition to aggregating helpful resources by topic, the improved Risk Control site also offers customers the opportunity to download materials or save them to the "Add to Favorites" section for easy bookmarking and future reference. The *Special Features* boxes highlight popular Risk Control products, newsworthy topics, emerging issues as well as external Web links to government and trade association sites.

For ease of use in finding information or materials, customers can now take advantage of an advanced, easy-to-use search function for more targeted search results. Policyholders have exclusive access to more than 1,500 tools and resources that can be sorted quickly by category, topic, product type, language or any customized combination.

To access the new features and enhancements, visit travelers.com/riskcontrol and log in to the Risk Control Customer Portal.

About Travelers

The Travelers Companies, Inc. (NYSE: TRV) is a leading property casualty insurer selling primarily through independent agents and brokers. Travelers understands that life and business are inherently dynamic and that the best way to serve customers is to deliver insurance in-synch with evolving risks. The company's diverse business lines offer its global customers a wide range of coverage in the auto, home and business settings. Travelers is a Fortune 100 company, with 2008 revenues of approximately $24 billion. The company has more than 33,000 employees. For more information on being in-synch, visit www.travelers.com.

Source: Travelers Companies, Inc.

Travelers Companies, Inc.
Jennifer Bagdade, 651-310-2883

Note: Courtesy of The Travelers Companies, Inc.

Exhibit 6.6

Traditional News Release: Cornell University's ILR School

Cornell University
ILR School

News Release

ILR's Employment and Disability Institute (EDI) awarded $5 million research grant
EDI will study transition of youth with disabilities from high school to work

For Immediate Release

Contact: David Brewer, Cornell University ILR School/EDI
drb22@cornell.edu, 607.254.4696

(Ithaca, New York) – Helping high-school students with disabilities move successfully into good jobs and go on to college poses special challenges for educators and disability professionals across New York state and the country. Cornell University's School of Industrial and Labor Relations' (ILR) Employment and Disability Institute (EDI) will partner with New York state on a five-year, $5.1 million research study to identify best practices that can help improve the transition process and inform state and national policy.

EDI received the $5.1 million research grant from The New York State Education Department's Vocational and Educational Services for Individuals with Disabilities (VESID). The study will examine the services provided by 60 schools in rural, suburban, and metropolitan districts across the state to youth with disabilities as they transition from high school to work, higher education, and community living.

The study also will evaluate the ways in which these schools collaborate with rehabilitation providers, assisted living facilities, and other community agencies to support transitions. VESID is providing funding to these schools through its Model Transition Project to help stimulate school-agency collaborations and provide more school-to-work transition services.

"Too many youth with disabilities are not accessing the vocational rehabilitation system before they leave high school because they don't often see the benefits, or they are getting into the system too late, which negatively affects their success," says David Brewer, EDI program lead for this research study. "We expect our research findings to address these concerns and ultimately help increase their options for employment and secondary education, and help turn around the high rate of unemployment that people with disabilities experience."

Brewer adds that this contract is the result of a 16+ year relationship with the state education department and builds on past disability-related work that the ILR School has been doing. He says the state did not accept any other bids for this project and selected Cornell because it is uniquely positioned to do this kind of study.

-more-

Advancing the World of Work   **www.ilr.cornell.edu**

continued . . .

Exhibit 6.6

Traditional News Release: Cornell University's ILR School ... *continued*

EDI/VESID research, page 2

EDI is one of the leading institutes of its kind offering research, continuing education, and consulting to companies, labor organizations, government agencies, schools, and communities throughout the U.S. and the world to accommodate and integrate individuals with disabilities. The ILR School is recognized as the world's leading higher education institution for teaching, research, and outreach focused on advancing the world of work.

-30-

Note: Reprinted with permission of Cornell University's ILR School

For example, instead of leading with "A national report issued today says that the number of Americans considered morbidly obese has risen to 9 million," open with "Americans are losing their fight with the scale."

- Use simple, one subject-one verb sentences. Radio listeners and television viewers get one chance to hear and understand what you say. The longer the sentence, the more difficult that is to do. If you have the urge to use commas, your sentence is probably too long and should be broken into two shorter sentences.
- Try not to use "who, which, or where" clauses in the middle of sentences. It's okay to use short clauses at the end of sentences, but it still may be smoother to make the clause a second sentence.
- Write it like you'd say it. Broadcast writing is for the ear, not the eye. It sounds natural and reflects the way people talk in everyday conversation. Unlike traditional print releases, it is okay to use personal language in the broadcast format. Use contractions (I'm, you're), shorter sentences, and, at times, incomplete statements without a subject or verb to express thoughts. There is one exception to the rule, however. Do not use "doesn't" for "does not" or "aren't" for "are not." If listeners don't hear the "t" sound in the contraction, the meaning of the word changes and then alters the story content.
- Keep the verbs active. This rule applies to all good writing, but broadcast media are more immediate than print.
- Attribute up front. Articles in print often note sources at the end of sentences. Broadcast writers tend to identify the source at the start of a sentence, often by title on a first reference. Again, this is more natural sounding since, in conversation, you would say "the director said," not "said the director."
- Spell out numbers and hard-to-pronounce words. Put *pronouncers* (phonetic spellings) of unusual or unfamiliar names in your scripts. You can spell out unfamiliar words but, if they are that unfamiliar, they shouldn't be in your script at all. Exhibit 6.7 lists some of the most common pronouncers.
- Package the message in broadcast style. Type the release using all capital letters, double space between lines, and don't use hyphens to split words at the end of a sentence nor split up a sentence if a second page is necessary.

Exhibit 6.7

Associated Press Pronouncer Guide

Pronouncers are used as phonetic guidelines for reading broadcast copy. They should be used with foreign phrases, unusual names and words, and familiar spellings that are pronounced differently than usual. Pronouncers are placed in parentheses immediately behind the word to which they apply. Using the Associated Press guidelines below, spell the word the way it should sound in lower case letters. Use hyphens to separate the syllables and write the accented syllable(s) in all capital letters.

Here are some examples:

The French phrase for "without worry"—sans souci (SAHN-soo-CEE)

The abbreviation for the State University of New York—SUNY (SOO-nee)

A different spelling of a common surname—Smyth (SMITH)

Vowels	Consonants		
a	bat, apple	g	got, beg
ah	father, arm	j	job, gem
aw	raw, board	k	keep, cap
ay	fate, ace	ch	chair, butcher
e, eh	bed	sh	shut, fashion
ee	feel, tea	ch	vision, mirage
i, ih	pin, middle	th	thin, math
oh	go, oval	kh	guttural, k
oo	food, two		
ow	scout, crowd		
oy	boy, join		
u	curl, foot		
uh	puff		
y, eye	ice, time, guide		
yoo	fume, few		

Note: Reprinted with permission of The Associated Press

Broadcast releases tailored for radio are often called radio news releases, or RNRs; those tailored for television are called video news releases, or VNRs.

Radio News Releases

RNRs vary in length—usually 30- or 60-seconds long—based on the preference of the radio stations to which they are being sent. However, they always include three components: a brief lead that introduces the subject and the spokesperson; the spokesperson's taped comments, which are called actualities or sound bites; and a closing that highlights a key aspect of the subject. Because the taped comments are in the middle, radio news releases are sometimes called "donuts." The length of actualities has become shorter through the years. Most stations prefer them to be 8 to 12 seconds long.

RNRs should avoid promotional language and only mention the sponsoring organization once or twice. While you can have the spokesperson read a prepared script, this is not advisable. It is best to conduct a face-to-face interview to ensure getting sound bites that sound natural and similar to those you would hear in broadcast news stories.

Video News Releases

For television, taped interviews can be combined with interesting visuals in a VNR. VNRs are produced to help companies get widespread exposure for themselves and their people, products, and services. But they cannot be TV commercials. Instead, they must present the company's key message in a more subtle way. VNRs can be produced in a variety of lengths, although 90 seconds is the most popular. They are mailed to newsrooms in videotape format or delivered by satellite. A single VNR can cost thousands of dollars, so you need to think carefully about some critical questions before starting production:

- Does the VNR have mass appeal? VNRs target a wide audience with information of general interest. If the target public is more narrowly defined, a VNR is probably not the best tool. VNRs on health, entertainment, technology, new products, food, and fashion are popular with television news producers.
- Is there a news hook, and are there credible sources and strong visuals? VNRs that feature comments from third-party sources—experts and specialists not affiliated with your company—may have more credibility; however, it is wise to position the organization's representatives as the experts, especially when the producer of the VNR is spending so much money to develop and distribute it. When you can, include footage that the media would otherwise have difficulty getting, and keep visuals of company logos or products to a bare minimum.
- Have we assembled a complete package? In addition to the fully produced VNR (also referred to as "a-roll"), include scripts written in broadcast-style separate sound bites and "b-roll." B-roll is the raw footage—just the visuals—with natural sound and no voice-over. Because of its flexibility, b-roll is becoming the favored format over the already-assembled VNR; if news producers want to use the story, but not in its entirety, they can read some of the script and use a sound bite, or they can show several seconds of the b-roll while an anchor reads an edited portion of the copy. Adding a Spanish version or sound bite to the package is a good idea, depending on the subject.
- How will we evaluate? You can hire a video clipping service, or use Nielsen Research's SIGMA electronic tracking system. VNR tapes are encoded with SIGMA, which can provide data on stations that used the spot, date and time of usage, total viewing audience, and how much of the encoded video was used.

When a nationwide hoax fostered reports of syringes found in cans of Diet Pepsi®, the soda company relied on b-roll as a major component of its crisis response plan. Shortly after the first news report (the story would lead newcasts for four days), the FDA conducted an exhaustive inspection of Pepsi's manufacturing procedures and ruled out any internal tampering. In an effort to capitalize on the FDA's report and calm the public's fears, Pepsi went inside one of its bottling facilities and videotaped the canning process footage, to show the close-to-impossible likelihood of internal tampering occurring during the bottling process. The footage was beamed by satellite to hundreds of television stations across the country and viewed by 296 million people.

While VNRs and other packaged video tools can be used effectively by public relations practitioners, they are not without controversy. VNRs were introduced at a time when newsrooms were being downsized; reporters turned to the ready-to-go stories as a convenient source of news, which led to the following questions:

- Is it appropriate for a VNR to appear in a newscast with the news station's logo superimposed?
- Should a VNR be aired without identifying the organization that produced it?
- How credible are the sources of VNRs and the footage in them?

NBC Nightly News once ran a story on the environmental dangers of logging in Idaho's Clearwater National Forest. The story included footage of dead fish in a stream—a stream that was actually located 400 miles away. An environmental group dedicated to ending logging of ancient forests on public land had given the tape to NBC.

Social Media Releases

The newest format of news release is the social media release, which combines the traditional print release with the multimedia opportunities that the Internet offers. The new format is somewhat controversial: some practitioners swear they are the wave of the future, while others believe they are an unnecessary fad. At the heart of the controversy seems to be the following question: "Why do we need the new format?" Are we using it to supplement the traditional print news release? Are we trying to make it convenient for media and customers to do "one-stop shopping" by providing information and multimedia in one place? Or are we experimenting with the format because the Internet is public relations' new playground? Probably all three.

SHIFT Communications, a public relations firm with offices in Boston and San Francisco, introduced the social media release in 2006 to, as it said, "evolve traditional press release formats for the dawning Social Media age." The template, which has become known as SMR v1.0 (social media release version 1), intrigued many public relations practitioners. Edelman, the world's largest independent public relations firm, soon introduced its own version. In a news release announcing Web-based software for producing social media releases, Edelman said, "The social media news release is a next-generation news release that combines traditional and emerging forms of communications." In 2008, SHIFT Communications announced its next generation of the social media release, SMR v. 1.5 (see Exhibit 6.8).

Exhibit 6.8

Social Media Release: Template

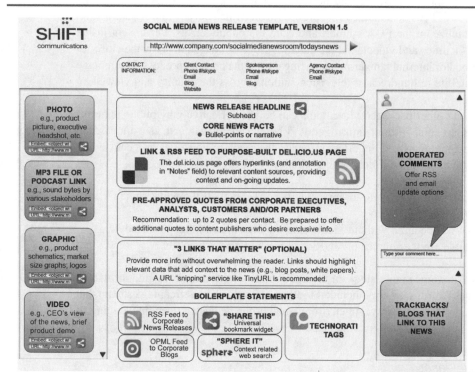

Note: Courtesy of Todd Defren, principal, SHIFT Communications

There are several main differences between a traditional media release and a social media release:

- The main content of the news release still follows the inverted pyramid style; however, bullets are used to list the facts, rather than the information being put in paragraph form. In addition, quotes and the boilerplate are listed under their own headings, rather than being part of the core news facts.
- Multimedia are used generously. Seventy percent of the journalists responding to the Bennett & Company survey said that they rely heavily on visuals. This may include logos, photos, graphics, and videos, as well as MP3s, and podcasts.
- Links are provided to make it easy for readers to access additional information or to share the news. These may include hyperlinks to relevant content sources, links to articles that have already been written on the news release topic, or links to social networking sites where information is posted and shared.

Exhibit 6.9 shows how the social media release template translates into an actual news release.

Exhibit 6.9

Social Media Release: SHIFT Communications

> 66 *SHIFT's eager can-do attitude & unique approach to media relations has resulted in great success to date. They know when a pitch works & when to adapt while always keeping the brand characteristics & core values in mind. SHIFT is strategic, passionate, fun & overall a great agency partner.* 99
>
> *Kate Laufer, senior PR manager, North America, Beam Global Spirits & Wine*

www.shiftcomm.com

News

CONTACT INFORMATION:

Parry Headrick
415.591.8402 office
415.246.8486 cell
pheadrick@shiftcomm.com
www.shiftcomm.com

PR Agency SHIFT Communications Tapped by Canadian Club and DeKuyper to Invigorate Brands with Social Media Strategies

October 27, 2008

NEWS FACTS

- SHIFT Communications announced today that it has been selected as the Consumer PR Agency of Record for Canadian Club®, the third-best-selling Canadian whisky in the world. SHIFT is also working on a project with DeKuyper®, the nation's top-selling line of cordials, to launch its Burst™ Bar Shots line.

- Both brands operate under the flagship of Beam Global Wine & Spirits, Inc. the fourth largest premium spirits company in the world, with nine of the world's top-100 premium spirits in its portfolio and approximately $2.5 billion in revenue.

- The SHIFT team will focus on increasing brand visibility by providing strategic counsel, Social Media consulting and aggressive media relations execution.

Please use this link to access a purpose-built del.icio.us page for more information about SHIFT Communications.

MULTIMEDIA ELEMENTS:

Download SHIFT   Download Canadian Club logo   Download DeKuyperlogo
Communications logo

QUOTES

- "Consumers operate under a completely different set of rules when it comes to sharing their product experiences, and SHIFT Communications understands these rules. It's an exciting time for both brands, between Canadian Club's 150th anniversary and the launch of Burst Bar Shots for DeKuyper. Working with SHIFT has given us an agency partner with the ability to dive in and meet a variety of needs—both traditional and non-traditional. SHIFT is strategic, passionate, fun and overall a great agency partner."
-- Kate Laufer, Sr. PR Manager, North America, Beam Global Wine & Spirits

continued . . .

Exhibit 6.9

Social Media Release: SHIFT Communications . . . *continued*

- "**Damn right** it's great to work with brands you're already familiar with and – in the case of Canadian Club and DeKuyper – enjoy responsibly. Large consumer brands are discovering that the conversations their customers have with one another directly correlates to their growth and reputation. We're looking forward to guiding these beloved brands through that process."
  -- **Todd Defren**, a principal at SHIFT Communications - click for **Defren's** LinkedIn profile)

Please contact **Parry Headrick** to arrange an interview and/or for additional quotes.

ABOUT BEAM GLOBAL SPIRITS & WINE

Inspiring conversations around the world, Beam Global Spirits & Wine, Inc., is building brands people want to talk about. Consumers from all corners of the globe call for our brands, including Jim Beam® Bourbon, Sauza® Tequila, Canadian Club® Whisky, Courvoisier® Cognac, Maker's Mark® Bourbon, Cruzan® Rum, Laphroaig® Scotch Whisky, Larios® Gin, Whisky DYC®, Teacher's® Scotch Whisky, DeKuyper® Cordials and Liqueurs, Knob Creek® Bourbon and Starbucks™ Liqueurs. Beam Global Spirits & Wine, Inc. is part of Fortune Brands, Inc. (NYSE:FO), a leading consumer brands company with annual sales exceeding $8 billion. For more information on Beam Global Spirits & Wine, its brands, and its commitment to social responsibility, please visit **www.beamglobal.com** and **www.drinksmart.com**.

ABOUT SHIFT COMMUNICATIONS

SHIFT Communications is an award-winning, privately-held national PR agency representing some of the best-known **high-tech and consumer technology brands**, including Akamai, Beam Global Wine & Spirits, Quantum, RealNetworks and Novartis. SHIFT pioneered the world's first **Social Media News Release** and **Social Media Newsroom**, changing PR forever. SHIFT Communications' 100+ employees are located in the **Boston** and **San Francisco**. For more information on SHIFT's high-tech public relations and consumer public relations services, visit **http://www.shiftcomm.com**.

`Add to del.icio.us`

`Digg this`

TECHNORATI TAGS:

SHIFT Communications | pr | public relations

SHIFT Communications is an award-winning, privately-held national public relations firm representing some of the best-known **high-tech and consumer technology brands**, including **Akamai, Novell, Quantum, RealNetworks** and **Shimano**. SHIFT pioneered the world's first **Social Media News Release** and **Social Media Newsroom**, changing PR forever. SHIFT Communications' 100+ employees are located in **Boston** and **San Francisco**. For more information on SHIFT's high-tech public relations and consumer public relations, visit **http://www.shiftcomm.com**

Full-Service PR | Media Relations | High Technology PR | Consumer PR
SHIFT LeadSensor | Blog Consulting | No Hype Policy

Site Map
©2008 SHIFT Communications, LLC. All rights reserved.

Note: Courtesy of Todd Defren, principal, SHIFT Communications

---

Because social media releases are distributed and housed on the Internet, it is important to make it as easy as possible for people to find them when conducting a search. Use popular keywords in the headline and lead. When selecting search phrases, keep in mind that half of all searches contain two or three words. Web sites such as wordtracker.com provide research on the most popular keywords. Keyword density, the number of times a keyword or phrase appears per block of text, also plays a factor in search results. Free keyword density calculators can be found on the Internet.

Timing

"It's all in the timing" is an expression that definitely applies to news releases. Your challenge is to stay on top of your organization's news and to share it with the media when it happens.

Daily newspapers are interested in "today" and "yesterday," broadcast media think about "this morning" and "this afternoon," and online media can report news minutes after it happens. You have a little more flexibility with trade publications and magazines that circulate less frequently. Whatever the case, the more recent or timely your development is, the more interest the media will have in it.

Many releases indicate they are "For Immediate Release," but, in reality, most releases should be written for immediate publication. There are occasions when an organization embargoes distribution of material. An *embargo* is a restriction that asks the media to hold information for release until a designated date. For example, companies officially launching a new product at a media event on a specific day establish embargoes with trade publications interested in writing about the product. Because many trade publications come out only once a month, providing information in advance helps them develop in-depth stories that can be published at the same time as those in daily or weekly newspapers. This gives everyone with an interest in the story an even news break.

Publicists sending out information about new CDs and upcoming films embargo with the media to time the release of information so that it coincides with the first day the CD goes on sale or with the motion picture's premiere. Embargoes are reserved for special situations like these, and should not be abused. Once media agree to an embargo, it is unethical for you to give a publication permission to publish before the embargo date. This does serious damage to media relationships.

Finally, know your media's deadlines. With the exception of hard news, daily newspapers usually want news releases on community events at least two weeks in advance. Special sections and Sunday editions have distinct deadlines, too. You need to get news releases to monthly trade and consumer publications at least a month or two in advance of the desired publication date. Depending on the publication, it could be several months in advance. Call the media you deal with and ask about deadlines before sending your releases.

Distribution

It's not just what your release says, but how you get it into the media's hands, that can make all the difference. Before sending a news release, become familiar with the existing media outlets that reach your target audiences and that cover your industry, and the communities your organization serves. Prepare and regularly update a list of print, broadcast, and online media and include the names of key reporters and editors working for those media. Know the news release subjects they are interested in, and stay aware of the kinds of in-depth story they like to publish and air that might spin off from a news release you send.

Much of the publicity you do will target radio and television news operations in local markets. Radio and television stations in cities large and small across the country have their own news departments, and they are often looking for news and human-interest stories for their newscasts. Public relations professionals primarily work with broadcast media assignment editors, who decide what stories are covered and assign stories to reporters each day (media alerts are generally sent to assignment editors; more on media alerts in chapter 7)); news directors, who oversee the entire news operation and are the primary contacts for setting up editorial meetings; and reporters, who cover specific beats and subjects and can be pitched directly with story ideas.

Check with your media contacts and honor their preferences for receiving news releases. In the Bennett & Company media survey, 91% of the journalists surveyed said they prefer to be contacted by e-mail. This was confirmed by the *PR Week* survey. When journalists were asked how they gather information about a company, nearly 71% answered "conversation or personal e-mail from a PR contact at the company," while nearly 50% answered "newswires."

Sometimes, the situation can dictate the method of delivery. A local company with news regarding a serious or emergency situation would probably use e-mail, text messaging, fax, a Web site, and maybe a quickly organized news conference to get the word out. If a situation has an immediate effect on many people in a large geographic area, or if a story has national interest, electronic distribution by a newswire and satellite delivery are efficient methods. The format of the news release may also dictate how it is distributed. Because of the large amount of disk space social media releases take up, they are difficult to send via e-mail. They are also more expensive to distribute through a newswire than sending a traditional print release.

Although the preference of receiving information via e-mail has steadily increased in recent years, give careful consideration to e-mail news release distribution. As mentioned before, never send information to media contacts by e-mail without first knowing their preferences. Include a strong subject line and headline to quickly convey the news aspect of the release, and make sure all the necessary contact information is provided.

Avoid mass mailing your e-mail releases. Editors may not even look at your release if the heading shows that the same copy went to 20 other editors at the same time, or if it is accompanied by a large attachment that wasn't requested. In fact, you should avoid attachments altogether. They may automatically be deleted by filters on the recipient's computer and, even if they aren't, many people don't open attachments owing to potential viruses. It is preferable to cut and paste the release into the body of the e-mail. You may also choose to write the information as a news summary (the beginning of a news release that contains the essential information) or as a fact sheet (who, what, where, etc.) and direct the receiver to a Web site that has the full text of the release in a traditional and/or social media release format.

ASSIGNMENTS

Assignment 6.1—The New Basketball Coach

Three months ago, Felice Shofar, head women's basketball coach at Metro College, resigned her position in a brief written statement without citing a reason for leaving. Luke Hammer, 48, a former quarterback with the Chicago Bears and currently the athletic director at Metro, immediately started a search for a new coach at the undergraduate, coed, four-year college located in Metropolis, IL, a city of 175,000.

The Metro search committee, chaired by Hammer, received and screened a total of 110 applications. Metropolis invited five of the applicants to the college for interviews and offered the position to Lucinda Smart earlier this week. Smart accepted the coaching position. She is the first African-American to coach the women's team at Metro.

You are the sports information director at Metro. For the past 10 years, the college's Division III women's basketball team has been nationally ranked and participated in four national tournaments, reaching the semifinals twice and winning the national titles last year. The *Metropolis Evening Sun* has given extensive coverage to the women's team—far better coverage than it has given to the men's team, which has had a losing record for 8 of the past 10 years. So, you know the local media will be interested in this story, and you begin work on a news release announcing that Smart has been hired. After receiving Smart's résumé from Hammer, you pull out the following details about her background:

Education: Joplin High School, Joplin, MO; BA Anthropology, Loyola, Chicago; MS Sports Management, College of the Hills, Forest Ridge, Pennsylvania.

Experience: Two years, assistant store manager, J.C. Penney's department store, Joplin, MO; three years, center, Women's All-Star Hoopsters touring team; two years, assistant basketball coach, College of the Hills.

In addition, you find out the following personal information: Age, 30; parents: Mr. and Mrs. Charles Smart, 2 Cedar Lane, Joplin; born and grew up in Joplin; single; one child, Peter, age 3.

You call Hammer to make a last minute check of details. He tells you that Smart's salary will be in the $70–80K range. You also learn in that conversation that Felice Shofar is now head basketball coach at a Division I university.

"I think I have most of the information I need, but I'd like to include a quote from you in the release."

"Sure," Hammer says. "Use this: 'We feel fortunate to be able to secure a person who is so highly qualified to lead our outstanding girls' basketball team. We expect great things from Cindy Smart, and we know she'll deliver the goods.'"

Exercises

1. Write a news release to be e-mailed to the *Metropolis Evening Sun*. Indicate that it is "For Immediate Release."

2. Write a news release for distribution to the Joplin media.

3. Write news releases for alumni publications produced by College of the Hills and Loyola.

Assignment 6.2—*Growing a Department Store Chain*

Coastal Department Stores, Inc., is a leading national retailer operating four regional department store chains throughout the country, mainly in the East and Midwest. In a move to broaden its reach, Coastal will soon be acquiring The Putnam Company. Putnam owns and operates Jordan's, one of the country's best known and oldest department store chains.

Most Jordan's stores are located in major cities including New York; Chicago; Washington, DC; and Boston.

You work for a public relations firm in its retail division, primarily handling media relations work. Coastal is one of your agency's accounts. Your supervisor calls a meeting with you and other members of the Coastal account team to discuss some big changes.

"You've probably been hearing some things about Coastal and some of its future plans. I just came from a meeting with some Coastal senior VPs, and they've announced their plans to move ahead with the acquisition of The Putnam Company. Coastal will pay about $10 billion for the acquisition and assume about $2 billion of Putnam's debt. Putnam recently opened 20 or so new Jordan's stores in the South and West, and in some larger secondary markets, but earnings from those stores did not meet financial expectations. That's where most of the debt is coming from."

You ask, "Does this mean, then, that Coastal will be taking over all the Jordan's stores? Coastal has a lot of its own department stores, so I'm guessing that some of those might carry the Jordan's name after this deal goes through?"

"Yes, that's pretty much what will happen with the four chains Coastal now operates, but there will be enough time to make the transition and ease the consumer into the change. Some of Coastal's department stores have strong brand recognition and loyalty, so there's real concern about changing the name and helping customers see that the quality and service they're used to won't change. In fact, it stands to improve with the strength of the Jordan's name and brand."

"I know that when these buyouts occur, sometimes there's an effort to refresh or even change an existing public image, or to make other changes that set them up to go after new audiences," you say. "Is that happening with Coastal and Jordan's?"

"Yes. Many of Coastal's regional department stores do well now, especially with housewares and kids clothing, but with this plan, Coastal's putting much more emphasis on women's and men's clothing and fashion, and bringing in more designer labels and names to attract a more upscale audience. Coastal's and Jordan's research has been showing that there is a fairly sizeable customer base who come into the stores and want to see more selection in clothing and cosmetics, not just their store brands and a designer name here or there, but more designer labels, like Calvin Klein and Kenneth Cole for men, and Donna Karan for women. And, they have the kind of discretionary income to purchase these brands. Everyone sees this as an opportunity to go more 'up market' and create a more upscale image for Jordan's."

"When is all this going to happen?" you ask. We'll probably be handling the media and press on this announcement, so it would be good to know the timing."

"Most of Coastal's stores will convert to the Jordan's name within a year. They'll also be freshening up the design of the stores to create a more contemporary, upscale look. You're right, they've asked us to write the initial media announcement about the acquisition and get that out to the right media fairly soon. There will certainly be more to do with media and around store opening events, and we'll need to do some planning and make some recommendations, but let's get started on this first news release to announce the buyout."

Exercise

Write two versions of a news release announcing Coastal's acquisition of The Putnam Company:

- a general release for distribution to business editors;
- a release for distribution to editors/media covering fashion and beauty.

Assignment 6.3—Announcing a Product Recall

Founded in 1940, the Play-Well Company has established a reputation as one of the leading manufacturers of quality toys and games for toddlers and children. Its product line includes items such as musical and crib toys for newborns, as well as a variety of preschool games and educational toys for children age 5 and older. One of Play-Well's most popular toys is Zoomers, a brand of battery-operated cars and vehicles that is designed for children to ride on sidewalks, grass, and hard surfaces. There are dozens of models, from motorcycles to trucks, for use by children 2 to 7 years old. Vehicle speeds range from 1 to 5 miles per hour.

Recently, Play-Well and the U.S. Consumer Product Safety Commission (CPSC) received complaints from parents and consumers about Zoomers. There have been 800 reports that the vehicles' electrical components have malfunctioned and overheated, not only when cars are being ridden, but also when they are simply parked or stored in the garage or home. A dozen children have suffered minor burns to the hands, legs, and feet, and 100 fires have been reported. Some homeowners have experienced property damage to houses and garages due to the fires, totaling $250,000.

After careful and quick deliberation, and with public safety as the top priority, Play-Well decides to conduct a voluntary recall of Zoomers products. You are asked to write the news release announcing the recall and schedule a meeting with Michael Hayes, vice president of consumer relations, to get more details.

"We need to move quickly on this recall and let people know right away which vehicles are affected and what they should be doing now to protect themselves and their kids," Hayes says. "We're working closely with the CPSC on this, as well."

"So, are we talking about recalling all Zoomers or just certain models?"

"The recall does not include any sold before November 2008, only those sold after that time. Still, that's a lot of Zoomers that could be affected, and you know that there are many model names, so this could get confusing. We're setting up an 800 number for people to call, or they can log on to our company Web site and find out if their model is being recalled. The company will make every effort to help consumers identify if their model needs repairs," Hayes says.

"Now, one of the reports I read did say that all models with two batteries are being recalled, so we need to make that point. We can also tell people to look for model names on each vehicle. I'm assuming that we also want to tell parents that they should disable the cars immediately and not let their kids use the vehicles until any repairs have been made."

"To go back to your first point, we are recalling all the models with two batteries, but some one-battery models are affected, too, so we need to make sure people know that," Hayes says. "And yes, stress that batteries should be removed immediately, and that consumers should contact a service center to schedule repairs. The service centers will install new electrical parts free of charge and do free safety checkups. Repairs can be scheduled by calling the 800-ZOOMERS number, or someone can go to the Web site, www.zoomers.com, and get a list of service centers in their area."

"That sounds good," you say. "I think I have enough information to draft the release. I know that legal and other senior people will need to look this over before it goes out, so I'll get started on this right away and have something to you in an hour or so."

Exercise

Write a news release to announce the Zoomers product recall for national distribution through PR Newswire.

References and Suggested Reading

Andrews, R., Biggs, M., & Seidel, M. (Eds.). (1990). *The Columbia world book of quotations.* New York: Columbia University Press.

Aronson, M., Spetner, D., & Ames, C. (2007). *The public relations writer's handbook* (2nd ed.). San Francisco: Jossey-Bass.

Barnes & Noble customers share the gift of literacy through annual holiday book drive (2008). Retrieved December 31, 2008 from http://www.barnesandnobleinc.com/press_releases/2008_october_27_hbd.html.

Bliss, E., & Hoyt, J. (1994). *Writing news for broadcast* (3rd ed.). New York: Columbia University Press.

Borden, K. (2002). *Bulletproof news releases: Help at last for the publicity deficient* (2nd ed.). Marietta, GA: Franklin-Sarrett Publishers.

Boyd, A., Stewart, P., & Alexander, R. (2008). *Broadcast journalism: Techniques of radio and TV news* (6th ed.). Woburn, MA: Focal Press.

Brody, E.W., & Lattimore, D. L. (1990). *Public relations writing.* Westport, CT: Praeger Publishers.

Carroll, V. M. (1997). *Writing news for television: Style and format.* Ames, IA: Iowa State University Press.

Edelman introduces Web-based tool for publishing social media news releases (2006). Retrieved December 3, 2008 from http://www.edeman.com

Goldstein, N. (Ed.). (2007). *The Associated Press stylebook and briefing on media law* (Rev. and up.). Cambridge, MA: Perseus Publishing.

Kerchner, K. (2002). *Soundbites: A business guide to working with the media* (2nd ed.). Superior, WI: Savage Press.

MacDonald, R. H. (1994). *A broadcast news manual of style* (2nd ed.). New York: Longman.

McIntyre, C. V. (2008). *Writing effective news releases: How to get free publicity for yourself, your business, or your organization.* Colorado Springs, CO: Piccadilly Books.

Mattel announces disaster relief support for China and Myanmar (2008). Retrieved December 3, 2008 from http://investor.shareholder.com/mattel/releasedetail.cfm?ReleaseID=311701

Media Survey 2008 (2008). *PRWeek,* March 31, 2008.

New Tide® with Dawn® StainScrubbers™ gives laundry a boost to fight some of the summer's toughest greasy food stains (2008). Retrieved December 31, 2008 from http://www.pginvestor.com/phoenix.zhtml?c=104574&p=irol-newsArticle&ID=1136193&highlight=.

PR agency shift communications refines social media release template with conversation aggregator, more democratization (2008). Retrieved December 3, 2008 from http://www.shiftcomm.com/Web20Releases/5222008.html.

Public Service Advertising Research Center, www.psaresearch.com.

Ries, A., & Ries, L. (2004). *The fall of advertising and the rise of PR.* New York: HarperBusiness.

Stumped for a Father's Day gift? Dads reveal movies to make their day in survey from Blockbuster. (2008). Retrieved December 3, 2008 from http://www.blockbuster.com/corporate/newReleases.

Technology continues to change PR practices. (2007). Retrieved December 3, 2008 from http://www.bennettandco.com/enewsletter/Social%20Networks%20Final%20100507.pdf.

Van Nostran, W. J. (1999). *The media writer's guide: Writing for business and educational programming.* Woburn, MA: Focal Press.

7

Other Media Formats

Soccer superstar David Beckham and Secretary of State and former First Lady Hillary Clinton don't really have "bad hair days," at least not in the eyes of the media. "I have come to expect that if I have a new haircut, it's front page news," Beckham says. And this from Clinton on the subject: "If I want to knock a story off the front page, I just change my hairstyle."

Don't expect your media relations work to be that easy. With so many organizations, people, and events competing day-to-day for headlines, you can't rely on a name, status or personal grooming alone to guarantee media coverage. It's a good bet that, if your CEO gets a "new (hair) do," the media won't care.

The fact is, the media are not watching every move the average organization makes. Reporters don't just sit around waiting for your company or client to do something worth reporting, except maybe during times of crisis. In general, the media won't know about goings-on in your company unless you tell them. Most of the publicity you get for your organization will result from ideas you come up with and pro-actively present as potential story subjects (Exhibit 7.1).

As chapter 6 pointed out, news releases are generally used to announce company developments to the media. Besides writing and sending announcements, public relations professionals should also host events, suggest story ideas, make spokespersons available for interviews, and provide photo opportunities. Media alerts and media pitches are important tools in this strategic publicity process. This chapter provides information on the proper use of media alerts and media pitches, how to write them to get a positive response, and what to think about when creating publicity photos and writing photo captions.

Media Alerts

While news releases can provide a starting point for more in-depth stories, many times they give an editor enough information to be published as written, or in some slightly edited or expanded form. In essence, you have already prepared the story for them.

Media alerts have a different purpose. Their content is not intended for publication. Instead, media alerts introduce the media to a potential story and invite them to cover it. Also known

Exhibit 7.1

What's the Story? A Nose for News

Public relations professionals must size up the news value of potential stories before suggesting ideas to editors. One important question is, how **significant** is the story? Does it have a dramatic effect on people? If a company plans to create hundreds of new jobs, or if it plans to lay off people, those stories are significant and newsworthy. The media like **conflict**. So, if your organization gets into trouble, there will be reporters at your door, even if you don't want them there. The media will cover disasters, activist group protests, union disagreements, and other such stories without much prodding from you. But, most of the time, public relations professionals find themselves trying to interest editors and reporters in subjects that aren't as hard-hitting or controversial. In those cases, consider the following factors to get your organization "in the news":

- *Localizing*. One of the best ways to get your company in the news is to tie in to the day's national events. Invite the media to interview one of your organization's "experts" who can comment on a national story that is unfolding.

- *Prominence*. If you are planning a campaign or a special event, involve a famous person, if you can. Actors, politicians, and well-known athletes connect themselves to charitable causes, which helps increase media interest. Every community has its own local celebrities, too, from the mayor to the beloved quarterback of the college football team, who can enhance the media appeal of your public relations program.

- *Timeliness*. Try to get news out when it happens. Getting the media to cover something that happened a week or two ago is difficult. Major company anniversaries (10th, 20th, 25th, etc.) are an excellent time to talk about the company's history, its notable successes, and its vision for the future. Consult *Chase's Annual Events* to find out if there is a national day, week, or month celebrated that you can use to promote your organization. Also, connect with trends. If more people are choosing to participate in job-sharing, where two people work part-time and share the duties of one position, let the media know about your company's job-sharing program, the benefits of flexible work schedules, and how that flexibility is supporting work–life balance for employees while improving organizational productivity.

- *Human interest*. People like to read and hear about other interesting people, and the media like to write about those people and their personal stories. For example, many not-for-profit health agencies sponsor annual road races or walk-a-thons to raise money for medical research and programming. To keep the media interested, they suggest new feature stories each year about noteworthy people participating in the event. Maybe one year it's a story about a young person running the race whose parent is afflicted with the disease. During the 10th year of the fundraiser, the focus might be on a runner or volunteer who has been involved every year since the event began.

- *The strange and extraordinary*. Remarkable achievements and quirky situations hold interest for the media. A person who beats the odds, breaks a record, or does something exceptional is a good subject for an article. At graduation time, high schools and colleges get media exposure by focusing on a high school senior who had perfect attendance or a college student who overcame major obstacles to receive her degree. To introduce *Dawn Princess*, the twin sister ship of *Sun Princess*, Princess Cruises reunited the cast members of the popular 1970s television show *The Love Boat*. Princess sponsored a national search for look-alikes to the show's original cast members, reinforcing the "twins" theme of the campaign. A bit off the wall? Sure, but the unusual contest generated extensive media coverage and contributed to a highly successful *Dawn Princess* launch.

as media advisories, media alerts are written to entice the media to cover your news conference, special event, or company announcement. If editors and news directors consider your event or development worthwhile, they assign reporters to cover and write stories about it. For example, organizations send media alerts to get coverage of news conferences that focus on company expansions and other hard news announcements, and to get coverage of special events and ceremonies where a new product is unveiled, a person is honored for exceptional achievement, or a building is opened or dedicated.

Media alerts and news releases do share some common features. Both include contact information that identifies your organization and the name of a person (often the public relations person) who the media can get in touch with if there are questions, along with that person's e-mail address, office phone number, and, preferably, a mobile phone number. Media alerts should be brief; they are never more than one page. Content must be clear, well written, error-free and presented in AP style. Like news releases, media alerts are distributed by e-mail and the Internet, by fax, and, less frequently these days, by U.S. mail. The distribution method you choose should be based on individual media preferences—how would they like to receive your information—and the urgency of the news.

There is no "one way" to format a media alert, as evidenced by the varied examples in Exhibits 7.2–7.4. Some present information in a simple, easy-to-read "Who, What, When, and Where" format, while others are written in paragraph form. The information included in the media alert depends on the situation. For example, when inviting media to a photo opportunity, you will need to include enough information to "paint a picture" of the potential visuals. The media alert in Exhibit 7.2 does this well: ". . . the exhibit highlights the natural habitat of otters and includes naturalistic rockwork, a free-flowing stream with a waterfall and extensive landscaping." This example also:

- includes "Media Advisory" and "Photo Opportunity" at the top of the piece, as well as a strong headline in bold to catch the editor's attention;
- highlights the local angle of a bigger story in the headline and throughout the piece;
- offers notable points that establish the success, history, and credibility of the TV show host;
- provides background information on the TV show and the zoo exhibit.

While the amount of information in this example is appropriate for a photo opportunity, other situations, such as news conferences, will require far less detail. Media alerts announcing a news conference, as in Exhibit 7.3, should be brief and not "tell all." They should give just enough detail to indicate that the event is scheduled, what and who it involves, and where and when it is taking place. If your media alert contains too much detail, news staff may find it unnecessary to send reporters since you've already given them enough information to write the story. As a result, what could have been a longer story ends up as a news brief.

A note about media events: As news operations cut back on staff, reporters are being asked to do more and might not have two hours on a given day to attend your news event. You should only think about holding news conferences and briefings in those circumstances when you have a major announcement to make, in emergency situations where the media will probably be coming to you any way, or when providing access to a company official or well-known

Exhibit 7.2

Media Alert: SUNY Fredonia and Buffalo Zoo

MEDIA ADVISORY — PHOTO OPPORTUNITY

Buffalo Zoo and SUNY Fredonia Partner to Bring Kids TV Show to Buffalo
"AquaKids" Episode to Educate Children about River Otters

WHO: - Tiffany Vanderwerf, Buffalo Zoo Curator of Education;
- Molly McKinney, host of "AquaKids";
- AquaKids television production crew, including an "audience" of several children.

WHAT: The filming of an AquaKids episode focusing on marine life native to Western New York. The Buffalo Zoo appearance will focus on the recovery of river otters, which through conservation efforts have seen a population increase in the Western New York region.

WHERE: The Buffalo Zoo's Otter Creek Exhibit, 300 Parkside Avenue, Buffalo.

WHEN: Monday, April 21, 2:30 p.m.

OVERVIEW: Aqua Kids is dedicated to educating children about the conservation of marine environments and the animals that inhabit them. In its seventh year of existence, it is targeted to children ages 7-14 and seen in 85 percent of markets across the U.S.

Molly McKinney, a 22-year-old senior communication major at SUNY Fredonia, has worked on this show since age 13 and traveled throughout the United States, Central America and the Caribbean on filming excursions. Since coming to Fredonia she has worked with the communications and biology departments to continue her work with AquaKids, and is concluding her undergraduate career by leading an episode focused on marine life native to the Chautauqua and Buffalo-Niagara regions.

SUNY Fredonia and the Buffalo Zoo are partnering to help Molly and her team in the production of this episode, and to further promote the recovery efforts of marine species native to the region.

Otter Creek opened in 2004 under Phase One of the Zoo's master plan. Modeled after Letchworth State Park, the exhibit highlights the natural habitat of otters and includes naturalistic rockwork, a free-flowing stream with a waterfall and extensive landscaping. When developing the Zoo's master plan, Buffalo Zoo President/CEO, Dr. Donna M. Fernandes, chose to add this aquatic mammal not only because of its playful nature, but because of its relevance to Western New York as a conservation success story.

To attend, please enter the Zoo through the main gate located on Parkside Ave.

CONTACT: Michael Barone, Director of Public Relations, SUNY Fredonia
716-785-7702 (cell); 716-673-3323 (office); Michael.barone@fredonia.edu

Jennifer Fields, Buffalo Zoo Public Relations Coordinator
(716) 995-6129; jfields@buffalozoo.org

Note: Courtesy of Michael R. Barone, director of public relations, SUNY Fredonia,
and Jennifer Fields, public relations coordinator, Buffalo Zoo

Exhibit 7.3

Media Alert: Florida Atlantic University

MEDIA ADVISORY FAU to Name Head Men's Basketball Coach

Press Conference to be Held at 2 p.m.

May 27, 2008

BOCA RATON, FL - Craig Angelos, Florida Atlantic University's athletics director, will introduce the new men's basketball coach at a press conference scheduled for 2 p.m. on Tuesday, May 27, in the Tom Oxley Center's Founders' Lounge, located on the Boca Raton campus, 777 Glades Road, Boca Raton.

The new coach will assume the helm of a program that has compiled a 46-46 record over the last three seasons. During that same time, FAU joined the Sun Belt Conference, which featured two teams in the NCAA tournament, of which, one advanced to the Sweet 16.

He will inherit a team that will return the team's top three scorers, Carlos Monroe, Paul Graham III and Carderro Nwoji, as well as 80% of the team's offense from 2007-2008 and 69% of the team's rebounding efforts. FAU returns seven scholarship players and signed three players during the November signing period.

Craig Angelos will introduce the new men's basketball coach at 2 p.m.

A streaming video of the press conference will also be available following the event at www.fausports.com.

Note: Courtesy of Nick Mirkovich

Exhibit 7.4

Media Alert: Multisorb

Media Advisory

WHAT: Opportunity to meet with Multisorb Executives at IFT 2007

WHERE: McCormick Place South, Chicago, IL Booth # 1972

WHEN: July 28-August 1, 10:00 a.m. to 5:00 p.m.

Multisorb Technologies, the leading provider of advanced active packaging solutions, invites you to meet with executives to find out more about their current product innovations and services.

Visitors to the Multisorb booth will learn how the company's moisture management technology is enabling food manufacturers to take advantage of the increasing demand for "clean label" products. Technical experts will be on hand to discuss the wide range of other active packaging solutions that help maintain food product safety, shelf-life and brand integrity.

Additionally, David Christian, Multisorb Director of Marketing and R&D, will receive the Riester-Davis lifetime achievement award to recognize his dedication to developing advancements in food packaging technology. Powers will also deliver a lecture on the benefits of a multidisciplinary technical background in developing successful food packaging technology. The lecture and award ceremony are scheduled for July 29, 2007 at 5:20 pm, directly after Food Packaging Division oral session 49 in room S504cd.

To schedule a booth appointment with a Multisorb executive at IFT, please click one of the links below to send an email, or call Joseph Blaise at (800) 555-5555.

- I would like to schedule an appointment at Multisorb's Booth #1972 (please specify date and time).
- I will not be attending IFT but would like to schedule a telephone interview (please specify date and time).
- I cannot schedule an appointment. Please send me a press kit.

Note: Reprinted with permission from Multisorb Technologies and ABI marketing public relations (names and phone numbers changed at request of Multisorb)

person who might otherwise be hard to reach. If your news has national and international impact, you might consider a Webcast to deliver your announcement via the Internet and to make it easy for media contacts, who can get the information without leaving their desks. In this case, you'd still need to send a media alert to let reporters and editors know that a virtual news conference is being planned. Appendix C includes information on planning news conferences, Webcasts, and other special events.

A few final points about media alerts:

- Proofread media alerts carefully before they are distributed. You don't want to embarrass yourself by leaving out a critical piece of information, such as the time or date of the event, or by misspelling the name of a company executive.
- Send media alerts a few days in advance of the news event; more lead time may be needed if travel is required, or if the media you work with prefer more advance notice. Most editors maintain a file for future stories. Even though a decision to cover your event usually will not be made until the day before or the day of your event, sending a media alert in advance can create some initial awareness and help media personnel in their efforts to stay organized.

There are mixed feelings among practitioners about the need for follow-up after media alerts are distributed. Many believe that you need to follow up to remind busy media contacts about the event, to make sure they received the material, and to further "sell" the event and its news value. Follow-up can also give event planners an idea of how many reporters to expect, which helps when determining room setup and when responding to pointed questions from bosses and clients about the expected media turnout. But some professionals say follow-up calls are a waste of time because the best response you can expect is "maybe we'll send someone, depending on what else happens that day." Another reason is many media contacts find follow-up calls and e-mails annoying.

The best advice is to know your media contacts and how each will react to follow-ups. When you do follow up, be polite and call at convenient times. A TV news director will not appreciate your call at 4:30 in the afternoon when the first newscast of the evening has begun or is just minutes away (unless, of course, you have breaking information about a potential danger to public health or an emergency situation that people need to know about ASAP). If using the telephone, state your case quickly and clearly. Introduce yourself, ask if your media alert was received, and if there are any questions about it. Be prepared to briefly explain your event and its news value for journalists who say they don't recall receiving the material, and arrange to e-mail or fax another copy of the alert. The typical follow-up call should last no more than a minute, maybe two, unless the person you are speaking with asks for specific information, or invites you to "sell" the story further. Speak to the individual needs of each media person and ask what you can do to help that person get the story he or she needs. A TV news program might, for example, want a few minutes alone with an event speaker just before or following the main program to get a comment that will be unique to that broadcast. Or, a reporter might be interested in the story but not be able to attend the event. In that case, he or she might ask for time to speak with someone by phone shortly after the event. You should do what you can to accommodate such requests.

Media Pitches

Read any newspaper or magazine, or watch any television news or talk show, and you will see articles, interviews, and news subjects most likely suggested or "pitched" by a public relations source. Here are three examples:

- a wire story on the food page of a daily newspaper about the entertaining chef of three food and cooking programs on a cable network;
- an article about the launch of the "first of a new generation" of video game systems in the science and technology section of a major news magazine;
- an interview on a national morning talk show with an author whose current book focuses on the need for better educated teachers in our schools.

In each of these cases, it's likely that the organizations and individuals involved pitched their stories. Each has a specific, "bottom-line" goal in trying to cultivate media interest. The cable network is trying to promote its food programs and boost viewership. The video company is looking to build consumer interest in its product and strengthen its reputation as a leader and innovator in that industry. The author is hoping to position himself as an expert on education and to stimulate book sales. But the media have no interest in what the organizations want; their goal is to provide news and information that will be of interest to readers and viewers.

In the case of the video game story, then, the astute public relations professional recommends an angle focusing on the impact this new video game will have on consumers and how it will revolutionize the industry. The company gets exposure indirectly by being identified as the product's manufacturer and through quotes from corporate marketing and product development executives. Emphasis is on the consumer product and the issues and trends surrounding it, not on the company and how wonderful it is for introducing this product.

That's the key to successful media pitching. You need to put your own interests aside, and concentrate on finding a news "hook" or angle that appeals to the media. Many times, that involves making your company and its product part of a "bigger-picture story." In the case of the video game company, that "bigger picture" is the growth of the video game industry and notable trends in video game technology. The company is really secondary to the story. Timeliness also strengthens your pitch. The talk show interview on teaching standards took place days before the start of a new school year, and the video story ran one week before the product hit the market. The media pitch in Exhibit 7.5 does a nice job of establishing a timely news hook.

The best results come from individualized pitches. Target a specific idea to a specific editor or reporter at a specific publication. The media like exclusivity—getting a story idea that no other publication is getting at that time and being the first to publish such a story. Consider your goals and target audience first and select a publication that greatly influences or is widely read by that group. Before making the media pitch, read the publication and become familiar with the types of story it likes to publish, preferred story angles, and the most appropriate editor or section to pitch. Such preparation will make your pitch stand out.

Exhibit 7.5

Media Pitch: Xerox

Hello Mr. X,

The World Health Organization reports the widespread transmission of the Avian Flu is almost certain. The U.S. Congressional Budget Office projects a worldwide economic slowdown as a result of 75 to 90 million infections and 100,000 to 2 million deaths.

A pandemic is largely a problem of people, not infrastructure. Companies typically have a plan for a fire in the warehouse or an earthquake but don't have a plan for a massive reduction in workforce and are not prepared to have the majority of their workforce working remotely for an extended period of time. Content is critical to the modern enterprise; integral not only to operational effectiveness but even to corporate viability. Without access to content and records, the majority of today's work simply stops.

Despite this impending disaster, there are specific ways businesses can prepare. John Doe, managing principle for Xerox Global Services, can offer commentary on how outsourcing records management can assist with employees accessing business-critical documents without crashing servers and ensuring that data is not lost.

If you are interested in a briefing with John Doe on how readers can prepare their organization, please reply to this email or reach me by phone at 555-555-1234.

Best,
Erica

Note: Courtesy of Xerox Corporation with Text 100 (names and phone numbers changed at request of Xerox)

According to *PR Week*'s 2008 Media Survey, half of the journalists surveyed said that the majority of pitches they receive do not relate to what they cover. Do not send the same pitch letter to different editors at the same publication. If you have questions about which editor to pitch, contact the publication (you might start with the editor you think is most appropriate) and ask for some guidance.

Effective pitches have three key parts: a creative and attention-getting first sentence; a body containing key facts that build interest in the story; and a brief closing with a clear "call to action."

- In the opening sentence, share a startling statistic, or present a hard-hitting fact that introduces your idea in an interesting way and makes an immediate connection with the editor and the publication. If you are framing your pitch around a lifestyle issue or a trend, start your letter by discussing the recent popularity of that issue or some significant aspect of that trend. Try to avoid being too self-serving in the lead paragraph. Your initial focus must be on the benefit of this story to the publication and its readers. Don't say that you know what a publication's readers want or need. There's nothing wrong with indicating your knowledge of who the readers are and why this story may be of interest to them at some point in the correspondence, but avoid general statements that seem pushy or presume you know more about the publication than an editor does.

- In the body, briefly expand the story angle and suggest credible sources in a few more sentences or using bullet points. Share statistics, anecdotes, and details that build interest and legitimize the story. In a media pitch on the new video games system, you could mention that the video game industry is a $6.3 billion business, and that analysts expect video game revenues to soon surpass motion picture revenues for the first time in history. These facts better position the new video game system as a more substantial news story. Pitches about people and human-interest stories include interesting facts about a person's background that show how that person is unusual or different from others like him. For issue and trends stories, offer the name and key credentials of knowledgeable sources and spokespersons who are available for interviews.
- There's no need to say too much in a last sentence or paragraph. State the goal of your media pitch (arranging an interview with a spokesperson, setting up a meeting to discuss the idea further, etc.). Indicate your plans for following up and reinforce your willingness to help arrange interviews, supply photographs, or provide any additional information.

Media pitches do not need to be lengthy in order to include all of the above information; they should be brief, but persuasive. They may be written in a business letter format and sent by mail; however, using e-mail is increasingly more common, as long as you play by the rules. Check with editors first to see if they welcome e-mail pitches, and think twice before sending unsolicited e-mail. When journalists in the *PR Week* media survey were asked how many unsolicited pitches they receive result in a story, nearly 64% of them said between 1% and 20%; 8.2% said "never." If you don't have an existing relationship with the reporter, consider making a phone call first to propose the idea and sending an e-mail to follow up.

When e-mailing media pitches, be sure to include an informative and catchy message subject line and headline. Also, don't keep sending follow-up e-mail messages to see how they liked your idea. Wait several days to a week and then call or send a brief e-mail message to check on the status of your pitch, and to discuss the merit of the idea further, if afforded that opportunity. When getting permission from editors up front to contact them by e-mail, ask them how follow-up should be handled.

Public Relations Photos

Ansel Adams, one of the 20th century's most beloved and renowned photographers, once said, "A true photograph need not be explained, nor can it be contained in words." Like Adams, public relations professionals should understand the impact of a good photograph. A visually interesting photo sent with a news release can make your story stand out to editors and help your chances of getting published. Publicity photographs used by public relations professionals generally fall into one of three categories:

- *Head shots*. These accompany news releases about people working for your organization. When an executive is promoted at your company, for example, it is common to send a news release and a head-and-shoulders or "mug shot" of that person to the "People in Motion" or "Company Matters" column published in the business section of the daily newspaper. Hometown newspapers, trade magazines, college publications, and association newsletters also use head shots.
- *Product photos*. Consumer magazines and trade publications often have sections on product news. If your company is launching a new product, updating an old product, or making changes to product packaging, send a product shot with your news release to add visual appeal.
- *Event and feature photos*. These include photographs taken before an event to attract attention and promote participation in the event, those taken during an event that can be published after the fact, and "people" or "action" photos that complement feature and human-interest stories. Theater companies send out photos of actors rehearsing scenes to publicize plays before they open and generate advance ticket sales. Organizations promote new construction projects by distributing photos taken of company executives shoveling dirt or surveying the site during a groundbreaking ceremony. A feature about the hands-on approach of a new corporate CEO might include a photograph of him or her in the factory examining a specific assembly line procedure with line workers.

Head shots and product photos are usually straightforward and static, although some product photos show someone using the product in its natural environment. In product photos, make sure the product name and company logo are visible. Most publicity photos, though, should be full of action. Avoid the "grip and grin" photo that shows people shaking hands and smiling at the camera. While these posed photos do occasionally get published, you will make a more positive impression on the media if your photos look natural and capture people while they are involved in an activity as it is happening. For instance, a keynote speaker at a fundraising dinner should be photographed while delivering the speech and talking with guests informally before and after the speech. Besides getting action into your photos, there are other rules to follow when producing photos for media publication:

- Know the media's photo needs and guidelines. Find out if the media you are working with accept photographs from outside sources. If they don't, ask if they assign staff photographers to take photos at newsworthy events, and what the procedure is for alerting them to photo opportunities. It is best to talk directly with editors about their individual needs and policies; most media directory listings also make note of a publication's interest in receiving photos. If you do send photographs, make sure you review publications first to see what kind of action shot they like to use. Whenever possible, offer exclusive photos to encourage publication.

- Create and reproduce high-quality photos. Prints that are washed out, have poor contrast, or some other technical flaw are unacceptable to the media. Unless you are well trained in photography, hire a professional photographer for major events and photo opportunities. Brief photographers before a shoot on the kinds of photo you and your target media are looking for, and how the photos will be used. Regardless of whether photos are taken by a professional or staff member, remember to include a photo credit with the picture.

- Avoid clutter and excessive promotion. Don't overcrowd your photos. The more people you try to cram into a shot, the less likely it is that your photo will have any action. Focus on two or three people who are relevant to the story and who can provide action in the photo to tell the story in a lively and creative way. The exception might be if the people shown are well known and involved in a major news event, but you still want those people talking with each other as opposed to staring straight ahead at the camera. It is acceptable to work your organization's name or logo into a photo, but do it subtly. You might set up the photo of a store grand opening so that the company sign is visible in the shot, but you would not want to have all the corporate executives in the photo wearing T-shirts and holding shopping bags imprinted with large company logos. Editors are interested in publishing news, not in promoting your company.

- Write descriptive captions, or *cutlines*. Send photos with two- or three-sentence cutlines that explain the action. Include contact information and a headline as you would at the start of a news release. When writing cutlines, use the present tense in the first sentence and any other sentences that describe what is happening in the photo. Don't waste this valuable space by stating the obvious. Background sentences providing additional detail and key facts about the news event can be written in past tense. Make only one reference to the company or client. Try to identify people based on the action taking place rather than on their location in the shot (i.e., pictured left to right are . . .), except in those situations where there are several people pictured and it would be awkward to do otherwise. The following is an example of a publicity photo cutline:

    ### LIONS CLUB FUND RAISER IS JUST "DUCK-Y"

    Kerry Ann Gleason, 4, points at hundreds of cute rubber ducks drifting by as she sits with her father, Robert, during the Camden Lions Club's 10th annual Labor Day Duck Derby fund raiser. Kerry's mother, Anita, and her brother, James, look on. The event, held on the Fulton River in Camden, raised $12,000 to benefit the club's many community activities such as youth sports and the Adopt-a-Park program.

- Select the most appropriate format. Ask about preferred format and size for photo submissions. The standard used to be glossy black and white prints, but many newspapers will now publish color pictures, and an increasing number of media outlets prefer digital picture formats, such as .jpg. In this case, find out the preferred resolution (the higher the DPI, or dots per inch, the clearer the picture) and maximum byte size (photos can be compressed to reduce their file size). You can also post photos on your Web site and let media know they can download photos there.

ASSIGNMENTS

Assignment 7.1—A Living History Event

You're a public relations manager for the Living Earth Museum. Your museum is part of a major research institution with a focus on earth science research and education. The museum's exhibits and programs focus on the history of the earth and its life, with an emphasis on the New England area where you are located.

The institution boasts one of the largest collections of fossils in the United States. This collection represents every major group of organisms from around the world over the past two billion years. In addition, the museum has on permanent display the Hyde Park Mastodon, one of the most complete mastodon skeletons found in the Northeast. Mastodons have been extinct for over 10,000 years.

As part of its outreach efforts, the institute provides resources for middle- and high-school teachers and a variety of outside-the-classroom experiences for students. In particular, the museum has an interest in drawing more families with younger children to its facility.

One afternoon, Shannon English, the museum's program coordinator, comes to your office to share an idea for an event that could help reach the young family audience.

"Our state fair is coming up, and that tends to draw people from across the state and even some nearby states, so I'm thinking we might have a great opportunity to set up a display. There'll be lots of families there and just lots of traffic in general. We could do a lot to make people more aware of us by being there for the run of the fair."

You say, "It sounds like a great place for us to get some exposure. Why don't we try to do something more than just an exhibit? Since we're an interactive museum, we should offer some kind of get-involved kind of activity, don't you think? It might be a great way to promote our mastodon exhibit. That's a big draw for us, and when people see it, they're usually pretty impressed."

"Kids really seem to think the mastodon's cool, and they like the fossil digging trips that we sponsor, so why don't we set it up to do that right at the fair?" Shannon says. "We could truck in loads of shale and invite people to jump in and get their hands dirty, so to speak. I mean, they'd be digging through 15,000-year-old sediment and maybe have the chance to find a mastodon bone fragment. I bet people would get into that. And no one would have anything else like it at the fair, I'm pretty sure. We could call our exhibit the Living Earth's 'Mastodon Big Dig' project, or something like that."

"I like that. I also think we could get some media interested, too," you add. The local TV stations are always looking for features about interesting goings-on at the fair, and this seems perfect. So, let's figure out how much all of this would cost before we make any commitments. I can devote some time to being there, but we also better make sure we have other staff available to take shifts at the exhibit."

Exercises

1. Write a media alert about the Living Earth's "Mastodon Big Dig" exhibit and interactive fossil-digging activity at the upcoming state fair. Assume that the state fair is occurring in the state where your college or university is located and that your exhibit would be housed in the Youth Building each day of the 10-day fair (feel free to make up dates).

2. You've identified a local TV reporter who's doing a special series called "All's fair at the Fair." She will do a story each day that brings attention to the more unusual, "can't miss" events and programs. Write an e-mail media pitch, with a link to an online story about the state fair exhibit and your museum's mastodon exhibit, to interest her in featuring the Living Earth Museum in her state fair series. ∎

Assignment 7.2—Promoting the "Road Rage" Expert

Your firm, Cary & Associates, located in the San Francisco area, does much of its public relations work for individuals. Clients include authors promoting new books and physicians looking to share their expertise about specific medical treatments or conditions.

As an account executive with Cary & Associates, one of your primary duties involves planning and executing publicity campaigns for several high-profile medical experts. One morning, you are called to a meeting with Louis Weeks, your boss and an account supervisor for the agency.

"We have a new client coming in shortly, and I would like you to work with her. I thought I should brief you about her before she gets here. Her name is Mariah Conrad and, believe it or not, she's a 'road rage' expert. Apparently, lots of people have trouble handling their anger on the highway and they need someone to talk to about it. She's building part of her practice around this specialty."

"Road rage, huh? I experience a little of that from time to time myself. This morning on my way to work, as a matter of fact. What else do we know about her?"

Weeks continues: "I've got her résumé here. Let's see, Dr. Conrad is 39, a licensed psychiatrist, and a hypnotherapist. She advocates using meditation and hypnotherapy to help drivers deal with their road rage. She's written a book, too. It's got a catchy title—*Don't Drive Yourself Crazy: Controlling Your Road Rage.* It's due out in a month or so. She's also started traveling around the country doing seminars on road rage at companies and at American Automobile Association offices. Oh, when I was talking with her on the phone, she said that one of the things she does with her clients is to first 'size up' their personality types. You know, like drivers who speed up when someone else tries to pass them. She diagnoses those drivers as having a 'competitive personality.' Interesting stuff, don't you think?"

"She's got some good credentials, that's for sure," you say. "What does she want us to do for her, do you have a sense of that?"

"I know she hopes to build up her practice, but she's also really interested in positioning herself as the leading authority on this subject. It's a pretty timely topic, and lots of people seem to be interested in it. Like you said, we all probably act like raging drivers at times. I know she's definitely interested in getting on some of the morning talk shows, like the *TODAY* show and *Good Morning America*. I bet we could get her on *Oprah*, too. We also talked about possibly working with her on a Web site. She'll be here in about a half an hour. It might be good for us to come up with some questions we'll want to ask, and then we can go from there."

Exercises

1. Write an e-mail pitch to interest a producer of NBC's *TODAY* show in scheduling an interview with Dr. Conrad. Your pitch should be no longer than three short paragraphs and include a strong message subject line to attract the producer's attention.

2. Write a media pitch to be sent to either *USA Today* or an automotive magazine such as *Car and Driver*. The goal of the pitch is to interest the publication in writing a feature story relating to Dr. Conrad and her work.

3. Prepare a media list of other national consumer magazines and television programs that might be interested in doing an interview with, or writing a story about, Dr. Conrad. Include the name of the publication or program, a mailing address and Web site address, frequency of distribution and circulation (or, for TV, how often the program airs and how many people watch the show); a brief description of its content and target audience; a key contact name, title, phone number, and e-mail address; and deadline information. ■

Assignment 7.3—Pitching the Virtual Workout

The social gaming experience (think Wii) has become a phenomenon, appealing to people of all ages and interests. This experience allows users to participate in a sport or game in a virtual way on their television screen. On the screen, users are inserted into a sporting event, such as a tennis match. Users participate in the match, virtually, by using a remote controller, simulating the swing of a tennis racket with the controller. It's not just fun—it also provides fitness benefits. As users move about the room playing the game and using the remote controller, they can work up a sweat and work off some pounds.

Realizing the potential of social gaming to offer an alternative to traditional workouts, VGames, a social gaming company, has designed a new product called VWorkout. Those using VWorkout can work with a virtual personal trainer, who walks them through a series of exercise options ranging from aerobics to strength training. Or, they can create their own workout experience and measure how their BMI (body mass index—body fat, based on height and weight) changes over time as a result of their VWorkout routines.

Your firm has been working with VGames to launch an integrated marketing communications program and create awareness of the VWorkout product. A primary audience is seniors, people 50+ who are looking to stay fit but would prefer to do it in the comfort of their own home, rather than going to a gym or participating in outside classes.

The company also has seen growing interest among assisted living facilities and even nursing homes, where seniors living in those facilities can work with staff to be easily trained on how to use the system. VGames provided VWorkout products to a test group of assisted living facilities and nursing homes. After the trial period, those facilities whose residents used VWorkout reported that people really enjoy using the games and that many residents have been able to lose weight and improve their health and emotional outlook as a result of their virtual workouts.

You are working on a public relations program to help build awareness of VWorkout among key audiences. This includes publicity efforts designed to generate exposure in targeted print and broadcast media.

Exercises

1. Write a media pitch on the VWorkout for *AARP The Magazine* that could be used in both the print and online version of the publication. AARP, formerly the American Association for Retired Persons, is "a nonprofit, nonpartisan membership organization for people age 50 and over . . . dedicated to enhancing quality of life for all as we age."

2. You propose that VGames coordinate a national publicity campaign targeting television programs to generate media exposure.

- In a memorandum, explain the plan you would follow in setting up this TV publicity campaign. Identify goals, audience(s) you would want to reach, strategy (what's the message you'd want to communicate, who should appear on the programs, and what would they do when appearing on the programs), any timing considerations (when should the campaign take place and why), and evaluation methods to measure the campaign's success. Attach a media list of 15–20 talk/interview programs you would target.

- Write a media pitch for television producers to interest them in airing a VWorkout segment.

References and Suggested Reading

Ansel Adams (n.d.). Retrieved on December 4, 2008 from http://www.brainyquote.com/quotes/authors/a/ansel_adams.html.

Beckham, D. (n.d.). Retrieved January 13, 2009 from http://thinkexist.com/quotes/david_beckham/2.html.

Clinton, H. (n.d.). Retrieved January 13, 2009 from http://thinkexist.com/quotes/Hillary_Clinton/.

Howard, C. M., & Mathews, W. K. (2006). *On deadline: Managing media relations* (4th ed.). Prospect Heights, IL: Waveland Press.

Hunt, T., & Grunig, J. E. (1997). *Public relations techniques*. Stamford, CT: International Thomson Publishing, 1997.

Marsh, C. (1996). *A quick and not dirty guide to business writing: 25 business and public relations documents every business writer should know*. Upper Saddle River, NJ: Pearson PTP.

Matthis, M. E. (2005). *Feeding the media beast: An easy recipe for great publicity*. West Lafayette, IN: Purdue University Press.

Parkhurst, W. (2000). *How to get publicity: Revised and updated for the Internet age*. New York: HarperBusiness.

Stewart, R. (1971). *Every picture tells a story*. [Record]. Location: Mercury.

8

Backgrounders and Features

Beyoncé Knowles, a music superstar and former member of the group Destiny's Child, attributes some of that group's success to controversy surrounding the "comings and goings" of group members. Some of the original group members quit over disputes with Matthew Knowles, Beyoncé's dad and the group's manager, and this helped generate more media attention. She adds, "I think in order for your group to be successful, your story has to be interesting."

The controversy aside, Beyoncé makes a good point. If you want more extensive media coverage, you need to position your story in an interesting way. Public relations materials such as backgrounders, feature articles, and opinion pieces can help you do that. These tools include facts, stories, and points of view relating to your organization and its people, and help you illustrate in a compelling way the impact your organization has on the community, an industry, or society in general.

There are many instances, as well, when media contacts need more detailed information than what is provided in a news release or a media alert. Once the media respond to your "new product launch" media alert, for example, they will need more background information on your company and the product to complete their stories. Or, your news release could prompt an invitation from a trade media editor to submit a longer article that shares one of your executive's thoughts on a timely industry subject.

But what kind of information should be included in backgrounders? How is writing a feature different than crafting a news release? This chapter will familiarize you with the types of backgrounder and feature written by public relations professionals, discuss how and why these tools are used in practice, and provide you with guidelines for properly structuring and writing these pieces.

Background Materials

Background materials come in many shapes and sizes, from one-page fact sheets to multiple-page corporate profiles. Background pieces are not written for publication; they are primarily intended to assist media writers when they are preparing their own stories. Updated versions should be kept on file and online at all times in order to respond quickly to media inquiries, especially during a crisis. All background materials should include contact information at the top of a first page, just like a news release, followed by a heading that clearly identifies the piece (e.g., "Company Fact Sheet," "Corporate Profile"). They should be written in a factual tone and not offer any opinions or conclusions. Background materials are:

- distributed at media events and news conferences to help reporters quickly grasp a subject and frame questions for spokespeople, and to provide them with statistics and other historical information for use in the stories they write;
- sent to reporters after a story is pitched to further explain the idea and convince an editor of the story's value;
- included in printed information packets about a company, a product, or a service distributed to prospective clients, customers, and other publics, and included in online press kits;
- provided to new employees to acquaint them with the organization, or to inform employees about critical issues or new policies being considered;
- used as secondary sources for the preparation of brochures, reports, and other public relations materials.

Fact Sheets

One of the most basic public relations pieces is the fact sheet. Fact sheets are brief documents that summarize key facts about a company, a product, an issue, or an event. They can help consumers, employees, media, and other audiences get a quick, basic understanding of a subject. Fact sheets can be presented in narrative or news-story form; list a series of key facts using bullet points; or follow a Q & A format and raise frequently asked questions about a subject followed by concise answers, as in Exhibit 8.1.

A company fact sheet often presents material under subject headings such as "Company Description," "Corporate Structure," "Key Personnel," "Products and Services," and "Corporate Mission and Philosophies." There are variations on these headings, as seen in the fact sheet in Exhibit 8.2, which features information on exhibits, admission, hours of operation, visitor amenities, and contact information.

Fact sheets are designed to inform. They briefly summarize the scope of an organization's services and influence, the features and benefits of a new product, the extent of a problem, or the significance of a social issue. They also highlight interesting and provocative facts to build interest in a subject. A reporter might see an unusual item in a fact sheet that provides an interesting story angle that's worth pursuing and use some of the fact sheet content to add more color to an article.

For example, fact sheets on BURGER KING® posted on the company's Web site (www.burgerking.com) list statistics on the total number of Burger King restaurants worldwide and company sales figures, as well as items such as "There are 221,184 possible ways for a guest to order a WHOPPER® sandwich." That's a potentially good "hook" for a feature story.

Exhibit 8.1

Q & A: Frito-Lay

Packaging Questions

We know that issues related to our packaging are really important to you. Here we answer the top questions from consumers like you.

Q: Can Frito-Lay packages be recycled?
A: Yes. Flexible plastic bags may be recycled into other products such as a wood substitute, which may be used for park benches, landscape decking, boat docks, and the like. For example, Frito-Lay bags have been used to make plastic trays at KFC restaurants in the United States.

Q: Which Frito-Lay packages can be recycled?
A: Frito-Lay items that can be recycled include:
-Dip cans - may be recycled in communities where aluminum is recycled
-Outer lid of dip can - may be recycled with other plastics
-Inner steel lid of dip can - may be recycled where steel items are recycled
-Salsa and dip jars - may be recycled as clear glass
-Salsa and dip jar lids - may be recycled where steel items are recycled
-Lay's® Stax® can and lid - may be recycled with other plastics

For recycling to be successful, recyclable materials must be separated and collected. Cans, paper and glass bottles tend to be more popular recyclable items than plastic. However, as more cities require and provide for separation of trash, opportunities for the use of recycled plastic will grow. For more information about the feasibility of starting plastic recycling, we suggest contacting your local city sanitation department.

Q: There is a lot of excess space in your packages. Can you reduce the packaging?
A: There is actually a very good reason for the excess space in our snack packages: The air at the top of the packages provides a "cushion" that protects the fragile chips against breakage in shipment and handling. Years of testing have resulted in this packaging technique, which protects the chips from breakage.

Because we are committed to decreasing the amount of solid waste produced, we have made some changes to decrease the amount of packaging material:
Lay's® brand and Ruffles® brand potato chips, once packaged in composite plastic bags, now are packaged in metallized plastic bags. This results in a 25% reduction of weight in the packaging material used for these two products and a reduction of more than 6 million pounds of packaging material per year from being placed in landfills.

FRITOS® brand corn chips has reduced the bag seal from the industry standard ½ inch to ¼ inch. This adjustment has resulted in a 5% reduction in Fritos packaging material from our landfills each year. We also are investigating reducing the seals on other chip products.

Note: Reprinted with permission of Frito-Lay

Exhibit 8.2

Fact Sheet: Jamestown Settlement

NEWS
FROM THE JAMESTOWN-YORKTOWN FOUNDATION
an agency of the Commonwealth of Virginia accredited by the American Association of Museums

www.historyisfun.org   P.O. Box 1607, Williamsburg, VA 23187-1607   toll-free (888) 593-4682   (757) 253-4838   Fax (757) 253-5299

FACTS ABOUT THE YORKTOWN VICTORY CENTER
Yorktown, Virginia

Theme: A museum of the American Revolution, the Yorktown Victory Center chronicles America's struggle for independence from the beginnings of colonial unrest to the formation of the new nation. Thematic exhibits and living-history programs relate the experiences of ordinary men and women who lived during the Revolutionary era.

Location: On Route 1020 in Yorktown; adjacent to Colonial National Historical Park, which encompasses Yorktown Battlefield, and 12 miles from Williamsburg. Six miles from Interstate 64, Exit 247.

Exhibit Areas: Events that led to the American colonies declaring independence from Britain are chronicled along an open-air walkway leading to indoor exhibits. The **Declaration of Independence Gallery** explores the document that articulated radical ideas inspiring decisive action. The **Witnesses to Revolution Gallery** presents the stories of a representative and diverse group of 10 people whose lives were profoundly affected by the Revolution. The **Converging on Yorktown Gallery** describes the multinational nature of forces that converged on Yorktown in the fall of 1781 and highlights the *Betsy* and other British ships scuttled or lost in the York River during the Siege of Yorktown. *A Time of Revolution*, an evocative 18-minute film set in an encampment at night during the Yorktown siege, dramatizes the musings and recollections of an array of individuals. **"The Legacy of Yorktown: Virginia Beckons"** exhibition examines how people from many different cultures shaped a new society and the development of the Constitution and the Bill of Rights. In an outdoor re-created **Continental Army encampment,** historical interpreters describe and depict the daily life of American soldiers during the last year of the war. A re-created **1780s farm** that includes a dwelling, kitchen, tobacco barn, crop fields, and herb and vegetable garden, shows how many Americans lived in the decade following the military end of the Revolution.

Historical Perspectives: Yorktown was the site of the climactic battle of the American Revolution. In early Fall 1781, Washington and Rochambeau had the British army trapped along the shores of the York River. The allied armies had all of the land routes blocked. The French navy blockaded escape by sea. Cornwallis had no option but to surrender to the combined forces.

- more -

Hours of Operation: Open 9 a.m. to 5 p.m. daily year-round, until 6 p.m. June 15 through August 15. Closed on New Year's and Christmas days. Allow a minimum of two hours for a visit.

2009 Admission: Adults, $9.25; children ages 6 through 12, $5.00. Discount for groups of 15 or more. Combination ticket with Jamestown Settlement: adults, $19.25; ages 6-12, $9.25. Annual pass with Jamestown Settlement: adults, $35.00; ages 6-12, $17.50. Parking is free.

Visitor Amenities: The gift shop complements and extends the museum experience with a comprehensive selection of books, prints, artifact reproductions, educational toys and games, jewelry and mementos. A snack and beverage vending area with patio seating is nearby. A museum admission ticket is not required to visit the gift shop or snack area. Hours of operation correspond with museum hours.

Administration: Operated by the Jamestown-Yorktown Foundation, an agency of the Commonwealth of Virginia accredited by the American Association of Museums.
Chairman: H. Benson Dendy III.
Executive Director: Philip G. Emerson.
Senior Director of Museum Operations and Education: Joseph A. Gutierrez, Jr.

Museum History: Opened April 1, 1976, as one of three bicentennial centers in Virginia. A major expansion and renovation of the Yorktown Victory Center culminated on April 11, 1995, with the grand opening of new exhibition galleries. In the 1990s, the museum's focus broadened to encompass the formation of a new government after the Revolution and to interpret the Revolution from diverse points of view. A renovated Declaration of Independence entrance gallery and long-term exhibition, "The Legacy of Yorktown: Virginia Beckons," debuted in October 2006.

Information and Photos: For additional information and photographs, journalists should contact Media Relations, Jamestown-Yorktown Foundation, P.O. Box 1607, Williamsburg, Virginia 23187-1607, (757) 253-4175 or 253-4114, deborah.padgett@jyf.virginia.gov or tracy.perkins@jyf.virginia.gov. High-resolution images are available for media use at www.historyisfun.org/museumimages.htm. Inquiries from the general public should be directed to (888) 593-4682 toll-free or (757) 253-4838, or www.historyisfun.org.

1/2009

Note: Courtesy of Jamestown-Yorktown Foundation

Backgrounders

Like fact sheets, backgrounders are informational pieces. Backgrounders, however, explain a subject in more detail than a fact sheet and are generally two or more pages long. Many are written like articles, in paragraph form, or use a "Q & A" approach. One of the most common and useful backgrounders is the *historical backgrounder* or *organizational history*. This piece gives a chronological account of the history of an organization, the birth and evolution of a product, or the origins of a program or issue. Because backgrounders usually are written for a long shelf life, care must be made to avoid using language that may date the piece. For example, use "1979" instead of "30 years ago" and avoid words such as "recently."

The American Red Cross backgrounder, shown in Exhibit 8.3, has good backgrounder form. The piece begins with the founding of the association and moves on to illustrate the growth of the organization, culminating with its main mission: "bringing aid to victims of disasters throughout the world." Instead of paragraphs, some historical backgrounders use a time-line approach. They begin with an introductory paragraph or two about how the company got started, and then list significant years from the founding of the company to present day, along with notable achievements during each of those years. Subheadings may be used, depending on the length of the piece; large amounts of text should be broken up to make reading easier.

Biographical Sketches

The biographical sketch, also known as a biography or a "bio," is a background piece about a person. Public relations writers should develop a file of biographies of senior managers and other key executives in the firm. This can be done by conducting staff interviews or by distributing a form that asks for written biographical information. It's a good idea to try to update bios once a year.

Biographies (Exhibit 8.4) acquaint reporters and editors with the expertise of company staff and executives and establish them as potential media sources. Public relations writers preparing publicity materials and newsletter articles on staff awards, promotions, and other employee news readily access bios to get needed background information for those pieces. Biographical sketches generally include:

- name, current job title, and a brief job description in the first paragraph;
- more specifics on job duties and activities, with an emphasis on special knowledge or practice areas;
- career history, including an overview of related positions with past employers, and other relevant work experiences;
- professional activities and education, such as memberships and leadership positions held in professional and trade organizations, certifications or accreditations (e.g., APR—Accredited in Public Relations), professional awards and honors, colleges attended, and degrees earned;
- community and public service work, including board positions held with not-for-profit agencies, charitable causes, schools, and other community organizations;
- personal information related to family and hobbies might be included, if that material is relevant and according to the wishes of the person.

Exhibit 8.3

Historical Backgrounder: American Red Cross

- Join Us »
- Give Blood »
- Donate Money »
- Volunteer Time »

About Us

Red Cross History

A Brief History of the American Red Cross

Clara Barton and a circle of acquaintances founded the American Red Cross in Washington, DC on May 21, 1881. Barton first heard of the Swiss-inspired International Red Cross Movement while visiting Europe following the Civil War. Returning home, she campaigned for an American Red Cross society and for ratification of the Geneva Convention protecting the war-injured, which the United States ratified in 1882.

Barton headed the Red Cross for 23 years, during which time it conducted its first domestic and overseas disaster relief efforts, aided the United States military during the Spanish-American War, and campaigned successfully for the inclusion of peacetime relief work as part of the International Red Cross Movement—the so-called "American Amendment" that initially met with some resistance in Europe.

Clara Barton

The Red Cross received its first congressional charter in 1900 and a second in 1905, the year after Barton resigned from the organization. This charter—which remains in effect today—sets forth the purposes of the organization that include giving relief to and serving as a medium of communication between members of the American armed forces and their families and providing national and international disaster relief and mitigation.

Prior to the First World War, the Red Cross introduced its first aid, water safety, and public health nursing programs. With the outbreak of war, the organization experienced phenomenal growth. The number of local chapters jumped from 107 in 1914 to 3,864 in 1918 and membership grew from 17,000 to more than 20 million adult and 11 million Junior Red Cross members. The public contributed $400 million in funds and material to support Red Cross programs, including those for

continued . . .

Exhibit 8.3

Historical Backgrounder: American Red Cross . . . *continued*

American and Allied forces and civilian refugees. The Red Cross staffed hospitals and ambulance companies and recruited 20,000 registered nurses to serve the military. Additional Red Cross nurses came forward to combat the worldwide influenza epidemic of 1918.

After the war, the Red Cross focused on service to veterans and enhanced its programs in safety training, accident prevention, home care for the sick and nutrition education. It also provided relief for victims of such major disasters as the Mississippi River floods in 1927 and severe drought and the Depression during the 1930s.

The Second World War called upon the Red Cross to provide extensive services once again to the U.S. military, Allies, and civilian war victims. It enrolled more than 104,000 nurses for military service, prepared 27 million packages for American and Allied prisoners of war, and shipped more than 300,000 tons of supplies overseas. At the military's request, the Red Cross also initiated a national blood program that collected 13.3 million pints of blood for use by the armed forces.

After World War II, the Red Cross introduced the first nationwide civilian blood program that now supplies nearly 50 percent of the blood and blood products in this country. The Red Cross expanded its role in biomedical research and entered the new field of human tissue banking and distribution. During the 1990s, it engineered a massive modernization of its blood services operations to improve the safety of its blood products. It continued to provide services to members of the armed forces and their families, including during the Korean, Vietnam, and Gulf wars. The Red Cross also expanded its services into such fields as civil defense, CPR/AED training, HIV/AIDS education, and the provision of emotional care and support to disaster victims and their survivors. It helped the federal government form the Federal Emergency Management Agency (FEMA) and serves as its principal supplier of mass care in federally declared disasters.

While closely associated with the federal government in the promotion of its objectives, the Red Cross is an independent, volunteer-led organization, financially supported by voluntary public contributions and cost-reimbursement charges. A 50-member, all volunteer Board of Governors leads the organization. The president of the United States, who is honorary chairman of the Red Cross, appoints eight governors, including the chairman of the board. The chairman nominates and the board elects the president of the Red Cross who is responsible for carrying into effect the policies and programs of the board. The American Red Cross works closely with the International Committee of the Red Cross on matters of international conflict and social, political, and military unrest. As a member of the International Federation of Red Cross and Red Crescent Societies, which it helped found in 1919, the American Red Cross joins more than 175 other national societies in bringing aid to victims of disasters throughout the world.

Note: Reprinted with permission of the American Red Cross

Exhibit 8.4

Biographical Sketch: eBay

Senior Management

John Donahoe
President and CEO, eBay Inc.

Download image

John Donahoe became President and CEO of eBay Inc. on March 31, 2008. In this role, John has global responsibility for growing each of the company's business units, which include eBay Marketplaces, PayPal and Skype.

John came to eBay in February 2005 as President of eBay Marketplaces, responsible for all elements of eBay's global ecommerce businesses. In this role, he focused on expanding eBay's core business, which accounts for a large percentage of the company's revenues. John also oversaw a number of strategic acquisitions, including Shopping.com and StubHub, and classifieds sites, such as Gumtree and LoQUo.

During the three years he served as President of Marketplaces, revenues and profits for this division doubled.

Prior to eBay, John spent more than 20 years at Bain & Company, a worldwide consulting firm based in Boston. Starting as an Associate Consultant, John rose to become the firm's CEO, where he oversaw Bain's 30 offices and 3,000 employees.

In addition to serving on eBay's Inc.'s Board of Directors, John is also on the Board of Trustees of Dartmouth College.

John received a Bachelor of Arts in Economics from Dartmouth College and an MBA from the Stanford Graduate School of Business.

Features

Features appear every day in the media, and editors look to public relations professionals for good feature story ideas. A feature story focuses on an interesting aspect of an organization and has much greater depth and more quotes than a shorter news story.

With some thought, you can take what seems like a basic news announcement and successfully pitch it as a feature. A school district wants to inform the local media about an award it received from the county for its classes and programs directed to senior citizens in the community. Instead of simply making that announcement and focusing on the award—which could have resulted in a three- or four-paragraph story—the district stresses a specific class in which high school students from the district help seniors learn computer skills. The result: a longer feature with the headline: "Lessons for young and old: Students help seniors learn computer skills." This feature angle puts less focus on the award, and more emphasis on a particular class that shows the positive results of teens and seniors working together.

A popular media feature is the ***personality*** or ***company profile***. The personality profile provides an in-depth look at a noteworthy person connected to your organization. A good time to pitch the media on doing a personality piece is when an individual gains recognition or reaches a milestone—your CEO wins an industry award for excellence in business management, or a volunteer begins 25 years of service to your not-for-profit agency. Company profiles are often done by the media during a significant stage in the company's history, such as the announcement of a major expansion, celebration of a 50th anniversary, or the launch of an innovative product or service.

Media features are usually arranged in one of two ways. The most common approach involves successfully pitching a story idea, providing additional background information, and suggesting sources for interviews. The reporter then writes the finished piece. There are times when you write a feature from scratch, after discussing the idea with an editor and getting her approval to submit it. This is often the case when you are working with consumer and trade publications that have small staffs. As stated in chapter 7, it is best to pitch one specific idea to one publication at a time. Before you spend the time and energy to write a feature, confirm that the editor is receptive to receiving and publishing it.

Types of Feature

Good feature ideas come from many sources. Read daily newspapers and magazines and monitor broadcast news programs and online publications to see how other organizations and your competitors get feature coverage. Some of the best features on people are found on newspaper sports pages, in men's and women's magazines (such as *GQ* and *Vanity Fair*), and in entertainment publications. Look through consumer and trade media to stay on top of lifestyle and business trends that you can tie to your organization's products and people. Some possible feature topics:

- ***Human interest***—stories about organizations or people making special efforts to help improve the quality of life for others, or about people overcoming challenges and obstacles. Example: a story from the American Greyhound Council about a special program that matches greyhounds, best known as racing dogs, with disabled people who need companions to help them open doors, turn on light switches, and manage day-to-day activities.
- ***Advice***—"how-to" stories that provide insight on better health, parenting, and other lifestyle issues. Example: in response to a trend showing sharp increases in childhood obesity, a personal trainer and successful author offers tips on how to help children establish better dietary habits.
- ***The unusual***—stories about interesting trends and fads. Example: more people are replacing red meat with exotic ostrich and buffalo burgers to cut down on fat, according to SPINS, a natural products market research company.

Writing the Feature

Features offer greater freedom for creative writing. Most traditional features should have a beginning, a middle, and an end, in contrast to news releases and news stories that follow inverted pyramid style. One of the more distinguishing elements of the feature is the lead. Whereas news release leads make a rather straightforward announcement, feature leads are designed to get the reader's attention and bring them into the story in an imaginative way. Some feature leads are quite effective using just a few words. Take this lead from a PR Newswire feature about a new book aimed at young boys:

> Today's kids don't read, especially boys.

In contrast, a ***descriptive lead*** is longer and more effectively paints a picture of someone or sets a scene, like this lead taken from a feature issued by MyFunCards.com:

> Even before you heard the first whispers of "Trick or Treat," stores skipped spooky and went straight to jolly and bright, setting up wreaths, trees and ornaments. Now it's December, and despite this early arrival of the holiday season, you're in a familiar situation: scrambling. The now not-so-distant bells on Santa's sleigh sound less like "jing-a-ling" and more like "tick tock." Nothing on your Holiday To-Do List is done, including item No. 1—"Make Holiday To-Do List."

Most people can relate to the scene described above. Using familiar references is an effective way to draw in the reader. This feature goes on to talk about the advantages of using e-card Web sites to send holiday greetings. Feature writing uses background information, descriptive language, revealing quotes, and lots of detail. A strong concluding paragraph will bring the reader full circle and reconnect with the opening paragraph, using either a statement or quote:

> Whether you're sending Happy Holidays one at a time, or wishing Merry Christmas to all at once, even the night before isn't too late.

By-lined Articles

The ***by-lined*** *article* is a feature targeted mostly to trade and business media. Its goal is to position your organization and its people as experts on industry issues and business challenges. These articles are called by-lined articles because they usually carry the by-line of someone in your company with particular technical expertise. They are often written, however, by public relations professionals after conducting research and an extensive interview with the expert.

The head of a credit counseling organization could develop a by-lined article for the local newspaper's "Business" or "Money" section on how to interpret credit card offers and choose the one best suited to a person's financial situation. *Public Relations Tactics*, a trade publication produced by the Public Relations Society of America, includes many by-lined, *"how-to" articles* by public relations professionals. These focus on everything from how to decide which social media tools are most appropriate for your organization to how to position yourself for career advancement. Technical articles are developed with these guidelines in mind:

- Pitch the story before you write it. Identify a newsworthy subject and a credible expert before you pitch an idea, and make sure the expert you've identified is willing to work with you on the article. Outline the subject briefly for the editor by telephone or in a written communication. Stress the timeliness and relevance of the subject, how the target audience will benefit from reading the piece, and why the writer is qualified to comment on the subject. If appropriate, suggest targeting the article to a special section or themed issue (you can usually get this information from a publication's editorial calendar). Once the media contact has shown serious interest in the article, confirm in writing the details you have discussed. Also, ask for the editor's ideas on specific points the article should cover.

Exhibit 8.5

By-lined Article: Xerox

L.A. Confidential: Secure Your Medical Records

By John Doe, Principal and Security Thought Leader, Xerox Global Services

When they cant sneak a few photos of unsuspecting celebrities in compromising positions, today's paparazzi are busy trying to get the next best thing: their medical records. The public's perpetual interest in entertainment news paired with an increasingly well-funded paparazzi, has resulted in a dramatic spike in the number of medical record privacy invasions. The going rate for such information is said to be a few thousand dollars per record.[1]

It looks as if financial gain proved too tempting for employees at UCLA Medical Center. More than 60 employees have been accused of illegally viewing and or leaking electronic medical records of celebrities.[2] This heightened awareness of the latest social phenomenon has many people questioning just how secure their individual records within healthcare organizations really are.

In terms of security this is – at its base – an access control problem. There are many solutions to this issue, some social, some technical. But all solutions come down to access and authentication. People will always be curious. In fact, some will actually exhibit nefarious behavior in some form or another in the workplace. Those that deliberately take records do so primarily because they don't believe they'll be caught. These individuals don't even consider the possibility that one incident could cost them their job. Many others will download or copy files unaware that they're not authorized to be in possession of the files. The key in both cases is to use technology wisely and educate employees so policies are understood.

continued . . .

Exhibit 8.5

By-lined Article: Xerox . . . *continued*

Healthcare organizations can start by establishing a chain of custody for their privacy-protected records. A chain of custody tracks access to critical content throughout its lifecycle in order to establish control and accountability. This is essential for a strong security implementation because employees will know that all of their actions will be tracked and improper use of content will not go without consequences. This policy also helps ferret out unauthorized access and assure privacy-protection.

It goes without saying that an organization must have a complete and accurate inventory of all privacy-protected information including paper and digital records. They must have role-based access control policies in place to make sure that only employees with a legitimate purpose have access to records and that control processes are setup to monitor and audit each system.

Healthcare facilities should take a second look at the multifunction devices sitting on each floor of their buildings. Aside from aiding employees with basic functions like scanning, copying, printing and faxing, these machines can act as a first line of defense against medical record miss-handling. These devices can be setup to work off of a card-based user identification system, requiring employees to swipe a valid ID badge and enter a PIN number before gaining access to the machine. A machine with an archival system can also track each scan, fax, copy and print made by an employee through this process and can be retrieved should that employee's actions ever come into question surrounding a medical records breach.

With digital and hardcopy patient information routinely flowing through a healthcare organization's operations – this activity that goes beyond the multifunction devices must also be carefully monitored. The solution? Enterprise content management. Healthcare facilities with an ECM system that turns hardcopy records into digital files and then tracks the deletion and manipulation of each document within the enterprise will have the ability to trace back missteps taken in the lead up to a security breach. Such a comprehensive system will not only help systems identify how a breach occurred – but will prevent future intentional incidents from happening, as employees will know that their every action can be traced. This audit trail and content repository is also crucial to remain compliant with regulatory requirements such as HIPAA.

Establishing a chain-of-custody by utilizing security functions on multifunction devices and setting up ECM solutions is the logical approach in enterprise environments where security is a mandate. Good employee awareness training and the deployment of the right technologies will improved workflow and yield greater efficiency and more secure operations. Good security is good business. The time to act is now.

[1]*Los Angeles Times,* Digging into Celebrity Medical Records Has a Long History, May 20, 2008.[2] ibid.[3] *Trade Secret Asset Management*, R. Mark Halligan, Richard F. Weyand, Aspatore Books, 2006.

Note: Courtesy of Xerox Corporation with Text 100 (name changed at request of Xerox)

- Conduct interviews. In addition to an interview with the expert, get information from relevant Web sites and secondary sources, and talk with others, such as trade association leaders and customers, to expand your knowledge of the subject and to get facts and reactions that strengthen your piece. This is especially important when writing **market impact technical articles** that detail how a new product or service will benefit an industry.
- Resist promotional writing. In a market impact piece, you might mention the product once or twice, but how-to articles should give general advice and information without making mention of the company or product. Although the article in Exhibit 8.5 is written by the principal for Xerox Global Services, the company's name is never mentioned within the article. Attribute statistics to industry sources, and support strong claims or predictions. Be concise and avoid criticizing the competition. The strength of this type of article is that the reader is likely to perceive the writer of the piece as the expert, which in turn will reflect positively on the organization. The organization's name can be mentioned at the end of the article, along with brief information about the writer.

Case Studies

Case studies, or **case histories**, are similar to technical articles in that they are written primarily for trade media. However, they differ in their approach. While technical articles offer useful advice without mentioning the product, case histories share success stories about products. Their strength lies in third-party endorsement. The case study distributed by the company Multisorb (shown in Exhibit 8.6) tells the story of how one of its products, Multisorb's StripPax System, provided a solution to the manufacturer of Mucinex, highly recognized for its Mr. Mucus advertising campaign. Case studies, like this one, present a problem and position a specific product as the best solution. They are detailed pieces that offer advice to companies facing similar problems. Case studies also can be great additions to your organization's Web site and your customer communication efforts.

Matte Releases

Although this format is called a "release," it is more of a feature than a news release. A **matte**, or mat, **release** is an article that is "publication ready." As seen in Exhibit 8.7, a matte release looks like a regular newspaper article, although it is actually promoting a product or service. It is already laid out, often with an accompanying photo, and can be used by a newspaper "as is." Syndication services, such as News USA and North American Press Syndicate (NAPS), distribute matte releases free to publications. Because these consumer-oriented features may deal with a variety of topics—from beauty to real estate to gardening—many editors use them to fill extra space in special sections of their papers. Matte releases are typically better suited for a national or regional campaign than a local one and can be costly, with prices running into the thousands of dollars.

Exhibit 8.6

Case Study: Multisorb

CaseHistory

System Reduces Cost, Improves Efficiency

Company enhances production and packaging efficiency with Multisorb StripPax System.

Since the launch of its Mucinex brand of expectorants, Adams Respiratory Therapeutics (Chester, NJ) has become a strong company in the OTC respiratory market. Thanks in part to an award-winning advertising campaign that introduced U.S. consumers to the company's animated Mr. Mucus mascot, Mucinex product sales have skyrocketed. The company—recently acquired by Reckitt Benckiser—needed to expand its manufacturing capacity and output to meet this increased demand.

Adams made a strategic decision to reacquire the manufacturing operations of the Fort Worth, TX, facility from Cardinal Health in July 2006. Adams's goal is to turn the site into a center of excellence by including state-of-the-art packaging lines to meet the needs of its adult oral-solid Mucinex products.

For one of its new packaging lines, Adams had used desiccant canisters and dispensing equipment to protect its Mucinex SE, Mucinex DM, Maximum Strength Mucinex, and Maximum Strength Mucinex DM products from drug-formulation degradation. To improve production efficiencies, however, Adams decided to switch to Multisorb's StripPax System.

The new system saved costs and added to much-needed production-line flexibility and mobility. Adams operations staff estimates that Multisorb's StripPax System provided approximately $25,000 in monthly costs savings, by minimizing material costs and increasing production efficiencies. Consequently, Adams foresees an annual cost savings of approximately $300,000.

RETHINKING PROTECTION

Chris Collins, a packaging engineer at Adams, said his team needed to ensure that new equipment and processes could handle the company's revised output requirements without

When desiccant canisters jammed its machines, Adams opted for packets.

expanding production foot space. "Our sales have gone up dramatically over the past couple of years, and we realized we had to take a hard look at our packaging systems," he says.

The other consideration for Adams was cost. To protect its products from moisture degradation, Adams was dispensing 1- and 2.5-g desiccant canisters in its adult oral-solid Mucinex bottles

using dispensing equipment. The per-unit cost of the canisters was a concern, especially with the anticipated increase in packaging volumes.

Adams was also experiencing some quality-control issues with canisters used during dispensing operations. "We had problems in the past with machine jams," Collins says.

Adams started looking at desiccant packets as an alternative to canisters. One of the options under consideration was the StripPax System from Multisorb Technologies (Buffalo, NY), which incorporates Multisorb's StripPax desiccant packets and APA-2000 Strip-Pax dispensing equipment. A simple review of the per-unit costs appealed to Adams.

DECISION AT PACK EXPO SHOW

The Adams packaging team met with Multisorb technical and sales representatives at the 2006 Pack Expo International show in Chicago. APA equipment was in operation at Multisorb's booth, and the Adams team was impressed with what it saw, particularly the APA-2000 StripPax dispenser.

"It was evident that Multisorb was an industry leader," says Kevin Johnson, an Adams associate operations ERP/DAX.

Given the manufacturing demands for Adams's production, the company needed to minimize the amount of time to switch over to the new equipment and

continued . . .

Exhibit 8.6

Case Study: Multisorb . . . *continued*

run validation testing and training. Adams outsourced testing to SMB Validation and Compliance Services Group Inc. (Kirkland, Quebec, Canada), a validation and pharmaceutical engineering firm that has long worked closely with Adams.

SMB developed User Requirement Specifications (URS) for packaging equipment suppliers that included the usage, speed, rate, and desired ROI and cost-savings based on Adams's needs. Multisorb responded to the URS, and SMB recommended Multisorb's APA-2000 dispensing unit. The decision was based on cost savings and the ability of Multisorb's technical staff to assist with validation, testing, and documentation. "We have validated Multisorb equipment in the past, and have been impressed with the company's high level of service and documentation practices," says David Buckley, validation engineer at SMB.

The APA equipment is designed to be used with StripPax packets, which are compact, nondusting packets that are accurately dispensed from StripPax dispensers at high speeds. Multisorb offers customized packets depending on the requirements for each drug formulation. For its adult oral-solid Mucinex line, Adams used 1-, 2.5-, and 5-g silica gel StripPax packets.

FACTORY ACCEPTANCE TEST

Working within a short time frame, Adams required additional validation

and factory acceptance testing (FAT) above and beyond what is typically involved for such equipment installations. "Adams wanted to minimize time spent on installation qualification by performing extensive testing during the FAT execution," Buckley says. "We produced FAT documents that tested all equipment functions, and Multisorb was very cooperative and facilitated the process at their location. They obviously knew what was required from a current Good Manufacturing Practices (cGMP) point of view, rather than just from an engineering point of view."

During the FAT testing, SMB performed high- and low-speed runs of multiple packet sizes, along with different bottle sizes (ranging from 100 to 625 cc). The qualified accepted reject rate was specified at 0.05%. The end result, however, was even better. "We actually achieved reject rate during multiple qualification runs of less than 0.01%," Buckley says.

In addition to cGMP, the testing was performed in accordance with Good Documentary Practices, and the documentation produced became part of the regulatory package, enabling it to be referenced rather than repeated once installed at Adams's facility. "The process was painless; not a single discrepancy came out of the FAT, which is highly unusual," Buckley adds.

The new packaging line became operational in May 2007, and so far the

results have impressed Collins and his team. "The efficiency and reliability of this machine is very good and dependable," he notes.

The APA-2000 StripPax dispenser is designed to dispense more than 300 units per minute, which is faster than Adams currently needs, but which will accommodate future requirements. Adams previously dispensed about 100 bottles per minute with its canister line, but based on new volume demands, the Multisorb dispenser runs at rates of up to 180 bottles per minute, with room for additional capacity in the future.

SMALL SIZE AND MOBILITY

The dispenser occupies a relatively small footprint and is separate from the unwind system. In Adams's facility, the dispenser operates in one corner of the line, and the unwind system stays out of the way until needed—a flexibility that maximizes available space.

The mobility of the unit has also proven to be an asset to Collins and his team. "We had some work to do on a conveyor, and we were able to take the machine off-line very easily, reducing our downtime," Collins says.

Managing the higher volumes has kept Collins extremely busy. As Adams prepares for new product launches, the switchover to this system has helped the company in its efforts to extract greater efficiencies as it ramps up production. ∎

MR. MUCUS

Adams Respiratory Therapeutics first launched its Mucinex product to the U.S. market in 2003. In 2004, it began the "Mucinex in, mucus out" concept, showcasing the animated character Mr. Mucus in television and print ads. Each advertisement typically featured Mr. Mucus and/or his friends living inside a cold-sufferer's chest, until they were expelled after the sufferer ingested Mucinex.

Increased brand awareness more than doubled unit sales of Mucinex by March 2005. An ad campaign in October 2005 introduced Mrs. Mucus under the theme of "Married to

Mucus" and, once again, the campaign boosted sales. In September 2006, Junior Mucus—the son of Mr. and Mrs. Mucus—was successfully introduced to consumers with the new Mucinex Mini-Melts product line.

In 2007, Adams launched nine products, including Maximum Strength Mucinex, Maximum Strength Mucinex D, Maximum Strength Mucinex DM, plus Mucinex Full Force and Mucinex Moisture Smart nasal sprays.

In addition to Mucinex products, Adams acquired the Delsym liquid cough syrup product line in 2006. After only one year of marketing, Delsym ranked No. 1 in Pharmacy Time's 2007 OTC Survey of Pharmacist Recommendations in both the adult and children's cough syrup categories.

Note: Reprinted with permission from *Pharmaceutical & Medical Packaging News*, a Canon Communications LLC Publication

Exhibit 8.7

Matte Release: National Crime Prevention Council

CRIME PREVENTION

7 Tips on Preventing Identity Theft

NewsUSA

(NU) - In the course of the day, you do many activities that put your personal information at risk — from writing a check at the store to charging merchandise in person or over the phone. You may not think twice about these transactions, but others might.

Identity theft — when a perpetrator assumes someone's identity for personal or financial gain, like stealing a credit card to make financial transactions in the victim's name — is the fastest-growing crime in America.

According to the U.S. Postal Inspection Service, there were almost 10 million cases of identity theft in 2004, which cost consumers $5 billion.

The National Citizens' Crime Prevention Campaign, sponsored by the National Crime Prevention Council, aims to educate consumers about what they can do to prevent identity theft. The council offers the following tips.

• Do not give out your personal information unless you initiate the contact or know the person or company with whom you are dealing. Also, never disclose personal information, such as a Social Security number or bank account number, in response to an email. Legitimate businesses will not ask you to do this.

• Do not disclose your credit card number to an online vendor unless it is encrypted and the site is secure. Look at the first part of the Web address on your browser. It should read "https://."

• Do not write your Social Security number or telephone number on checks or credit card receipts.

• Remove all documents with personal information from your hard drive before discarding your computer or sending it in for repair.

• Shred discarded documents, including preapproved credit card applications, bank statements, store receipts and utility bills. "Dumpster divers" can gain access to your personal information if such items are thrown in the trash.

• Cancel all credit cards that have not been used in the last six months. Open credit is a prime target for thieves.

• Order your credit report at least twice a year and report any mistakes to the credit reporting agency in writing.

If you are a victim of identity theft, contact your local police department as soon as possible. If your identity was stolen in one jurisdiction but used in another, you may have to report the crime in both jurisdictions.

To learn more about preventing identity theft, visit the National Crime Prevention Council's Web sites at www.weprevent.org and www.ncpc.org.

Note: Reprinted with permission of *NewsUSA*

ASSIGNMENTS

Assignment 8.1—Alcohol Awareness Month (B)

As discussed in chapter 3, Assignment 3.2, you are a public information specialist with the Council on Alcohol and Drug Dependence. The council is a not-for-profit agency whose mission is to educate people on the dangers of substance abuse and to prevent individuals, especially young people, from abusing alcohol and other drugs.

You have been asked to plan and implement public relations activities during Alcohol Awareness Month in April, to increase knowledge of the risks associated with binge drinking. Binge drinking involves consuming large quantities of alcohol in a single session. The primary target audience is college students, who are among the largest populations involved in binge drinking. Research shows that college students who are binge drinkers tend to miss classes and have poor academic performance; many leave college before finishing their studies. Binge drinkers are more likely to engage in unprotected sex, damage property, and get in trouble with the law.

One of your strategies for Alcohol Awareness Month is to provide information on binge drinking to local communities and campus media in your area, in hopes that they will cover the issue in some depth. A key tactic is preparation of written background materials for information kits and the council's Web site.

Exercises

Gather relevant facts and information on binge drinking and prepare the following written materials:

- a three-page backgrounder on the history and impact of the binge drinking problem on U.S. college campuses from the 1980s to today;

- a 500-word by-lined article for publication in daily or college newspapers on the dangers of binge drinking. This piece should carry the by-line of LaToya Glover, the council's executive director.

Assignment 8.2—United Way Feature Stories

The United Way of America (UWA) is a national system of volunteers, contributors, and local charities that helps meet the health and human-care needs of millions of people. Its mission is to "improve lives by mobilizing the caring power of communities."

The UWA provides research, training, advertising, and other support services to the 1,400 locally based United Ways (UWs) in cities across the country. The main focus of the local UWs is to raise money, which is then distributed to UW member agencies in those areas. These member agencies include a variety of organizations, from those that fight hunger or work to strengthen families, to others that assist older adults or help youth at risk. Many member agencies that receive UW funds are the local chapters of nationally known social and human service organizations such as the Salvation Army and American Red Cross.

You have recently started an internship with the UW in the city or area where your college is located. Langston Hill, the UW's director of communications, tells you about a meeting he has just come from with the editors of a local weekly newspaper.

"As you know, we recently did a survey that showed many people in the area don't have a complete picture of the United Way's role, where our fundraising dollars go, and how the money we raise is used to help all kinds of people in the community," Hill says. "So, I shared those findings and suggested that the paper start running a series of articles on the different member agencies the United Way supports. They liked that idea, and said they would have no problem with us writing the articles, as long as they could edit them as they saw fit. They also want us to send them some United Way background materials."

"Do they want the articles to give an overview of the agencies and what they do, or would they prefer some other kind of focus?" you ask.

"The articles need to talk about the mission of each agency, but it will probably be more interesting if we identify a more distinct angle. For some of the agencies, UW funds are used to support one particular program, so we'd want to focus on that. In other cases, we might make it more of a human-interest piece. You know, talk about people who benefit from the agency's programs, or even a story from the perspective of local agency volunteers who are making a difference. Of course, we need to make sure that the agency's connection to the United Way is mentioned in the article, but these can't be promotional pieces for us. The focus should be on the member agency and how it helps the community, and then we can weave in somewhere how the services they provide are made possible by UW funding," Hill says.

"I gather that these articles should have feature-type leads, lots of good quotes. These are feature articles, really. How about length?"

"Yes, they definitely want us to write in feature style. They said to shoot for about 500 words. No more than two pages, double-spaced. As you've probably figured out by now, I'd like you to take on this project. I think it would be a good experience for you, and help you learn more about us and the agencies we serve. And, it will give you some excellent interviewing and feature writing practice, too."

"I would definitely agree with that," you respond. "I'll get started on it today."

Exercises

1. Write a two-page backgrounder focusing on the key accomplishments and community impact of the local UW chapter in your area.

2. Select a UW agency in your area, and write:

   - a two-page feature story on that agency for publication in the UW article series explained in the case;

   - a one-page biographical sketch of the agency's executive director.

Assignment 8.3—Harnessing Renewable Energy

Sunergy Inc., established just one year ago, is a growing business in your city specializing in the residential and commercial installation of solar energy panels. Solar panels are used to produce electricity from sunlight, helping homeowners and businesses to lower their energy and electricity costs, and to reduce the impact of global warming.

You recently joined Sunergy as the company's first public relations manager. Alex Scala, Sunergy's president, has called a meeting with you to talk about this new role and his thoughts about using public relations more fully to advance the company's business objectives.

"A big part of this company's mission," Scala says, "is to help educate people and counsel them on the benefits of solar and wind energy. Obviously, we're running a business here and we need to be profitable, but we founded the company because we also feel very strongly about the need to protect the environment and create healthy communities powered by clean energy. So, this isn't just about business for us; it's about the future."

"That's one of the reasons I was attracted to this job, because everyone seemed genuinely committed to the cause," you say. "What kind of public relations work have you been doing so far?"

"Not too much. We've had some minimal coverage on the business pages of the local newspaper, mostly to announce that the company had been launched and to announce new staff. We launched a Web site, but at this point, it has pretty basic information—a statement about the company, staff bios, a few customer testimonials, but it needs a lot of work. I think, in general, there's probably so much more we could be doing to reach out in the community and help people better understand why these alternative energy sources are so important. Doing that, too, helps us get our name out there in a more subtle way, but still connects us with potential customers."

"Some ideas are already starting to come to mind," you say. "Just to be clear, you want to target the residential homeowner but also the business owner. Those are the key publics?"

"Yes, in general. But I'd welcome any thoughts you might have about how to narrow those broad groups and maybe do some more specific targeting. I'm open to suggestions. I would like to see a plan at some point that lays out public relations strategies, but right now, there are some immediate projects that I could use your help with. I think we need to do more with our Web site, content-wise, and we really don't have any printed materials we can give to people as we talk about the company and the importance of renewable energy," Scala says.

"I have been looking at the Web site, and I think we should have pages and a section of the site that speak specifically to facts about renewable energy. We can create some kind of a fact sheet that not only lives on the Web site, but that you can download and distribute in printed form, if you need to. I'm also thinking that you can be a credible source on this subject, because you have a degree in environmental science and you've done some teaching and research on renewable energy. We should explore ways to showcase your knowledge of this subject."

Exercises

Conduct additional research on the subject of renewable energy and the benefits of using solar and wind energy. Then, write the following pieces:

- a fact sheet, presented in Q & A form, on this topic that could be included on Sunergy's Web site;

- a by-lined article (use Alex Scala's by-line) on solar/renewable energy for placement in a weekly publication produced in your city that includes listings of homes for sale as well as other articles of interest to home buyers and homeowners.

References and Suggested Reading

Aamidor, A. (2006). *Real feature writing* (2nd ed.). Mahwah, NJ: Lawrence Erlbaum Associates.

Ali, L. (2001, May 21). A date with destiny. *Newsweek.*

Bivins, T. H. (2007). *Public relations writing: The essentials of style and format* (6th ed.). New York: McGraw Hill.

Domestic and global facts (2008). Retrieved December 4, 2008 from http://www.bk.com/companyinfo/corporation/facts.aspx.

Feature news (2008). Retrieved December 4, 2008 from http://www.prnewswire.com.

Stress-free season's greetings are a click away (2008). Retrieved December 5, 2008 from http://www.prnewswire.com.

What is a mat release? Retrieved December 4, 2008 from http://www.matrelease.com.

9

Web Sites and Social Media

Homer Simpson, the loveable, doughnut-eating dad of the long-running animated TV series *The Simpsons*, doesn't seem to have a clue about digital media. Consider his remark, "Oh, so they have Internet on computers now?" Spanish sculptor and painter Pablo Picasso did not like computers much, as you can see from this quote: "Computers are useless. They can only give you answers" (Picasso).

Whatever someone knows or doesn't know, or thinks, about computers, the Internet and digital technology, they are integral to the work you will do as public relations professionals in the 21st century. On any given day, you can probably expect to send e-mail to a reporter or a colleague, access a search engine or blog, update a Web site, or perform some other online function. But computers don't do the thinking for you. They can't write your e-mail message in good form and style, design your online research approach, or develop your social media strategy. Used effectively, and not as a total substitute for the face-to-face contact that builds strong relationships, online and Web-based communication, and the strategic use of new and social media, can have tremendous impact and open your organization to audiences like no other channels can. This chapter covers two of the most common types of Internet writing: Web sites and blogs.

Web Sites

When you need information on a company or organization, whether it's an address or product data, you most likely go to the company's Web site. The Internet is here to stay, and most companies and organizations must have an online presence. Public relations practitioners are typically involved in developing copy for their company's Web site. Writing for the Internet and the World Wide Web requires an approach that is somewhat different from that applied to traditional print media and public relations literature. This section discusses those style differences, and gives direction on developing Web sites that will engage your audiences and best serve your organization's goals.

Exhibit 9.1

An Introduction to Web 2.0

As we entered the 21st century, organizations were seen as progressive if they had a Web site. As the Internet grew in popularity, more and more companies jumped on the bandwagon and developed an Internet presence. However, in many cases, that presence was one-dimensional and focused more on disseminating information rather than communicating with target publics, and, as public relations practitioners know, publics will find a way to talk even if the company doesn't provide the outlet. Enter Web 2.0.

The term "Web 2.0" is frequently used to describe the vast amount of Internet applications that enable people to network and form online communities, forums where people with similar interests and like-mindedness can come together to share views and seek information. The public relations firm Hill & Knowlton has developed a process called MAIL that provides a roadmap for public relations practitioners engaging in social media: **m**onitor what is being said about your organization, **a**nalyze what you've heard, begin to **i**nteract with others on social networking sites, and become a **l**eader in the conversation. Here are some of the more popular sites to get you started:

- **Facebook (www.facebook.com)** is the No. 1 social networking site worldwide. Originally limited to college students, the site is now open to people of all ages who create "user profiles."
- **MySpace (www.myspace.com)** was previously the most popular social networking site. The site is especially popular with musicians, who can upload their music and expose other users to it.
- **YouTube (www.youtube.com)** features homemade and professional videos and commercials uploaded by individuals and organizations.
- **Flickr.com (www.flickr.com)** consists of photo albums uploaded by individuals and organizations.
- **LinkedIn (www.linkedin.com)** is made up of user profiles that are business-oriented and focuses on professional networking.
- **Ning (www.ning.com)** is a site where people can form their own social networking communities.
- **Twitter (www.twitter.com)** enables people to keep in touch with each other by sending short messages, called "tweets," that answer the question, "What are you doing?"
- **Technorati (www.technorati.com)** is a search engine specifically for blogs.
- **Digg (www.digg.com)** allows people to vote, or "digg," on blogs and articles on the Internet, which move up the ranks based on popularity.
- **Del.icio.us (www.delicious.com)** is a site for bookmarking your favorite blogs and Internet sites.
- **Wikipedia (www.wikipedia.com)** is a collaborative, Web-based encyclopedia that allows users to create and edit information.

Popular sites for creating, housing, and searching for individual blogs are **blogger.com**, **wordpress.com**, **typepad.com**, and **xanga.com**.

Writing for the Web

Visitors to Web sites tend to scan text rather than read it word-for-word. What does that mean for the public relations professional writing copy for a Web site? Keep it short—even shorter than most copy you write for other public relations materials—because most Web readers want to absorb information quickly and they won't labor over every word. Plus, reading text on a computer screen is much harder on the eyes and takes longer than reading the same text on paper. Here, then, are some guidelines for Web-based writing:

- Keep your sentences and paragraphs short. It's better to write several short paragraphs than two or three long ones.
- Use headlines and subheads, and write in a direct and conversational tone.
- Break general text categories down into sub-categories. For example, an "About Us" or "Company Profile" section may be divided into smaller sections on company history, financial data, and senior staff biographies. The reader can access the main "About Us" page for a brief summary and a list of bulleted sub-categories. They can click on the sub-categories to go to separate pages with more detailed information on those subjects, or to go directly to that content if the information is presented on one long page . . .
- Think about the computer screen when you are developing Web content. Nielsen (2006) found that people read Web pages in an "F-shaped" pattern—scanning the top part of the page from left to right, scanning the next level of content from left to right, and then vertically scanning the left side (often where navigation is located). Some pages may need to be longer, especially if you know that certain visitors are receptive to reading more on one page.

Conceiving and Designing the Web Site

According to Michael Pranikoff, director of emerging media at PR Newswire, the rule of thumb for developing messages for the Internet is to make the content easy to access, easy to view, and easy to use. Your Web site should have style and substance—a writing style that suits Web readers, as well as content and graphics that are easily accessible and will entice people to read, spend some time at your site, and share what they've found. Some critical Web site design factors:

- Establish goals for the site. Have company-wide discussions about the site and what its purpose should be. Will it primarily be an information resource, or is the focus to showcase and sell products and services?
- Target specific audiences. Aiming your site at a large, general audience will attract many visitors who may only come to your site once or twice. Focusing on smaller, defined groups will lead to more return visits by a greater number of people in the long run.
- Size up your competition. Do some research and see what your competitors are doing on the Web. Try to make your site different and consider new and interesting ways to present standard information. In addition to listing and describing its product line, Asics running shoes includes a shoe fit guide on its Web site, educating potential customers about the right way to select a running shoe and then matching their needs with Asics products.
- Create and register a short, easy-to-remember address, or **URL** (Uniform Resource Locator). Many sites use the organization's name, one key part of the name, an identifiable abbreviation (e.g., aspca.com for the American Society for the Prevention of Cruelty to Animals site), or a keyword that relates to the site's content (e.g., cancer.org for the American Cancer Society's site).

- Prepare a blueprint of the site content, also known as the information architecture. Organize content into broad categories that include useful information for your audiences and make it easy to navigate your site. As noted previously in this chapter, many organizations include an "About Us" section that includes background on the company, its history, and its people. The information architecture you create should be based on the goals of your site and the types of information that your Web visitors want to find and that you want to provide. Many college or university Web sites, for example, organize pages and content around audience—current students, prospective students, faculty and staff, alumni and friends, parents, etc. This way, whether you are a member of one of those groups or someone looking for information as it relates to your interests as an alumnus or prospective student, you'll know where to click and then go.

- Create a strong front page, or home page. The ***home page*** is often the first page visitors see when they access your site, so it needs to be attention-getting and attractive. As illustrated in the example in the previous bullet, when visitors come to your home page, they should see right away how the site connects to their interests, and identify quickly how to access information they seek within the site. Include brief text introducing visitors to the site, and display a table of contents that outlines what visitors will find in the site. Many sites have a navigation device called a toolbar at the top or left side of the home page. The toolbar includes two- or three-word descriptions of site content. Visitors can click on an item in the toolbar and be taken to that page or section of the site. Exhibit 9.2 shows the home page for KnowHow2Go.org, a site aimed at showing low-income students how to achieve their dreams of going to college. The site features its core message—the four steps to college—on its home page, and the navigation toolbar makes it clear where target publics should go for more information that applies specifically to them.

- Think carefully about visuals. If you include photos, you might want to think about showing people that the target audience can relate to or identify with. Be sure the visuals you use have been properly formatted for the Web so that they take the least amount of time to download.

- Be attentive to smart design. Web designer Roger Black, a former art director for *Rolling Stone* magazine and the *New York Times* and author of *Web Sites that Work*, suggests that information on Web pages should be presented in small sections for easier reading. Use bigger type and only one or two typefaces for a consistent look, and try to avoid setting type in all caps or in reverse. He also says that black, white, and red—with black type on a white background—are good, basic colors that will make your site highly readable.

- Assess the site's impact, and update content regularly. Provide a mechanism for visitors to give you feedback on the site and how it could better serve their needs. Add fresh content and material as often as you can, and look for opportunities to introduce new sections. Someone who visits your site several times and sees the same material on the home page from a month or two before might not return soon, if at all.

Exhibit 9.2

Home Page: KnowHow2Go

Note: Reprinted with the permission of Lumina Foundation for Education, Inc.

Multimedia

Today's successful Web sites go beyond text and static images. Using multimedia will make your site interesting, provide additional information to your publics, and increase return visits. In addition to still photos, consider using audio and video applications. Audio may include speeches or broadcast interviews; video may feature commercials or demonstrations of how to use a product. **Podcasts** and **vodcasts** can make a site even more interactive and offer a personal connection to your target publics.

A podcast, which gets its name from "iPod" and "broadcast," is part of a series of audio downloads to which visitors to your Web site can subscribe; vodcasts are video downloads. These applications can help position the expertise of your organization by delivering helpful advice on a regular basis. The Student Loan Network (www.financialaidpodcast.com) offers a weekly podcast on scholarship availability, financial aid, student loans, and careers. On the Weber grill Web site (www.webernation.com), grilling enthusiasts can view free grilling classes as vodcasts. Be sure to archive past podcasts and vodcasts for visitors just discovering your Web site.

Online Media Rooms

According to *PR Week*'s 2008 Media Survey, 89% of journalists responded that they get information about a company through the company's Web site, so you want to make sure that the information they're looking for is there. An online media room will not only make it easy for journalists to access information about your company, but will expose your target publics to the information, as well. Many organizations create a special area within their site that includes news releases and other content of primary interest to the media. This makes sense, because public relations professionals are using online techniques more frequently to deliver news and pitch ideas to editors and reporters. How can you make your Web site and online communications "media friendly"?

- Set up your home page with a "Media Information" or "Press Room" button, within the toolbar or menu, that links media contacts quickly to news materials.
- Make information easy to find. The most common way to list news releases is in reverse chronological order, with the most current release first on the list. You might also set up a search function to make it possible for media contacts to find something by subject or by entering keywords. Categories make it easier to search.
- Give them more than just news releases. Offer other Web site content, such as biographies of your executives that highlight their special knowledge and expertise on timely issues; company and product backgrounders; industry data; and links to industry and related sites. Include artwork that reporters can easily download, such as company logos, product shots, and photos of your CEO and senior staff.
- Add an interactive component. Include a form that media contacts can fill out to request an interview with an expert from your organization on a specific topic.

Blogs

Blogs are an extension of Web sites that allow organizations to talk to their target publics in a more personal, conversational way. Many companies now have a blog component on their Web sites. They may be written by the CEO, a group of senior managers, or employees, and the topics may range from corporate responsibility to favorite cookie recipes. "Marriott on the Move" (see Exhibit 9.3) is written by Marriott Corporation CEO Bill Marriott and covers topics such as diversity, education, and the environment. The McDonald's "Value in Practice" blog includes information on nutrition and well-being, and sustainable supply chains. The award-winning blog of Kodak, "A Thousand Words," offers employees a venue for sharing their interests and "stories about imaging and its power to influence our world."

No matter who is writing the blog and what the topic is, there are some standard guidelines that are important to consider:

- Pick a good name for your blog, one that reflects the organization and its core message: for example, General Motors' "Fast Lane" and Kodak's "A Thousand Words."
- The design of your blog should complement your corporate Web site, but not be identical. David Meerman Scott, author of *The New Rules of Marketing and PR*, says this sends a nonverbal message to readers that the blog, while sponsored by the organization, is more than just "corporate speak."

- Consider carefully who will write your blog and how often postings will be made. Blogs are a time commitment. If one person can't make the time, perhaps a group can share posting responsibilities. Some of the most popular, independent bloggers post up to 20 times a day; corporate bloggers typically post once or twice a week, even daily.

- Write your blog as if you were in a conversation. That's what blogging is all about. Unlike the strict formats used for news releases and many other public relations materials, blogs are about "freedom of voice." When people read your blog, they should feel like you're talking directly to them. Use personal language, such as "I," "we," and "you," and let your personality shine through. Of course, good writing basics such as proper grammar usage and correct spelling still apply. The length of your blog will vary on the topic of the blog and what you have to say. Research has shown that Internet users have short attention spans, but that doesn't mean your blogs have to be brief. On the other hand, don't ramble on if you have said all you want to say. As one blogger put it, "My own thoughts are that a post is done when it's done."

- Comments make up the very heart of blogs. Consider how you will handle them. Blogging software will allow you to choose whether you want comments to your blog to be posted automatically or to go through a moderation process where they must be approved. If you choose the latter, identify who will handle the moderation.

Exhibit 9.3

Blog: Marriott on the Move

◀ Listen

Celebrating World Environment Day
Posted: June 2, 2008 3:48:24 PM

June 5 marks a very important day to encourage environmental awareness - it's called World Environment Day. I've told you before about many of our global initiatives like our partnership with the Brazilian state of Amazonas and our efforts to reduce fuel and water consumption globally. While efforts like these are in place at our properties, many of our Marriott hotels around the world have taken it upon themselves to create their own local initiatives to help protect the environment. Let me share some of these fantastic efforts.

Amman Marriott associates watering a tree in Marriott Forest

In the Middle East, where we just announced that we will be more than doubling our number of properties, the associates at the Amman Marriott hotel planted trees to establish the "Marriott Forest" on a piece of land provided by the Jordanian Desertification Society.

Also in the Middle East, our Marriott Executive Apartments and our Courtyard by Marriott hotel in the Green Community of Dubai are doing some great things. They have created an organic garden in a special landscaped area. Each associate who wants to take part is given one meter of the garden to tend. The property's goal is to produce over 100 kilograms of fruits and vegetables each month, which will be cooked and served in the hotel. Other hotels around the globe are also beginning to grow their own organic gardens as this is becoming a very popular trend.

And here, in the U.S., our hotels are working within their communities, too. The associates at the Evergreen Conference Center and Resort in Georgia frequently participate in clean-ups of roads and shore lines. The hotel is even working on developing written water conservation plans to help manage state water levels as they continue to adjust to local drought restrictions.

In other regions of the world, Marriott hotels are implementing great environmentally friendly practices, too, like our Sanya Marriott Resort in China that has installed solar panels. Our Melbourne Marriott hotel in Australia had the distinction of being named the first green five-star hotel in Melbourne. The JW Marriott Mumbai hotel in India was named The Most Environmentally Friendly Hotel of the Year in India last year. And the Portland Marriott Downtown Waterfront and Philadelphia Airport Marriott both achieved Green Seal certification.

All of these are terrific examples of what's called "glocal" - thinking globally and acting locally. That has always been the model we've followed at Marriott and now our hotels are applying that philosophy to protect the environment.

I'm Bill Marriott and thanks for helping me keep Marriott on the move.

Note: Courtesy of Marriott International

Whichever approach you choose, you will need to also identify who will be responsible for responding to comments and make sure the responses are prompt.

Components

The anatomy of a blog makes each blog unique and also helps to promote its presence on the Internet:

- When you post a blog, a ***date stamp*** with the date and time you posted it will automatically appear at either the top or bottom of the post. The most recent blog will appear at the top of the page. Search engines rank the most recent postings higher.
- Just as Web sites have their own URL, so do blog postings. Every time you publish a post on your blog, a ***permalink*** for that specific posting will automatically be generated. For example, the permalink in the Marriott blog is http://www.blogs. marriott.com/default.asp?item=2208945.
- Because of the varied topics blogs cover, placing blogs in ***categories*** will make it easier for readers to find the subjects that interest them most. Visitors to the McDonald's blog may be interested in nutrition, but not sustainability, so instead of sifting through all the posts, they can click on the nutrition category and get the information they really want. Categories also help search engines locate your blog.
- Similar to categories are ***tags***. While categories are broad, tags can be very specific and reflect the content of the post. They are an integral part of the search engine process. Think of them as the keywords you type in when conducting an online search. For example, the Marriott post is categorized under "Environment," but tags may include "World Environment Day," "Marriott Forest," or "glocal." People typing in these terms in a search engine will find a match in this post.
- The community of blogs, known as the ***blogosphere***, is based on the idea of sharing information. ***Trackbacks*** acknowledge other bloggers and inform readers of your blog to visit other blogs on the same subject. When you enable your blog software and include a trackback on your blog, the author of the blog you are citing or talking about will receive a notice, called a "ping." Trackbacks are an important part of developing relationships with other bloggers on the Web and gaining visibility for your blog.

Ethical Considerations

The founder of Ebay, Pierre Omidyar, once said, "The remarkable fact [is] that 135 million people have learned they can trust a complete stranger." Social networking communities are built on trust, and there are severe ramifications for those organizations that break that trust. The Word of Mouth Marketing Association (WOMMA) cautions that "consumers come first, honesty isn't optional, and deception is always exposed." Some organizations have harmed their reputations by jumping into the blogosphere unprepared for the scrutiny that occurs there.

For example, Wal-Mart gained a lot of attention when a couple driving an RV across country and staying in Wal-Mart parking lots overnight chronicled their journey in a blog. However, that attention turned negative when the blog was discovered to be a "flog," a fake blog. While the couple and their journey were real, the fact they were receiving compensation for the RV, meals, and other expenses was not disclosed. In fact, the journey was the product of Working Families for Wal-Mart, an advocacy group created by Wal-Mart and the Edelman public relations firm. All three organizations involved became the target of criticism; Edeleman's president and CEO, Richard Edelman, apologized for the lack of transparency, adding, "I am completely committed to doing better, not only for our firm but also the PR industry."

Following ethical guidelines will not only save your organization from negative comments, but it also may position your company as a leader. Scott (2007) suggests paying close attention to the following issues:

- Transparency. Use your own name when writing a blog or posting comments, and reveal any connection between a company and the blog it sponsors.
- Privacy. Don't disclose information that was given to you confidentially or use information without permission.
- Disclosure. Acknowledge any possible conflict of interest. Be upfront about any relationship you have with an organization or product you are writing about.
- Truthfulness. Quite simply, don't lie.
- Credit. Don't steal ideas and words from other bloggers; instead, give them credit through a trackback and foster the conversation.

Organizations that have blogs, especially if they are being written by several people, should provide guidelines to ensure all writers are aware of their ethical responsibility. WOMMA has developed an "Ethical Guide for Bloggers," which can be seen in Exhibit 9.4. Exhibit 9.5 offers advice on handling a cybercrisis.

Exhibit 9.4

WOMMA's 10 Principles for Ethical Contact by Marketers

Guidelines

Remember: Consumers come first, honesty isn't optional, and deception is always exposed.

1. I will always be truthful and will never knowingly relay false information. I will never ask someone else to deceive bloggers for me.
2. I will fully disclose who I am and who I work for (my identity and affiliations) from the very first encounter when communicating with bloggers or commenting on blogs.
3. I will never take action contrary to the boundaries set by bloggers. I will respect all community guidelines regarding posting messages and comments.
4. I will never ask bloggers to lie for me.
5. I will use extreme care when communicating with minors or blogs intended to be read by minors.
6. I will not manipulate advertising or affiliate programs to impact blogger income.
7. I will not use automated systems for posting comments or distributing information.
8. I understand that compensating bloggers may give the appearance of a conflict of interest, and I will therefore fully disclose any and all compensation or incentives.
9. I understand that if I send bloggers products for review, they are not obligated to comment on them. Bloggers can return products at their own discretion.
10. If bloggers write about products I send them, I will proactively ask them to disclose the products' source.

Note: Courtesy of WOMMA, Word of Mouth Marketing Association (www.womma.org)

Exhibit 9.5

Handling a Cybercrisis

Dissatisfied consumers and employees can enter an Internet chat room or blog and, within minutes, begin airing complaints and spreading rumors about a company and its products and services. Quick support has been rallied online for major boycotts and protests. Negative Web sites crop up that are solely devoted to criticizing an organization and its policies.

When a college professor felt he didn't receive good customer service after complaining to Intel that there was a flaw in its Pentium computer chip, he took his complaints to the Internet. Despite growing negative publicity, Intel decided not to acknowledge the problem and chose not to notify its customers or offer a recall. The cybercrisis continued to escalate, and, six months later, IBM announced it was halting shipments of PCs containing the faulty Intel chip. Finally forced to respond, Intel ran full-page newspaper ads apologizing for not handling customer complaints properly; the company also offered a free replacement Pentium.

Dissatisfied customers, disgruntled employees, and activist customers may turn to the Internet for more than just posting negative comments—they may create a rogue Web site. Ford Motor Co. found itself the victim of an Internet attack when the Association of Flaming Ford Owners posted a site demanding the recall of 26 million cars and trucks. McDonald's also was the target of a cyber-attack when the McInformation Network created a Web site called McSpotlight to provide the media and public with information on a lawsuit McDonald's had brought against two people who published a fact sheet featuring negative comments about the fast food chain on the Internet.

Managing the cybercrisis begins with actively monitoring what people are saying about you on the Internet. In addition to the daily chat room monitoring you can do sitting at your office computer, consider hiring an automated online monitoring service such as eWatch or CyberAlert to do a lot of the work for you. eWatch, for example, monitors thousands of Usenet groups and electronic mailing lists, hundreds of public discussion areas hosted by services such as Yahoo! and Google, and thousands of Web publications for information on topics you designate. What should you do when faced with a cybercrisis?

As with any crisis, have a plan. The Internet provides instant communication, and damaging comments can spread fast, not just to other consumers but to reporters and the financial community as well. Responding quickly, then, is critical. Having prepared strategies in place for potential cybercrises makes that quick response much easier.

- Defend yourself, but don't aggressively attack. If you know for a fact that claims being made online about your company are misinformed or false, make every effort to educate people and set the record straight. Don't go on the attack or try to shut down a negative site. Investigate the situation, open a dialogue to find out exactly what people are thinking, and then post information on your Web site and use listservs and third party experts to help correct misperceptions and regain support.

- Be ethical, and admit to mistakes. Never go into a chat room and pose as someone else to get information or try to influence people. If anyone finds out that you actually work for the company, this will certainly make the situation worse. And, keep an open mind. There may be times when a legitimate concern is brought to your attention in cyberspace. Do the right thing and work to solve the problem.

- Keep a watchful eye, even after the crisis is over. Once someone puts negative material on a Web site, it can stay up there for a long time. After the first crisis dies down, it is possible for the controversy to get reignited when new visitors access the information. Stay alert to those possibilities.

Promoting Your Online Presence

Once you develop your Web site or blog, you'll want people to visit, revisit, and talk about it. Don't assume that people will just find your site, however. Prepare a plan that outlines how you will proactively make target publics aware of your site and what it has to offer.

The simplest way to make your site known is to include its URL in all publicity and promotional materials such as news releases, brochures, newsletters, advertising, product packaging, company letterhead, and business cards. There are a number of inexpensive ways to create visibility for your site using the Internet, as well:

- Register your site with popular search engines. Go to the search engine's home page and fill out the requested information, which includes a brief description of your site and selected search keywords. While some search engines offer free registration, others may charge a fee. Be sure to include search engines that are specifically for blogs; Technorati.com is the most popular.
- Use a Web site announcement service such as Submit-It or Web-Promote. For a low fee, these services will register your site for you with major search engines, online directories, and yellow pages.
- Arrange for other relevant and high-traffic sites to offer free links to your site. You can do this by talking directly with people who manage those sites or by enlisting a service. Including trackbacks on your blog will also widen your site's exposure, as will asking bloggers who write about similar topics to include you on their "*blogroll*," a list of their favorite sites.
- Include the site address with your signature on e-mail correspondence. Set it up so people can click on the address and automatically go to your site.
- Create exposure for your site in newsgroups and chat forums. Closely monitor newsgroups and chat rooms for a period of time to make sure they are appropriate, and then look for opportunities to work subtle mentions of your site into related discussions. When you do join the conversation, however, make sure you are following ethical guidelines for transparency and disclosure.
- Include social media tags—tiny icons representing various networking sites—on your blog postings and Web site articles and news releases. Readers who like what they're reading can then share the material to their online communities. Also provide a way for visitors to e-mail the material to others they think would find it interesting.
- Allow visitors to subscribe to your site. Really Simple Syndication, or **RSS**, offers a way for readers to be automatically notified whenever the site is updated. RSS can also enable visitors to subscribe to podcasts, vodcasts, e-zines, and blogs.
- If your organization has a blog, feature a link to it on the home page of the organization's Web site.

Intranets

Whereas the Internet connects the vast area known as cyberspace, intranets work within an organization. Described as an organization's private Web site for employees, intranets provide electronic access to all kinds of information, from company policies to sales reports. Intranets are designed with electronic devices called firewalls that limit access to employees only. Many companies say that intranets more fully empower employees and increase productivity by providing fast and easy access to information they need to take initiative and do their jobs more effectively. They are especially helpful in facilitating the flow of information within organizations that have more than one geographical location or have employees working off-site.

Internal Web sites can reduce day-to-day operating costs and save companies money, too. Intranets make it possible for a company's project managers from around the world to "meet" and discuss projects online, which eliminates the need for frequent in-person meetings and reduces corporate travel expenses. Putting the company's policy guidelines or other manuals online can save tens of thousands of dollars, if not more, in annual printing costs.

Intranet experts and administrators point to several factors that contribute to good intranet design. These include getting management support at the start of the process and maintaining that support; defining what you want your intranet to accomplish; testing a pilot site to get employee feedback before launching the official site; and making employees aware of the site before its launch and training them on its use.

Wikis

Wikis are collaborative Web sites—Web pages that a group of people can access and contribute to or edit. Wikis can be used in many ways to bring together people and ideas about a subject. Savvy public relations practitioners can create a wiki as a clearinghouse for industry information, to fill a need in the marketplace, or act as a "thinktank" to address a problem. They can also be used internally as part of an organization's intranet to gain input on proposed policies or edit draft documents.

Perhaps the best-known public wiki is Wikipedia.com, the online encyclopedia written and edited by its visitors. Public relations practitioners should be familiar with Wikipeda.com for a couple of reasons. Each entry includes many links—blue words, which link to other entries on the subject; and red words, which indicate a topic that has not yet been written about. Those topics may provide an opportunity for public relations practitioners to submit an entry. Practitioners should also be aware of what is said about their companies on the site and request that any inaccuracies be corrected. Be sure to go through the proper channels, however. Wikipedia has strict guidelines on the involvement of public relations practitioners contributing and making edits to entries, which should be neutral and unbiased.

ASSIGNMENTS

Assignment 9.1—Blogging for Autism

 According to Wikipedia, autism is defined as a brain development disorder that impairs social interaction and communication and causes restricted and repetitive behavior, all starting before a child is 3 years old. It's estimated that there is a prevalence of one to two cases per 1,000 people for autism. The number of people known to have autism has increased significantly in the past two decades. Most children with autism are not able to live independently after becoming adults, although some can be successful.

You work as an assistant director of communications for the Autism Society of America (ASA), the nation's leading grassroots autism organization, dedicated to improving the lives of all people affected by autism. You've been talking with your supervisor, Kim Holloway, executive director of communications, about using more social media to support your public relations and outreach efforts. This morning, you have a meeting with Kim to talk more about this subject.

"I've been giving this a lot of thought, and taking a look at what's out there, and I think we could really benefit from starting a blog," Kim says. "I know we've been using an e-newsletter to reach out to families and others in the autism community, but this could be another way to provide information, but even more personally."

"A blog could work for us," you say, "but it requires someone to oversee it and post to it regularly. We'd also have to figure out what, exactly, we want it to do, the kind of content and features we'd like it to have, and who we really want to reach with it."

"Generally, I'm thinking parents and families are the main target," Kim says. "Younger parents and even younger siblings who have a brother or sister with autism, and who are definitely living more in the online world, would probably find it useful, maybe even cool. We could think about having video, and there would need to be some interactive elements."

"Okay, if we think we might want to go in this direction, why don't I start developing a plan of attack. I'm guessing that, since we're having this conversation, you probably want me to get pretty involved in this, right?"

"Now that you mention it, yes! You do have your own personal blog—I check it out every now and then—so you obviously have the blogger perspective. I just think you could get really excited about an ASA blog, and that's the kind of person I want managing it. Why don't you put some ideas together, and get back to me in a week or so?"

Exercises

1. Develop a plan for the ASA blog to include: (a) an introduction that explains the opportunities a blog presents to advance ASA's mission and communication efforts, as well as the challenges/issues that must be addressed that could impact the blog's success; (b) goals and audiences to be targeted; (c) general ideas for the structure and organization of the blog, including content and special features; and (d) methods that could be used to measure the blog's effectiveness.

2. You're preparing to launch the ASA blog. You need some text to introduce the blog and get people excited about visiting it. Write introductory text (no more than 150–200 words) that visitors would see on the front page of the blog site.

Assignment 9.2—*Promoting a Pop Music Star's Cause*

Nick Brideau is a popular singer, songwriter, and musician who some critics have compared to musicians Dave Matthews and John Mayer. His style has been described as ranging from "mildly alternative" to folk rock-ish, making him popular with everyone from college students to baby boomers. Brideau's last three CDs went platinum, and he has become one of the top concert tour draws in the past three years.

You are Brideau's publicist. He's asked you to meet with him to talk about the release of his next CD, *Hiding in Plain Sight*, and his growing involvement in supporting the fight against AIDS in Africa. Sub-Saharan Africa has been more heavily affected by AIDS and HIV infection than any other part of the world. The devastation of AIDS is being felt by families who are losing their primary income earners and whose average life expectancies are dropping from 62 to 47 years.

"So, we've got the new disc coming out in a few months, and I know you've started creating some buzz about it. That's great. What I haven't told you—mostly since I've just made a decision about it—is that I really want to use some of the sales from this CD to help the AIDS in Africa cause."

You say, "I know that your last trip to Africa a few weeks ago was pretty eye-opening. When you came back, you couldn't stop talking about it. I think your fans will probably like the fact that you're doing this."

"Well, I think people know that this is not just me trying to get some publicity. I've been involved in this cause for a while, and now that I've spent more time seeing its impact up close, I definitely want to do more," Brideau says.

"Okay, so do you have any specifics in mind?"

"I'm thinking 5% of CD sales. I've been talking about this with the record company, and we're working out the details. They seem okay with that number. I want the money to help the people affected—improving the hospitals and paying salaries for more health care workers since there's a big shortage. Many kids are losing their parents, so I'd like some of the money to be used to help provide for them."

You add, "I know that some of the songs on the new CD were inspired by this issue and that some of the music has an African sound and feel. You did some amazing things with drums and percussion in a few songs. We can bring that in to the mix, too."

"Yes, definitely. Of the 12 songs, I'd say half of them are inspired in some way. The first single—*For Africa*—is really about the epidemic. Any way, I'd really like to make a big splash about this, especially on the Web. I'm thinking some special Web pages, a video where we can talk about what's happening in Africa, you know the drill. If we could put the video on YouTube, that could reach a lot of people and help make more people aware. Hey, I also know we need to promote a CD, but I don't want to lose focus on the cause."

"Sounds good, Nick. Let me start mapping out a plan, and I'll get back to you fairly soon with some ideas."

Exercises

1. Conduct any additional research on AIDS in Africa and gather some facts that could be used for your Web and publicity efforts.

2. Develop a script (can include audio as well as visual elements) for a video that could be used on the Web and placed on YouTube. The video should be no longer than 90 seconds and should focus on the AIDS in Africa issue, with some mention of the new CD and how it will raise funds to help combat this epidemic.

3. Write the following media materials to announce the latest CD, including:

   - a news release for Nick Brideaus's Web site;
   - an e-mail pitch that could be sent to a major music magazine to help cultivate a feature story.

Assignment 9.3—The Olympics Podcast Series

You work for one of the oldest and best-known financial services firms in the world. The company offers an array of insurance, investment, and retirement planning products and services. Over the years, the company has found value in sponsoring sports events, including major golf tournaments and college football. It has now decided to sponsor the next summer Olympics, which coincides with the company's 100th anniversary.

As a member of the company's communications and public relations team, you and members of your work group—who specifically focus on Web and digital communications—attend a meeting with Matthew Grasso, senior director of public relations. He has been asked to coordinate sponsorship and related communications activities.

"We're seeing this sponsorship as a tremendous opportunity for us. It's a major financial commitment, but the Olympics give us visibility to the world and generally get a TV audience of two billion. Plus, we have the added bonus of connecting all of this with our 100th anniversary. The public relations value will be great. And, it plays into the themes of excellence and realizing dreams, which are certainly relevant to what we do."

Grasso continues: "We're going to need a dynamic Web presence that shows our involvement in the Olympics but that does much more than that, too. There should be features and content that people want to see and that will give them a reason to come to the site and spend some time there. Obviously, this provides another way for us to bring potential customers who are important to us—especially men in the 35–54 demographic—into our Web universe, so we're hoping that, besides the good will this can generate, it will also build awareness and interest in our services."

"I'm thinking about the 100th anniversary," you say, "and there are so many things we could do around that. How about a podcasting series—you know, something like the '100 greatest Olympic moments' sponsored by us. We could feature these twice a week, starting the year before the games and leading up to the games. It could be one way to keep people coming back to the site."

"I like that idea a lot," Grasso says. "Put together some thoughts on how we might do this, playing on the '100 greatest moments' or some other idea. Of course, we're going to need a plan for the Web site, as well. We should think through a conceptual approach for the site, what the information architecture might look like as it's laid out on the home page, and so on. Let's work on that, and get back to me in two weeks or so with some preliminary recommendations."

Exercises

1. Working with a partner, develop a proposal for Grasso that includes the following:

    *   a suggested theme line for your company to use in conjunction with the Olympics sponsorship. This will be used on the Web site and in all public relations and materials produced for the sponsorship;

    *   recommendations for the Web site approach and design, including: (a) statement of goals; (b) description of, and justification for, the conceptual approach you suggest

taking with the site, to include the information architecture/general content areas of the Web site; and (c) ideas for the presentation/design of the home page;

- recommendations for the podcast series, building on the "100 greatest moments" idea or some other approach. State the goals of the series and explain the conceptual approach you decide on; use some examples to illustrate the content/focus of specific podcast segments; and draft a script for a sample podcast segment. ■

References and Suggested Reading

1000words.kodak.com.

Black, R. (1997). *Web sites that work.* Berkeley, CA: Adobe Press.

Bradley, S. (2007). *Is there an optimal post length for blogs?* Retrieved December 17, 2008 from http://www.vanseodesign.com/blog/blogging/is-there-an-optimal-post-length-for-blogs/.

Clark, J. L., & Clark, L. R. (2001). *Cyberstyle: The writer's complete desk reference.* Cincinatti, OH: South-Western College Publishers.

Financial aid podcast.com.

Gillin, P. (2007). *The new influencers.* Sanger, CA: Quill Driver Books.

Holtz, S. (2002). *Public relations on the net* (2nd ed.). New York: AMACOM.

Levine, M. (2003). *Guerilla PR wired: Waging a successful publicity campaign on-line, offline, and everywhere in between.* New York: McGraw Hill.

Maney, K. (2005). *10 years ago, e-bay changed the world.* Retrieved December 17, 2008 from http://www.usatoday.com/tech/news/2005-03-21-ebay-cover_x.htm.

McDonnell, S. (1998). *The everything internet book.* Holbrook, MA: Adams Media Corp.

McNamara, R. (n.d.). *In Quotez* (computers). Retrieved December 6, 2002 from http://www.geocities.com/Athens/Oracle/6517/computer.html.

Media Survey 2008. (2008). *PRWeek* March 31, 2008.

Middleberg, D. (2000). *Winning PR in the wired world: Powerful campaign strategies for the noisy digital space.* New York: McGraw-Hill.

Nielsen, J. (2006). *F-shaped pattern for reading web content.* Retrieved December 15, 2008 from http://www.useit.com/alertbox/reading_pattern.html.

Picasso, Pablo (n.d.). *Pablo Picasso.* In Computers quotations. Retrieved December 6, 2002 from http://www.wisdomquotes.com/cat_computers.html.

Scott, D. M. (2007). *The new rules of marketing and PR.* Hoboken, NJ: John Wiley & Sons, Inc.

Seibert, T. (2006). *Edelman apologizes for Wal-Mart 'flog.'* Retrieved December 17, 2008 from http://www.mediapost.com/publications/index.cfm?fuseaction=Articles.showArticleHomePage&art_aid=49698.

Shiva, V. A. (1997). *The internet publicity guide.* New York: Allworth Press.

Web content report. Chicago, IL: Lawrence Ragan Communications, Inc.

Witmer, D. F. (1999). *Spinning the web: A handbook for public relations on the Internet.* New York: Addison Wesley, 1999.

WOMMA's practical ethics toolkit (n.d.). Retrieved December 16, 2008 from http://www.womma.org/blogger/.

10

Business Correspondence

It's been said that death and taxes are the only certainties in life. Public relations practitioners can add a third item to that list: writing business documents. Statements such as "Send me a memo on that" or "Great idea, why don't you put that in writing?" are part of everyday conversations between public relations professionals and the people with whom they work.

To meet the challenge of good business writing, consider these comments made by Kathy Griffin, of stand-up comedy fame and star of the television show "My Life on the D-list," and American motion picture producer Samuel Goldwyn of Metro Goldwyn Mayer (MGM). Griffin says: "I hate it—it is tedious. When I write for my act . . . I write bullet points. I cannot sit in front of a computer. That is not my style." And from Mayer: "I read part of it all the way through."

Both statements have relevance to business writing. While you should expect to spend some time working at a computer as a public relations professional, the use of bullet points can help make your business correspondence easy to read. Plus, those who receive your e-mail and other correspondence should be able to read these documents quickly and with ease "all the way through" and to clearly understand what you are trying to communicate. Also, without written documents in place, decisions made at meetings or great ideas shared in hallway conversations may be forgotten. Putting them in writing is the professional, smart, and safe thing to do.

Much of the time, business correspondence is factual and straightforward. There are, however, occasions when you must include persuasive appeals. In general, simplicity and clarity are essential to improve the chances of your message being read and understood.

Memoranda

Memos are documents that pass along information inside an organization. The most basic memos are brief—a few paragraphs to a page long. Since memos today are often distributed in electronic form, it's even more critical to keep them brief and easy to read. Memos are used for the following:

Purpose	Example
Inform about new developments.	Some important changes have been made to the company profit-sharing plan that you need to know about.
Inform about upcoming events.	Next Tuesday is "Take Your Son or Daughter to Work Day," and we want to encourage you to take part in that special day.
Confirm verbal decisions and agreements.	As we discussed this morning, I will begin planning the June 10 Webcast.
Provide program and activity.	The annual meeting is one month away, so I thought I should update you on our progress in planning this event.

Every memo is written (1) to someone; (2) by someone else; (3) at some point in time; (4) about some subject. These are the four items that should be included in the standard memo heading:

Memorandum

To: Deborah Pearson
From: James Curry
Date: November 15, 2008
Subject: Annual Meeting Progress Report

There are variations of the heading. Some organizations begin the memo heading with the date or always include job titles. It's a good idea to include job titles when the sender and recipient are not well acquainted.

When writing memos, use proper spacing: single space between sentences within a paragraph, and double space between paragraphs. Leave some white space between the last line of the heading and the first paragraph of the memo. Paragraphs may be indented, depending on the style your organization prefers. Regarding the content of memos:

- Clearly state the memo's purpose in the first sentence. Don't waste time on details that prevent the reader from quickly seeing your reason for writing, as the following paragraph does:

  A few days ago, I called and left a voice mail message for you about a project I am working on. I need to speak with you and get some information that will help me write an article for the employee newsletter on the employee diversity training workshops.

A better opening paragraph gets right to the point with fewer words:

  I would like to arrange an interview with you to talk about the upcoming employee diversity training workshops. The information will be used to write an employee newsletter article.

- Emphasize the most important points in the body of the memo. Write short sentences and paragraphs. Use "I," "you," and "we" to keep it direct and personal:

  First, I would like to get a quote from you on the value of these workshops to employees and what the company hopes to achieve by running these workshops. I also need some additional facts:

  - the days, times, and locations of the workshops;
  - the content and format of the workshops—what will employees learn and in what activities will they take part?
  - measures you will use to evaluate the success of the workshops.

- In the closing, say what you will do next or what you want the receiver to do. If a deadline is being imposed, it can be wise to mention that early in the memo, too, so that the receiver doesn't miss it. Avoid using general statements such as, "I look forward to hearing from you." Make your call-to-action specific:

  I need this information by Friday, June 9. Please e-mail your responses to me by that date. Thank you.

  OR

  I would like to meet or talk with you by phone for 20 to 30 minutes sometime during the week of June 5–9. I will call you this Friday, June 2, to arrange a convenient day and time for the interview.

There are times when a longer memo is justified. Many public relations professionals create *planning memos*, which present program plans in memo format to others within the organization. The same memo heading is used, but the document tends to be longer. Each program planning element is detailed, from the situation analysis to evaluation methods. A short paragraph at the beginning of the memo introduces the content that follows, and a brief conclusion reinforces the strengths and benefits of the plan. Subheads are used to separate each section. Planning memos also make greater use of numbered items, graphics, and bullet points to make the content easy to read and certain items jump off the page. For example, use numbers when listing program goals, highlight strategies in italics, and list key tactics under each strategy with bullets.

Letters

A French philosopher once said, "I have made this letter longer than usual, only because I have not had the time to make it shorter" (Boone, 1999, p. 57). This is not the way to go for business letters you write. Well-written letters are clear in their purpose, to the point, and generally follow the content guidelines for good memo writing. They provide information and verify arrangements, but are directed primarily to external audiences. Public relations letters, for example, confirm price quotes and production timetables with printing companies, or respond to dissatisfied customers and offer apologies for a negative experience. Letters follow a specified format:

- *Heading*. This includes the date, followed by a single-spaced block that includes the name, title, company, and address of the receiver. Leave a single space between the date and the person's name. Your company and address are unnecessary in the heading since most letters are distributed on letterhead, with the company name and address clearly visible.
- *Salutation*. Use "Dear Mr. or Ms." or accepted formal titles such as "Dr." or "Professor," never "Dear Sir or Madam." It has become more common to use the person's full name, as well (e.g., "Dear P. Jones," "Dear Pat Jones"). First names are fine for letters being sent to familiar business associates.
- *Body*. State your reason for sending the letter in a brief first paragraph. Other paragraphs are short and present key ideas. It is okay to use bold type or underscoring to highlight a point or two, but don't overdo. Like memos, single space between sentences in a paragraph, double space between paragraphs.
- *Closing and signature*. "Sincerely," "Best Regards," or "Best" are common "closing" words. Leave room for your signature below the closing and type your name (or, insert an e-signature, if you're sending via e-mail) below your signature. If you have a title, type it beneath your signature.

The business letter format can be seen in Exhibit 10.1.

Exhibit 10.1
Business Letter Format

[Your company letterhead]

[Date]

[Name of recipient]
[Title of recipient]
[Company of recipient]
[Address of company]
[City, State, Zip code]

[Salutation]:

[First paragraph: Reason for sending the letter]
[Second paragraph: Present key ideas, bullet points could be used]
[Third paragraph (if needed): Additional details]
[Last paragraph: Summary/concluding information]

[Closing],

[Signature of sender]

[Typed name of sender]
[Title of sender]

In addition to basic business letters, public relations people write specialized letters that are more persuasive in tone. These pieces are called "direct mail," because they are targeted and mailed to a specific audience. Direct mail includes *appeal letters*, *sales letters*, *pitch letters*, *new business letters*, *customer response letters*, and *thank you letters*:

- *Appeal letters*. These are typically written by not-for-profit organizations to solicit donations, members, or some other kind of support. Smith (2007) states, "The only difference between effective appeal letters and junk mail is the recipient's interest in the topic," so it is critical to carefully analyze your target public when writing this type of letter. Exhibit 10.2 offers additional tips.
- *Sales letters*. Similar to an appeal letter, a sales letter needs to speak to the reader; it should be customized and personal. In the opening, the letter must immediately grab the attention of the customer by offering a clear benefit; it should address the customer's need and focus on a clear solution. Joanne Krotz calls this "WIFM," or

Exhibit 10.2
Effective Fundraising Letters

How do you get potential donors to align with your cause and become motivated to give? *Fundraiser Insight*, a fundraising magazine, offers these tips for writing fundraising letters with impact in its e-book, *Writing Knock-out Fundraising Letters:*

- Begin by being clear about your audience. Are you writing for existing donors or new donors? Think about why these donors should care about the cause, how they might be personally touched by it, and how you can make them feel the urgency of your request.

- Explain what your organization does and how important it is to the people it serves. Add quotes from people who your organization helps to illustrate the difference you are making in their lives.

- Use storytelling to inspire and engage. Share a real-life success story to let the reader see what is possible with his or her support, or a dramatic experience that demonstrates how great the need is.

- Stress the benefits of financial support and clearly articulate how donations are used to improve lives or make a situation better.

- Focus on the positive, not the negative. Don't over-emphasize the problems your organization faces. Instead, help donors realize how their support can lead to positive change.

- Present a shocking or surprising fact to get your audience's attention or, as appropriate, incorporate a current news headline that connects with your fundraising campaign. Mothers Against Drunk Driving (MADD) did that when Paris Hilton was charged with driving under the influence, using the headline "Help MADD stop the 500,000 Paris Hiltons" to draw attention to the high incidence of drunk driving.

- Show how a specific donation amount can have a direct benefit. For example, "Your $25 gift will feed a dog in our shelter for x# of weeks."

- Make it easy for donors to give. Send self-addressed (stamped, if possible) envelopes, and make sure that contact names and phone numbers, as well as Web site URLs, are visible and easy to find.

- Get your fundraising material noticed by using an odd-sized mailing envelope. Consider printing an eye-catching graphic or a provocative teaser copy line on the envelope that can help you stand out and prompt people to open your mailing.

"What's in it for me?" In her article "How to Write an Effective Sales Letter" on www.microsoft.com, she offers 11 tips for how to effectively follow an opening that focuses on WIFM:

- *Build trust*. Include endorsements and testimonials, especially from customers who may be well known.
- *Get to bona fides*. Briefly present your credentials—explain who you are, what you do, and why you are good at it.
- *Make it memorable*. Add useful information that your customer can refer to later; this will increase the shelf life of your letter and allow for future consideration.
- *Emphasize good looks*. Pay attention to the visual aspects of your letter and design it for maximum impact.
- *Include a call to action*. Let the customer know what to do next and explain the follow-up process.
- *Include an incentive*. Offer a discount or something free.
- *Resist "mail merge."* Try to send specialized letters based on your customer's sales history and preferences.
- *Forge connections*. Use your letter to build a relationship, not just to push your product or service.
- *Test*. Send out at least two versions of the letter and see which one garners more response.
- *Hit the right notes*. Write the way YOU speak. If you normally present yourself casually, write casually.
- *Calculate the response rate*. Make sure you can handle the response to your direct mail (e.g., filling product orders) BEFORE you send it.

Exhibit 10.3 shows an example of a direct mail piece aimed at regaining a lost customer.
- ***Media pitches***. These letters or e-mails present story ideas to media and are fully discussed in chapter 7.
- ***New business*** *or* ***prospecting letters***. These are used by public relations firms to introduce themselves to potential clients. Prospecting letters introduce the firm and the writer, include background information about the potential client and reasons why public relations services are needed, suggest a few ways in which public relations can benefit the prospect, and request a face-to-face meeting.
- ***Customer response letters***. You may also write letters in response to legitimate customer complaints or other criticisms of your organization. In their book *Writing that Works: How to Communicate Effectively in Business,* Kenneth Roman and Joel Raphaelson suggest that it is best to be courteous rather than defensive when responding to all complaints. When writing these letters:

  - In the first paragraph, acknowledge the person's complaint. Don't accuse someone of overreacting. Show that you are aware of the person's concerns and be respectful of his or her feelings.
  - In the body of the letter, tell the person how you plan to respond to the complaint. Indicate specific steps to be taken and when those steps will be taken, as well as

other decision makers who will be consulted. In addition, offer apologies for any inconvenience or upset the situation may have caused. If there's a chance a situation may prompt a lawsuit, you should consult with the organization's legal staff before publicly acknowledging any fault.

- In a closing paragraph, point out that you welcome future suggestions and feedback and that you value that person's continued business and support.

There are situations where a concern or complaint is unjustified or is based on inaccurate information about company policy or procedure. In those cases, state your company's position in a polite and straightforward manner and make an effort to clarify any misconceptions.

- ***Thank you letters***. A "thank you" goes a long way when building and maintaining relationships. Take the time to thank donors for their support and customers for their business. Write thank you letters promptly and use them as an opportunity to reaffirm to readers that their decision to donate money or purchase a product was a wise one.

Exhibit 10.3

Direct Mail: Netflix

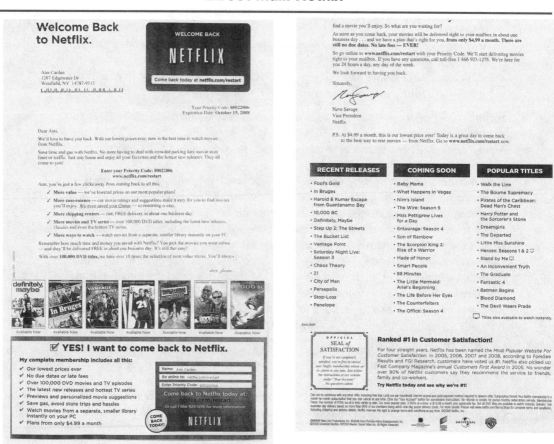

Note: Reprinted with permission of Netflix, Inc.

For example, when thanking donors, give an example of how the money was used. Thank yous also go a long way in strengthening relationships with co-workers who do exceptional work or with colleagues who give you some helpful advice. In those instances, while a brief e-mail message or verbal thank you can usually serve the purpose—it's good practice to thank people regularly on the job—a handwritten note on a thank you card in certain instances is a nice gesture, as well.

E-mail

Much of your day-to-day business communication is now being done through the use of e-mail. While most professionals expect to get e-mail messages during the course of the work day, you should not just assume that your message will be welcomed. A sure way to alienate media contacts is to keep sending e-mails for which they didn't ask. In response, they may activate a mechanism to automatically block any messages coming from your e-mail address. E-mail works best when you:

- First, decide if e-mail is the best choice. Some messages are better sent by other methods. If, for example, you are extending an invitation to a conference speaker or attempting to get a local company to sponsor your community event, a more formal letter, printed and mailed on your organization's letterhead, might be required. Once contact is made, e-mail becomes a good follow-up tool. In these days of e-communication and digital media, we often forget the value of a telephone call or personal contact. If you need a quick answer, or if you have a sensitive matter to discuss, a phone conversation or a face-to-face meeting is usually the best choice.
- Carefully choose your recipients. Place the recipients whom you are directly addressing the e-mail to in the "To" field. If it is necessary to keep someone else "in the loop," that recipient should be placed in the "Cc" field. Use special caution when replying to an e-mail: you may not need to send your reply to everyone who received the original e-mail. For example, if you reply to an e-mail that was sent to a listserv, your response will go to everyone on that listserv, not just the sender.
- Include a strong subject line that connects with the receiver's interests. The media and others you deal with receive loads of e-mail each day. A well-conceived subject line can make your message stand out. If you are trying to get a business reporter to take an interest in something your company has done, write a subject line that uses business-type words or clearly states the benefit to readers: "ABC, XYS companies announce merger."
- Include a salutation. Refer to the person to whom you are writing the e-mail the same as you would in person. If you normally use the person's first name, then start your message with "Dear Michael." Otherwise, use the appropriate courtesy title with the person's last name.
- Keep your message brief. Get to the point quickly in the first paragraph. Limit your message to a few short paragraphs, except in those instances when someone has requested more depth.
- Follow the rules of good writing. One of e-mail's benefits is its speed of delivery, but that doesn't give you the license to be hasty and sloppy when preparing messages.

Exhibit 10.4

E-mail Etiquette

Words actually make up less than 10% of the messages we send. The rest of the message is communicated through other factors, such as body posture, gestures, eye contact, facial expressions, and how we use our voice. With e-mail messages, or any written message, we don't have nonverbal and vocal support. So we must rely on words alone.

Although e-mail is quick and convenient, don't make the assumption that writing e-mail messages is any different than writing a letter you would send through "snail mail." When drafting an e-mail message for someone other than a close friend, be professional and follow these guidelines:

- Use correct spelling, punctuation, and grammar. It's easy to click on that reply button and write a quick message. That doesn't mean you can be sloppy. Write in complete sentences and use correct grammar. Use spell check and the dictionary. Avoid using exclamation marks. When writing business e-mails, don't use text messaging abbreviations. You can't assume, for example, that the receiver will know that "2MI" means "too much information."

- Use capitalization correctly. Follow the same rules for capitalization that you would in any other written communication. If you type your e-mail using all capital letters, it will make the receiver feel like he or she is getting yelled at. On the other hand, if you don't use any capital letters, even at the start of sentences, you may be sending a message that you have low self-confidence.

- Don't use smiley faces. Another way we have attempted to make up for the lack of nonverbal and vocal cues in e-mail is through the development of a series of cute online symbols used for emphasis and emotion, such as :-) for "happy" and :-(for "sad." . . . Do you really want to include one of these in a business e-mail? Enough said.

- Proofread carefully. Once your message has been drafted, take a critical look at it. Be objective and try to read it through the eyes of the receiver. Is there any confusing language? Is there any content that could be misinterpreted?

- Make the message easy to read. Using the above guidelines will help improve the clarity of your message. To improve readability, indent paragraphs or double space between them. Keep sentences and paragraphs short. A paragraph in an e-mail message doesn't have to be longer than two sentences.

- Protect the thread. The thread is the series of messages that has been exchanged since the original message. When replying to a message, continue the thread by clicking on "reply" rather than starting a new message. The thread contains important background information that will help put the new message in context for the receiver.

- Don't be hasty. Because e-mail is so quick and convenient, we are tempted to reply to messages right away. Not only will this affect how well written your message is, but it also may cause regrets later on. If you're upset over an e-mail message you receive, or if the message has an angry tone, don't react immediately. Take some time to think over the response, or consider if a response is even necessary. Once you hit the send button, there's no getting that message back

- Avoid "flame wars." Hasty responses may result in "flame wars." Flames are "verbal" e-mail attacks. If you are on the receiving end of a flame, consider the merits of ignoring it. Getting into arguments over e-mail is often a futile effort. Flames consume time and inbox space.

- Keep private things private. Never think of e-mails as personal and confidential. Companies have the right to monitor their employees' e-mail practices; messages can remain on your computer system (yes, even after you delete them), and they can be forwarded to other people. When composing an e-mail message, make sure you are comfortable with the information being shared with others.

Write in complete sentences, use spell check, and take time to proofread. Hold back on the use of cute online symbols (e.g., :-) to relay humor. They are fine for personal e-mail, but inappropriate for professional communications. Guidelines for e-mail etiquette are featured in Exhibit 10.4.

- Always add a signature. Your e-mail address may not always accurately indicate who is sending the e-mail, so always include a "signature." Your signature may consist of just your name or your name, title, company, address, phone, Web site, and e-mail (the information that would typically be on the company's printed letterhead). Many e-mail senders have begun adding quotes or images at the end of their signatures. While these add-ons might be fine for people with whom you are well acquainted, it's probably best to keep them out of most of your business e-mail.
- Think twice about sending attachments. There is nothing more frustrating than receiving an attachment file that you cannot open. In some instances, such as those times you are providing information to a reporter, you should ask first if it's all right to send an attachment. Before sending it, find out if you are using compatible word processing programs, to ensure that the receiver can open the file.

Voice Mail

Most of us have had the following experience: You're checking your voice mail and suddenly you hear the name or voice of a person famous for long-winded messages. Because you're busy, and you suspect this is another unessential message, you instantly press the delete button. Unfortunately, there may have been vital information in that message, but, because the person rambled on, you never listened long enough to hear it. If used properly, voice mail can be an effective way to communicate, and a good way to get important information to large groups quickly and simultaneously. How can you make the best use of voice mail?

- State your message in 30 seconds or less. Write down what you want to say before you send voice mail. Identify yourself, briefly explain why you are calling, and quickly mention the information most relevant to the receiver. Leave your name and phone number if you are the contact person, or let people know how they can find out more about the subject.
- Leave out all the details. Focus on main points and refer people to written documents, Web sites, or other sources that can provide more specifics. If your intention is to get a return phone call, there's no need to say everything. Share the main reason for your call and express your interest in talking further about the matter. Suggest the best time to call back within the next day or two.
- Return calls promptly. When you are the receiver, be courteous and get back to someone as soon as you can. Your quick response ensures that others will give your voice mail the same considerations. When you're out of the office for a few days or longer, revise your voice mail message to let people know that you are away, when you will return, and who they can speak with regarding an urgent business matter. You also can leave a mobile phone number, if you want people to be able to reach you.

ASSIGNMENTS

Assignment 10.1—The Samaritan House Appeal

As a new public relations and development assistant for The Samaritan House, your duties include planning special events, handling publicity and media relations, and writing most of the fundraising campaign materials. The Samaritan House, a social service agency established in the early 1900s, has more than 300 operations in cities nationwide. The International Association of Good Samaritans is the parent organization that coordinates all The Samaritan Houses. The Samaritan House in your city is one of the largest in the country, with 350 employees, 25 social service programs, and an annual budget of $11 million. In addition to running several homeless shelters and soup kitchens in your area, The Samaritan House offers alcohol and drug rehabilitation programs and a learning center where disadvantaged individuals can learn computer and other job skills.

While many of those who use the services are low-income elderly and single-parent families, a growing number are middle-class adults who recently lost a job owing to major company downsizing in your area. Some of these individuals have found new jobs, but at much lower salaries, which is making it difficult to keep up with their bills. Others have failed to find work in a market where the unemployment rate has steadily increased in the past two years. As a result, The Samaritan House has seen a 10% jump in the number of people using its services in the past year.

One of your main tasks at this time is to create solicitation materials to raise money for the annual Thanksgiving dinner, one of The Samaritan House's major events. People with nowhere to go or who can't afford to prepare a holiday meal for themselves and their families are treated to a delicious turkey dinner with all the trimmings. The major source of funding for the dinner is financial donations from individuals and local businesses. A donation of $2 will feed one hungry person; $20 will feed 10 people; $28 will feed 15 people; $38 will feed 45 people; and $120 will feed 60 people. Your research of previous dinners produces some additional facts:

- Last year, 2,000 people enjoyed The Samaritan House's Thanksgiving dinner in your city. Many of those in attendance were single mothers with children under 10 and senior citizens without spouses or whose children live a great distance away. This year, The Samaritan House in your city plans to serve more people on Thanksgiving Day. In addition to serving those who come to The Samaritan House, it will also be delivering a hot holiday meal to more than 1,000 men and women who can't leave their homes owing to age, illness, or disability.

- During its existence, The Samaritan House has fed tens of thousands of people on Thanksgiving. The Samaritan House serves three hot, nutritious meals every day of the year in its dining room to hungry people in your area. This year, in total, The Samaritan House in your city has served more than 300,000 meals to hungry people.

- Community donations are vital for this event and provide more than 75% of the total funding needed. Individual contributions are important this year because of cutbacks in government funding, reductions in the area's business work force, and the slumping economy, which are all contributing to increased financial need and increased demand for services.

- This year, like every year, many volunteers from throughout the community will share part of their Thanksgiving Day to help prepare and serve the meals.

Exercises

1. Write a direct mail fundraising letter to prospective, first-time donors who have not supported the Thanksgiving dinner in the past. This letter will be sent via U.S. mail with a promotional piece on the Samaritan House and its services.

2. Write a direct mail fundraising letter to individuals who made a donation to support the Thanksgiving dinner last year, encouraging them to support the event again this year.

3. Write a follow-up e-mail message that can be sent to the "previous donor" audience one month after the printed piece is mailed. Include a subject line for your e-mail message.

Assignment 10.2—Layoffs at ExpressAir

Skyrocketing fuel prices and a slowing economy have caused major financial problems for the airline industry. In the past several years, a few airlines have gone out of business, and most have experienced reductions in staff in an effort to achieve financial stability.

You work for ExpressAir, a mid-sized carrier with about 10,000 employees. Despite the airline's best efforts to cut costs, the company's CEO, Ashley Kenyon, in consultation with her senior leadership team, has decided to initiate layoffs of 750–1,000 employees. As the senior public relations officer, you're asked to work on an internal e-mail to be sent to all staff, from the CEO, announcing the layoffs. You speak with her to get more of the details.

"As you know, we've held off on doing any major layoffs this past year, when some of our competitors did decide to reduce staff. Since we're known for being more 'no-frills' and keeping our costs generally lower than most other airlines, we've been able to maintain good ticket sales, until now. The effects of the unstable economy and higher fuel prices have taken a toll. We just can't manage it any longer and survive for the long-term unless we let some people go. It's a tough decision to make. But it's just not good business for us to keep operating this way," Kenyon says.

"Who is this affecting? Is it just pilots and flight attendants, or are we talking about corporate staff, as well?" you ask.

"This will include pilots, flight attendants, and ground crew, as well as managers and staff working in corporate headquarters. We're looking to cut back service to and from some of our lower-yielding routes. Some of the destinations on our schedule currently have more frequent flights than are necessary for the number of passengers we tend to have on average. Since we'll be cutting back service in several areas, that means we'll need fewer employees in those areas. We're also retiring about 50 of our planes over the course of the year, which will help us save money on fuel and maintenance."

"I know we've tried to cut costs in other ways, to prevent us from having layoffs. Some people might be wondering if those and other measures haven't been working, and why we've chosen to lay people off versus something else."

Kenyon says, "I think it's important to stress that we did raise ticket prices a year ago and ran a number of promotions to try to boost ticket sales. That had some modest success, but the fact is, people just don't have the discretionary income these days and they're cutting back on personal travel, especially air travel. Our ticket sales have continued to drop, and, in the last six months, we had losses of about $20 million. Our projections show that we don't expect any turnaround in the next 12 months, either. Fuel accounts for anywhere from 30 to 50% of our operating costs right now, which is very significant."

"Okay, I think I've got enough here to start working on a draft. I know we want to move quickly, so I'll have a draft for you in two hours or so. Did you say when this is taking effect?"

"We'll probably start contacting affected staff in the next 30 days or so, and should complete the layoffs in the next three months. We need to move quickly to help get us try to get back on more stable financial footing.

Exercises

1. What, if any, additional information would you like to have from the CEO to develop this announcement, as well as any other communication relating to the layoffs?

2. Identify the key message points that you would want to include in this internal communication and that should be consistently communicated by ExpressAir in the next few months.

3. Write the internal e-mail message to be sent to all ExpressAir staff announcing the lay-offs. Include an appropriate subject line.

Assignment 10.3—The Shopping Bag Complaint

You work in the public relations department of Tees & Flannels, a national retail clothing chain. Tees & Flannels sells casual and outdoor clothing that appeals mainly to teens and college students. One day, Jacob Zellers, the company's public relations director, shares with you an angry e-mail message sent by a parent whose daughters recently purchased clothing at one of your stores:

Yesterday, my 12- and 14-year-old daughters bought some T-shirts at your store. I was shocked by the high prices they paid for the shirts, but I was even more disturbed by the images on the shopping bag—a young man stripped naked to the waist with two young girls on each side of him. The three of them are rolling around on a couch in a very suggestive manner.

This picture, in my opinion, is completely inappropriate, considering that 12- and 14-year-olds like my daughters are your typical customers. What messages do my girls get when they go to your store and get bags like this? Clearly, the young people on this bag are up to no good; from the dirty grin on the young man's face, it's clear he has other things on his mind besides clothes. Is it really necessary to show half-naked people on your shopping bags and to promote sexual behavior among adolescents in this way? Not only is it unnecessary, it's irresponsible.

I did talk about this with my daughters and I explained that this kind of advertising is not acceptable because it treats girls as sexual objects. Honestly, they are puzzled by it all and don't really understand why your store would use this kind of picture on its bags. Frankly, I have a hard time grasping that myself. I ask you to stop using these bags and to please reconsider the kind of sexual images you are conveying. My feeling is, this letter will probably get a quick read and then just filed away somewhere, but I needed to express my concerns nonetheless. Please, please be more sensitive to your impressionable young customers, and be more sensitive to the concerns of parents like me who, I should add, supply the money that teenagers use to buy your overpriced clothes.

Sincerely,

Michael Chalmers

After you read the e-mail, Zellers replies: "We need to respond to Mr. Chalmers' concerns. I would like to send a response to him clarifying our corporate position on the bag's design. Let's also be sure that we're sensitive to his feelings and that we give him a personal response. I don't want this to look like a form letter."

"Have other customers been complaining about the bags?" you ask.

"Some have, but it hasn't been a huge number," explains Zellers. "The bags have been in the stores for about three months, and we've only had a few complaints. Most people don't seem to care one way or the other and, if they do, they're not telling us about it."

"So, what is our position on this?" you ask. "Obviously, these images target our young audience, so there is value from a marketing perspective, but I don't think that argument will carry much weight with Mr. Chalmers. I mean, the people shown on these bags aren't doing anything that's clearly sexual, really. How old are the models, anyway?"

"All of them are at least 18. The young man is actually 22, and the two young ladies are both 21. They just look young, that's all," answers Zellers. "There has been talk of hiring older-looking models in some of the recent marketing meetings. I'm not sure where those discussions will lead, but we are talking about the issue. Basically, our position is that the bags show a bunch of kids having a good time. It's some friends getting together and goofing around, period. Yes, the images are fun and wild and even a bit sexy, but the idea is to show the fun and excitement of youth, not to promote teen-age sex. That's the wrong interpretation of what we're aiming for with the bags."

"It will be a challenge to write this response, but I'll take my best shot," you say.

Exercise

Write an e-mail response to Mr. Chalmers' concerns about Tees & Flannels' shopping bags. Include a subject line.

References and Suggested Reading

25 quick tips for attracting readers (n.d). Retrieved December 15, 2008 from http://www.fundraiserinsight. org/articles/25-fundraising-letter-writing-tips.html.

Alred, G. J., Brusau, C. T., & Oliu, W. E. (2006). *The business writer's handbook* (10th ed.). Boston: St. Martin's Press.

The AMA style guide for business writing. (1996). New York: AMACOM.

Argenti, P. A., & Forman, J. (2002). *The power of corporate communication: Crafting the voice and image of your business.* New York: McGraw Hill.

Berger, A. A. (1993). *Improving writing skills: Memos, letters, reports and proposals.* Thousand Oaks, CA: Sage Publications.

Boone, L. E. (1999). *Quotable business*, 2nd edition. New York: Random House.

Business letter format. Retrieved November 30, 2008 from http://teacher.scholastic.com/lessonplans/ Format.pdf.

Davidson, W. (2001). *Business writing: What works, what won't* (Rev. ed.). New York: St. Martin's Press.

Dobrian, J. (1997). *Business writing skills.* New York: AMACOM.

E-Mail etiquette (1998). Retrieved November 30, 2008 from http://iwillfollow.com/emailetiquette.pdf.

Krotz, J. (2008). *How to write an effective sales letter: 11 tips.* Retrieved November 30, 2008 from http://www.microsoft.com/smallbusiness/resources/marketing/customer-service-acquisition/how-to-write-an-effective-sales-letter-11-tips.aspx#Howtowriteaneffectivesaleslettertips.

Roman, K., & Raphaelson, J. (2000). *Writing that works: How to communicate effectively in business* (3rd ed.). New York: HarperResource.

Seglin, J. L., & Coleman, E. (2007). *The AMA handbook of business letters* (3rd ed.). New York: AMACOM.

Smith, R. D. (2007). *Becoming a public relations writer* (3rd ed.). Mahwah, NJ: Lawrence Erlbaum Associates.

11

Reports and Proposals

Noted statesman Winston Churchill, the United Kingdom's leader during World War II and a Nobel Prize-winning writer, once said, "This report, by its very length, defends itself against the risk of being read." He also cautioned, "Please be good enough to put your conclusions and recommendations on one sheet of paper in the very beginning of your report, so I can even consider reading it." Another world leader, U.S. President Barack Obama, has said: "A good compromise, a good piece of legislation, is like a good sentence or a good piece of music. Everybody can recognize it. They say, 'Huh, it works. It makes sense.'" These are all good pieces of advice and observations when writing reports and proposals. This chapter reviews the many reasons public relations professionals prepare reports and proposals, the components of these documents, and how to write so people will read them.

Reports

Reports are written to inform clients and senior managers about the results of public opinion studies and other research efforts, to provide in-depth assessment of a campaign or project, and for other business purposes. Many of the same guidelines for writing memos, e-mail messages, and other business correspondence apply to reports. Brevity, clarity, and simple language help to make these documents most effective. Research and annual reports are two of the most common types of report used in public relations.

Research Reports

A model for report writing is the ***research report***, which includes the following sections:

- Cover page, with a title that summarizes the focus of the report and includes the name(s) of those submitting the report and the date of submission.
- Table of contents outlining the report sections and their page numbers.
- Executive summary that highlights significant findings, conclusions, and recommendations in one or two pages. Even though this section is at the beginning, it should be

written after you have completed the rest of the report. The executive summary should be so inclusive, yet concise, that the reader could read only this section and understand the substance of the entire report.

- Introduction that explains the purpose of the report, the history of the research problem, research methods used, and limitations of the study.
- Body of the report, which presents detailed findings. If survey results are shared, findings are best presented in percentages rather than numbers (e.g., 30% said "yes," 50% said "no," 20% said "no opinion"). Charts and graphs make the data easy to read and understand.
- Analysis and conclusions. The report writer must interpret the data, pull out the most significant findings, and discuss their implications.
- Recommendations on how the organization should proceed based on the research findings.
- Supporting materials. These can include copies of questionnaires or related media articles that add perspective to the subject.
- Bibliography that lists the sources used in compiling the report.

Annual Reports

Another type of report written by public relations professionals is the annual report. Annual reports review the financial performance and accomplishments of an organization in a given year, and define strategic direction for the future. For-profit companies that trade stock publicly are required by law to produce specific financial information for their shareholders, investors, and the financial community. This information often is included in an annual report, which can double as a promotional tool written with stockholders, employees, and other key publics in mind. Not-for-profit agencies are not obligated to produce annual reports. Many do, however, because of increasing public scrutiny of charitable groups and how they spend fundraising dollars. The annual report is a way to build donor confidence in their cause and their financial management.

Formats for annual reports vary. A large corporation may create a lengthy, magazine-style report with four-color photographs and splashy graphics. Not-for-profit groups, sensitive to the way administrative dollars are spent, might create less slick reports printed in black and white, or two colors. Online versions of annual reports are included on many organizations' Web sites. Annual reports, as with any other printed piece, should reflect the character of the organization.

Most annual reports contain common elements: (1) a theme: for example, Tandy Corporation/Radio Shack used the annual report theme line "We've Got Goals" in conjunction with its "You've Got Questions, We've Got Answers" advertising campaign theme; (2) a letter to shareholders from the CEO addressing the company's performance in the past year, key challenges, and future goals (Exhibit 11.1 is a good example taken from a Burger King annual report, the theme of which was "The Adventure Begins"); (3) detailed financial facts, figures, and statements; (4) information on the company, its people, and its products or services, with an emphasis on the past year's innovations; and (5) an examination of critical issues the company faces and how it plans to tackle those issues in the future. Other than the financial data, public relations writers, or the firms they hire to work on these time-consuming pieces, usually write most sections of the report, including the letter from the CEO. When producing annual reports:

- Be honest. This is less a "tip" than it is a necessity. Annual reports are factual, straightforward documents. Maintain a positive tone, but never hide negative news or distort financial information in the company's favor.
- Be creative and interesting. Break the mold and try something new. Foodmaker, the parent company of Jack in the Box restaurants, presented an annual report in comic-book form, which was well received by stockholders and financial analysts. Wichita Children's Home won praise by presenting its report through the eyes of a child living at the home, with type that looked like a child's handwriting. Calavo Growers, a leader in the avocado industry, has exhibited great creativity with its annual reports, having issued one designed as a passport and another designed as a storybook.
- Be easy to read. Avoid overloading people with highly technical terms and facts. Focus on main points and use simple, easy-to-understand language. Write in active voice and use photos, charts, and other visuals.
- Be mission-driven. Annual reports connect with the company's goals. The Wichita Children's Home saw its report as a tool for educating people about the home's importance to abused children, and as a vehicle to recruit new donors. The report is credited with a 5–10% increase in funding.

Proposals

Proposals are designed much like standard reports, but they do more than provide facts, findings, and suggestions; they aim to convince the reader to take a specific course of action. In order to do that, they must be written in a persuasive manner. Arthur Asa Berger, in his book *Improving Writing Skills: Memos, Letters, Reports and Proposals* (1993), states that, in general, proposals are most persuasive when they:

- appeal to the self-interest of, and have clear benefits for, all the involved parties;
- use your reader's ideas and beliefs to your advantage, by knowing what the reader is looking for before you develop and submit the proposal;
- deal with short-term or long-term benefits, or both if appropriate; focus on long-term benefits if short-term costs are great or vice versa;
- emphasize cost efficiency by showing that the proposal leads to a payoff or to increased savings;
- have a writing style that expresses confidence in the value of your ideas without being too arrogant;
- show how your proposed actions or solutions are better than all others suggested.

Public relations professionals write proposals for any number of reasons. A common use of proposals is to "sell" senior managers and others within an organization on the benefits of making charitable donations, sponsoring a new event, or initiating some other program, in an effort to secure support and resources needed for that project or initiative. For example, after

Exhibit 11.1

CEO Letter to Shareholders: Burger King Holdings, Inc.

TO OUR

SHAREHOLDERS

**Our business has never been stronger, our future never brighter.
And the best is yet to come as the *Burger King®* adventure continues.**

By any major financial or operational metric, Burger King Holdings, Inc., delivered record results and significant achievements in fiscal 2008. Profits grew by 24 percent amid sharply rising commodity prices and a challenging consumer environment. We accomplished this through our people—employees, franchisees, and suppliers—all working together to drive our brand forward each and every day, and their unwavering dedication to deliver on our *Have It Your Way®* brand promise globally.

Our laser focus and commitment to progressive improvements enabled us to continue our grand adventure—serving great tasting food at affordable prices in 71 countries and U.S. territories. Our adventure is defined by our *True North Plan* and its four strategic growth pillars—products, marketing, operations, and development. This year we continued our winning streak, posting significant improvements and setting new records.

IN OUR SECOND FULL YEAR AS A PUBLIC COMPANY,
BURGER KING HOLDINGS, INC. POSTED:

:: **Record worldwide revenues of $2.46 billion,**
up 10 percent from fiscal 2007
:: **The 18th consecutive quarter of worldwide
positive comparable sales**
:: **Exceeded last year's best in a decade
traffic performance**
:: **Record worldwide average restaurant sales (ARS)
of $1.3 million, up 9 percent from fiscal 2007**
:: **A net restaurant gain of 282—the highest net
restaurant growth in eight years**
:: **Record earnings per share of $1.38, up 24 percent
from our adjusted earnings per share in fiscal 2007,
again exceeding our long-term growth target**

We expect this exciting global adventure to continue for the next several years. For fiscal 2009, we will open even more restaurants; step up our company-owned restaurant reimaging initiative; roll out the first *Whopper Bar*™; continue to innovate and launch high-demand products; excite consumers with new promotional tie-ins and creative advertising; effectively execute on our operational platforms; and, of course, give back to the communities we serve. We are uniquely positioned to deliver best-in-class results based on our multiple growth drivers and our steadfast desire to be the best in the industry.

In fiscal 2009, we expect to open 350-to-400 net new restaurants worldwide by expanding in key markets including China, Brazil, Eastern Europe, the Middle East, and North America. Our plans call for us to reimage even more company-owned restaurants with contemporary designs and décor with many of our franchisees making similar investments. We're also accelerating efforts to reduce our environmental footprint, reducing the size of the restaurants and introducing more energy-efficient equipment. We expect all of these development opportunities to significantly grow our top-line and increase profits.

Our innovation process—refined over five years of successful menu strategies, product R&D, and new kitchen equipment—continues to satisfy the demand of both indulgence-seeking and value-minded guests. Our product offerings are intended to increase our broad-based appeal and to fill in existing product gaps in breakfast, snacking, and desserts. We are very excited about upcoming launches, including *BK Breakfast Shots*™, *BK Burger Shots*™, mega Angus burger, soft-serve ice cream treats, and *BK®* Smoothies. All these great tasting products are aimed at driving traffic and increasing ARS.

14 :: Burger King

continued . . .

Exhibit 11.1

CEO Letter to Shareholders: Burger King Holdings, Inc. *. . . continued*

EXECUTIVE TEAM

Top row left to right: Anne Chwat, Gladys DeClouet, Chuck Fallon, Armando Jacomino, Russ Klein
Middle row left to right: Julio Ramirez, John Chidsey, Raj Rawal
Bottom row left to right: Peter Robinson, Pete Smith, Peter Tan, Amy Wagner, Ben Wells

Our robust marketing calendar is filled with innovative and cutting-edge promotions and tie-ins aimed at attracting even more SuperFans and SuperFamilies across the globe. Our marketing leadership continues as we align ourselves with properties such as the *NFL, The Pink Panther™, Star Trek™,* and a soon-to-be-announced new gaming partner! Our brand strategies are designed to drive increased brand awareness and social relevance leading to incremental guest visits.

We continue to improve the guest experience by executing on our operational platforms and the roll out of new technologies. Guest satisfaction scores are at all-time highs, but we are committed to exceeding these results. Restaurants with higher scores correlate strongly with higher sales and profits. Worldwide, notable technological improvements in fiscal 2009 will include the continued implementation of new point-of-sale systems and the versatile flexible broiler. Additionally, in the U.S., we will continue the roll out of our new pricing tool designed to make market-driven pricing decisions and *Bluetooth®* headsets to enable faster and more accurate customer service. We are dedicated to running cost-effective, highly efficient operations aimed at improving guest satisfaction, and as a result, greater profits.

We are also increasingly proud of the efforts and commitments to give back to the communities we serve. Through our *Have It Your Way®* Foundation, we have granted thousands of scholarships, helped children with life-threatening illnesses, and supported youth programs. And our franchisees also continue to positively impact their communities through active participation in many local philanthropic efforts.

With our focus on our *True North Plan* and its strategic global growth pillars, we are well-positioned to continue our positive momentum into fiscal 2009. We recognize consumer pressures will likely continue, but we have taken appropriate steps to position the brand profitably. We are ready to serve consumers' increasing demand for quality and convenience as they look to us to provide great value while creating significant value for you, our shareholders.

I'm sure you agree that's an adventure worth pursuing.

John W. Chidsey
Chairman and
Chief Executive Officer
October 8, 2008

2008 Annual Report :: 15

Note: Printed with permission from Burger King Corporation

doing some research, you decide to recommend a local radio program sponsorship to create a higher profile for your organization. In exchange for a paid sponsorship, your organization is mentioned on the air. All mentions include brief text, of your choice, explaining who you are and, often, your organization's tagline or slogan. To justify the expense, you create a proposal to introduce the promotional idea and explain the challenges it addresses or opportunities it presents; identify goals that the sponsorship would help you achieve and the key publics you could reach through this sponsorship; explain details of the radio sponsorship, with background information on the audience it reaches and what you get in return for the paid sponsorship, along with costs; identify evaluation techniques (how will you measure impact and the return on investment); and give a conclusion that reinforces the benefits of the sponsorship to your organization, and why you should invest in this opportunity versus others like it.

In addition to internal proposals like this one, public relations professionals in all settings (firms, companies, nonprofit organizations) work on proposals directed to a variety of external groups, including prospective clients, potential business partners, vendors, and foundations that award funding for projects.

New Business Proposal

Public relations firms develop new business proposals to present their credentials to prospective clients and demonstrate how their services can help the clients' businesses. The format of this kind of proposal is quite similar to research reports; however, three sections increase in their importance, especially when written for a prospective client:

- Recommendations should address the components of the public relations plan discussed in chapter 3: goals, objectives, target publics, strategies, tactics, budget, time line, and evaluation methods. Effective campaign proposals demonstrate a strong connection between the recommendations and the research presented in the body and analysis/conclusions sections of the report.
- In the supporting materials section, you may want to include a sampling of creative materials to entice the reader.
- The executive summary should be written last and will summarize the reason for the campaign, research findings and analysis, recommendations, and, most importantly, why you are the best choice to handle the task. The executive summary should end with a strong, persuasive statement: "ask for the sale" and position your proposal as the best alternative to address the situation at hand. Potential clients should read the summary and be "wowed."

Request for Proposals

At some point in their career, public relations practitioners will most likely have to either write or respond to a request for proposal, or RFP.

RFPs invite companies to participate in a selection process in order to gain new business. Organizations might issue an RFP to outside businesses when seeking public relations assistance to develop a new logo, conduct opinion research, plan a special event, or implement a campaign.

The information requested in an RFP will vary depending on its purpose; however, it usually will include:

- background on the organization issuing the RFP;
- a summary of the problem or opportunity facing the organization;
- a description of the project;
- public relations goals and objectives or expected results;
- scope of services being sought;
- selection criteria;
- a budget and/or fee schedule;
- time line for evaluation and selection;
- guidelines for submitting the proposal;
- legal considerations, such as the term of the contract, disclosure, confidentiality, or conflict of interest.

If you are planning a meeting, conference, or special event, you might choose to submit your RFP electronically. Many hotels and convention and visitors bureaus have an RFP section on their Web sites that allows planners to fill in information such as meeting specifications, room needs, and food and beverage requirements.

Public relations firms responding to RFPs should pay strict attention to detail, provide the information that is asked for, and adhere to the guidelines for submitting the proposal. Depending on the selection criteria, be prepared to:

- highlight your firm's experience, as well as the experience of individual practitioners within the firm;
- provide an overview of the firm's resources (i.e., staff, financial, equipment);
- give examples of past performance that may relate to the RFP to which you're responding;
- describe the firm's approach to business and how you work with clients;
- pay special attention to additional capabilities you can offer the client that could be a competitive edge, such as specialty areas.

Grant Proposals

Not-for-profit professionals seeking outside funding for projects design **grant proposals** and submit those to corporations and foundations. Some funding sources provide forms and exact criteria for completion of grant proposals, while others simply tell you to submit a proposal. In general, well-written grant proposals make their case with concise and persuasive language, and incorporate statistics and other hard evidence to justify the funding request.

The Corporation for Public Broadcasting (CPB) reviews annual grant requests and provides major funding to public television and radio stations. The CPB provides tips for grant proposal writing on its Web site (www.cpb.org/grants/grantwriting.html). It lists four components of a grant proposal: (1) the narrative, or body, of the proposal; (2) the budget, with specific cost projections; (3) supporting materials as requested by the funding source, such as case studies and letters of support for your request; and (4) authorized signatures from appropriate, high-ranking officials within your organization. The narrative, structured much like a public relations program plan, should answer the following questions:

- What do we want? (A clear statement of the funding need.)
- What public concern or issue will be addressed and why? (Background on the problem and reasons the proposal should be supported.)
- Who will benefit and why?
- What goals and measurable objectives can be accomplished?
- How will results be evaluated or measured?
- How does this funding request relate to the funder's purpose, objectives, and priorities?
- Who are we and why are we qualified to meet this need? (Includes credentials of key staff involved in the project as well as the organization's résumé.)

The CPB stresses the importance of identifying and clearly explaining the "hook." The hook aligns your request closely with the purpose of the funding source. As stated on the Web site, this is "a critical aspect of any proposal narrative because it determines how compelling reviewers will perceive your proposal to be."

ASSIGNMENTS

Assignment 11.1—Examining Social Media

According to *WebProNews*, social media can be defined as those online technologies and practices that people use to share opinions, insights, experiences, and perspectives. Social media can take many different forms, including text, images, audio, and video. These sites typically use technologies such as blogs, podcasts and wikis that make it possible for users to have dialogue and interact (specific examples of social media can be found in chapter 9).

You work as an intern in your college's communications office (or, the setting could be another organization that you select or that your instructor designates). Your supervisor has asked you to lead a special project to help the institution get a better handle on social media and how this can be used most effectively in support of key institutional goals.

"Clearly, reaching prospective students is always important to us, but I'm also thinking about audiences like alumni and parents, people in the community who are important to our survival, and maybe even our current students, who we need to stay connected with," your supervisor says. "I know there are lots of social networking options these days, and that many of us, including myself, aren't totally tuned in to what's out there and how it works, and whether we should even care about it."

You say, "It probably would be a good time to do an inventory, identify what we're doing now, and not doing, and see what kind of results we might be getting and if those can be measured. Just because 'everyone's doing social media,' it doesn't necessarily mean we should be, too, or at least to the extent that everyone might think."

"Right, that's a good way to state it. On the other hand, we need to be competitive and visible, and, especially with younger people, if we're not on the social media radar, then I'm afraid we're missing some opportunities," your supervisor says. "Doing an inventory is a great idea, but we also need some direction. What should we be doing, what makes the most sense, strategically, and how do we decide where to place any investment of time and money in social media. If you could come up with a report and recommendations, that would give us an excellent starting point."

Exercise

Prepare a report that includes the following:

- introduction that describes how social media and social networking can be used to support and advance the organization's goals;

- summary of social media currently being used by the organization and its impact (how it is working, specifically to support and advance goals). If the organization is not using social media at all or in any significant way, state that fact and discuss the implications;

- recommendations on other social media that the organization should be using. Justify your choices, and keep in mind the organization's limitations with regard to staffing and financial resources (can these recommendations realistically be executed—do we have the money and people to make it happen?);

- conclusion that recaps major points and reinforces the benefits/strategic value of your social media recommendations.

Assignment 11.2—Law Firm's Community Relations Program

Fleischman, Craig, Gurdak, and Heasley is the second largest law firm in a city of 400,000 people. The 75-year-old firm employs 50 attorneys and has an executive committee comprised of eight senior partners. Among its specialties are corporate and tax law, wills and estate planning, and real estate law. Two of the firm's partners have extensive experience with legal cases relating to medical malpractice, right-to-die, and other health-care issues, and another has developed a national reputation for her expertise in environmental law. The firm's clients include large and small businesses, hospitals, banks, school districts, engineering firms, as well as individuals. Recently, the firm has been trying to build its client base of professional men and women nearing retirement age who have special legal and estate planning needs.

Many of the firm's attorneys are graduates of Yale, Georgetown, Columbia, Duke, and other leading law schools. Firm partners and associates are active in pro bono work; a major focus is providing free legal advice to local persons with AIDS. A few of the attorneys have taken leadership roles on the boards of directors of civic, cultural, and nonprofit groups such as the local symphony and the United Way.

One year ago, the firm hired Stephen Michaels as its first-ever marketing and client relations director. Michaels worked previously for a large advertising agency in the area as a copywriter and marketing specialist. Most of his first year with the firm has been spent doing market research, developing brochures and informational materials, and getting to know the firm and its clients. He also created a Web site for the firm and an e-newsletter for internal audiences. As his responsibilities expanded, Michaels realized he needed additional staff, and the firm agreed to provide budget monies to hire a marketing communications assistant.

Michaels hired Lisa Chen, a recent college graduate with a degree in public relations. Chen meets with Michaels the second day on the job to discuss an important project.

"Up to this point, I've been focusing most of my efforts on marketing, but I think we could be doing a lot more in the public relations area," Michaels says. "That's one of the main reasons I brought you on board, Lisa, since you have that kind of background. I think the time has come for us to develop an ongoing public relations program for the firm, and I'm going to ask you to take the lead on this. I'm more of a marketing person than a public relations person so I'm looking to you to provide some strategic direction."

"I'm glad you have that kind of confidence in me," Chen replies. "From what I can tell, the firm hasn't done too much public relations programming. I'm curious, how do you think the senior partners view public relations?"

"Many of them don't understand what public relations is and how it can be used effectively. I think there are a few who still don't see why we even need a marketing program. They think the firm sells itself. On some level, they're right, since much of the business and corporate work they do comes from client referrals. But the market is much more competitive now, which is something they do understand. The partners here are still cautious about the kinds of promotion we do. We don't do much advertising, we send out news releases once in a while, and we've got little presence in the local media. I should add that our key competitors seem to pop up in the press quite often."

"It's interesting that you say that. I notice that the client study the firm just completed reinforces this 'lack of presence' you're talking about."

"Yes. We surveyed our clients and asked them what they thought about the firm and how it is perceived. What we found is that our clients think the work we do for them is top-notch and that the firm is well respected in legal circles, but they don't hear or read about the firm all that much, and they'd like to see us having a higher profile in the community. That's why I think public relations can be valuable since it directly addresses those kinds of concerns."

"I'm hearing, then, that you'd like me to come up with some public relations ideas for the firm. Do you want me to focus strictly on publicity activities or do you want some suggestions on how to build our profile in the community?"

"A mix of both would be good. Any ideas you have that will help us be more visible to our clients, to prospective clients, and to other key publics. But I'd like you to limit your recommendations to five or six public relations activities that provide a good starting point for the firm. If we could only get involved in six public relations activities or projects right now, what would they be? Don't worry about going into a lot of detail—just give me a general description of the activity, what it involves, and why we should do it. The partners will be interested in knowing how public relations will help the firm grow and contribute to the bottom line, so each activity you suggest needs to be explained and justified with those interests in mind. Since this is more of a preliminary proposal to help give me a better idea of how to begin, why not put your suggestions in memo form—two or three pages at the most should do it—and get those to me in one week."

Exercise

Work in teams of two or three to discuss start-up public relations activities for the law firm and to write the proposal for Michaels. Follow the guidelines for proposal writing explained in this chapter. When explaining recommended start-up activities, be sure to indicate the publics targeted for each activity.

Assignment 11.3—Harnessing Renewable Energy (B)

As the new public relations manager for Sunergy. Inc., a company specializing in the residential and commercial installation of solar energy panels, you have been working on some materials to help educate homeowners in the community about the benefits of solar and wind energy (see chapter 8, Assignment 8.3).

Alex Scala, Sunergy's president, met with you to discuss some start-up projects, including updates and additions to the company's Web site. You recommended creating a new section for the Web site to include facts and general information on renewable energy. You recently completed a fact sheet that now appears on the Web site and that is included in Sunergy marketing packets given to potential customers. You also placed a by-lined article (carrying Scala's by-line) on solar and wind energy issues as they relate to homeowners in the weekly home buyers publication distributed in your area.

"I've been really happy with the progress you've been making, and I think we're starting to head in the right direction with our Web site," Scala says. "Now that we've addressed some immediate needs, I'd like to go back to something we started talking about when we first met, that is, thinking about a broader public relations program for the company."

You say: "I've been giving this a lot of thought since we first talked, and some ideas are already starting to come to mind. Just to be clear, you want to target the residential homeowner but also the business owner. Those are the key publics?"

"Yes, in general. But I'd welcome any thoughts you might have about how to narrow those broad groups and maybe do some more specific targeting. I'm open to suggestions," Scala says.

"What about research? Should I be considering that as I think about this program?"

"Well, to be honest, I'd rather be using the budget we have on other kinds of projects and activities," Scala says. "As we bring in new customers, we've been asking them how they heard about us, and most of them say word-of-mouth or some kind of personal interaction with one of our staff, an existing customer, or someone else who knew about us. We also know that, in general, our customers have made decisions to install solar panels primarily due to cost savings and how it helps the environment. That's probably no big surprise, but it's something we should keep in mind, nonetheless."

"Okay. I'll start working on this project and come back to you with a proposal that we can use as a jumping point for more discussion."

Exercises

1. Prepare a public relations program proposal for Scala. Your proposal should include program goals and publics to be targeted, as well as recommended strategies and tactics. Include a brief section that explains how you would measure the effectiveness of your proposed program.

2. Scala tells you that he wants to design a simple annual report for the company that can be posted on Sunergy's Web site. While the report would include some information on the company's success in its first year and the work it has done in the community, a key goal is to use the report as another tool to help educate people about renewable energy and its benefits, emphasizing how the use of solar and wind energy can protect the environment. Conduct additional secondary research and then write a letter from Scala (no more than 400 words) for the annual report that focuses on the growing importance of renewable energy in the 21st century and how this can have a positive impact on our environment.

References and Suggested Reading

Alred, G. J., Brusau, C. T., & Oliu, W. E. (2006). *The business writer's handbook* (10th ed.). Boston: St. Martin's Press.

AMA style guide for business writing. (1996). New York: AMACOM.

Argenti, P. A., & Forman, J. (2002). *The power of corporate communication:Crafting the voice and image of your business*. New York: McGraw Hill.

Basic elements of grant writing (2000). Retrieved November 30, 2008 from http://www.cpb.org/grants/grantwriting.html.

Berger, A. A. (1993). *Improving writing skills: Memos, letters, reports and proposals*. Thousand Oaks, CA: Sage Publications.

Davidson, W. (2001). *Business writing: What works, what won't* (Rev. ed.). New York: St. Martin's Press.

Dobrian, J. (1997). *Business writing skills*. New York: AMACOM.

Report quotes (n.d.). Retrieved January 10, 2009 from http://thinkexist.com/quotes/with/keyword/report/.

Roman, K., & Raphaelson, J. (2000). *Writing that works: How to communicate effectively in business* (3rd ed.). New York: HarperResource.

Seglin, J. L., & Coleman, E. (2007). *The AMA handbook of business letters* (3rd ed.). New York: AMACOM.

The adventure continues: Burger King Holdings, Inc. fiscal 2008 annual report (2008). Retrieved November 30, 2008 from http://media.corporate-ir.net/media_files/irol/87/87140/BurgerKing_2008_AR_FINAL.pdf.

12

Advocacy Writing

"As a rock star," says Bono, lead singer for the rock group U2, "I have two interests—I want to have fun and I want to change the world. I have a chance to do both." It can be argued that all public relations writers are advocates for change of some sort, and that all public relations writing advocates something in an attempt to influence or persuade. There are, however, specific tools—*letters to the editor*, *op-ed articles*, *position statements*, *talking points* and *speeches*, *public service announcements*, and *public relations advertising*—you can use to more strongly establish a public position or express a point of view.

Letters to the Editor

Letters to the editor are primarily targeted to the opinion–editorial sections of print media. This includes newspapers, as well as many magazines. They have multiple purposes:

- When a negative or inaccurate story (or another letter to the editor) about your organization appears in the media, a well-written response can help your organization lessen the bad publicity or correct false information.
- Letters are used to respond positively to media coverage, as well. A hospital public relations person, for example, could send a letter to commend a reporter's series on health care or a health issue, and then use that platform to create further awareness of the hospital's services and to present the hospital as an information resource.
- Whether an article was positive or negative, letters to the editor can "fill in the blanks" and provide information that was not included in the media's coverage.
- Not-for-profit organizations write "thank you" letters to an editor after major fund-raising events to thank the community for its support.
- Organizations can promote a cause they have adopted or bring attention to important issues in their industry that may affect the community.

Newspapers are not required to print letters to the editor, but almost all of them do. Some suggestions for writing letters to the editor:

- Keep the letter short, about 250–300 words. Most newspapers publish letter guidelines on the op-ed page, so follow their rules.
- Each letter should begin with "Dear Editor" or "To the Editor," and conclude with the name, title, and organization of the sender. Sometimes, writing letters on behalf of senior managers and CEOs (with their knowledge and approval, of course) and signing their names can carry more weight and help you get published.
- The first paragraph of the letter should reference the specific article or issue to which you are responding. Mention the headline and date of the article. Other letters written about major issues should quickly identify the subject and indicate why this subject is timely.
- The remaining few paragraphs of the letter should give more background on the subject, making reference to hard facts and statistics when possible. Then, express your opinion or reaction, and conclude by summarizing your main point.
- Maintain a positive tone in the letter. Avoid name-calling and harsh criticism. When responding to a critical or inaccurate story, focus your energy on "setting the record straight" and creating a positive impression about your organization. Consider the consequences of "burning your bridges" with the reporter and publication.

Exhibit 12.1 illustrates the correct physical format and concise writing style of a letter to the editor. It addresses the reason for writing the letter in the first sentence, provides background in the subsequent paragraphs, and concludes by summarizing the main point.

Op-ed Articles

Op-ed articles are longer versions of letters to the editor that allow you to comment on a subject in more depth. There are times when your response to an article or your opinions about an issue will be welcomed in a longer opinion piece, especially when the subject is timely or controversial. Op-ed pieces also are a good way to gain exposure for your organization and position people within it as experts. In the article "And Now a Word from Op-Ed," David Shipley, the deputy editor for the *New York Times'* op-ed section, describes the format this way:

> Op-Ed is different from the editorial page in that it does not represent the views of anyone in the editorial division, even its own editors. It is different from letters in that it is not a venue to debate articles that have appeared in The Times.

With an estimated 1,200 op-ed submissions arriving weekly, Shipley says an op-ed is more likely to be selected to appear if the writer offers a fresh perspective or presents a topic that has not already been covered in the editorial section.

Op-ed pieces, which get their name from being "opposite the editorial" page, are set up much like technical articles in that they include the by-line of the company expert qualified to talk about the issue. Like technical articles, op-ed pieces should identify key message points or arguments and then use facts, statistics, and supporting evidence to back up those views. The end of the article, besides summarizing main points, should leave the reader with a clear

Exhibit 12.1

Letter to the Editor: National Association of Counties

The Voice of America's Counties

July 21, 2008

To the Editor:

I would like to take this opportunity to express my deep gratitude to Multnomah County Commissioner Lisa Naito for her hard work and dedication this past year as chair of the Justice and Public Safety Steering Committee of the National Association of Counties (NACo).

The committee is responsible for developing NACo policy regarding federal legislation and policy pertaining to criminal justice and public safety systems, including criminal justice planning; law enforcement; courts; corrections; homeland security; community crime prevention; juvenile justice and delinquency prevention; emergency management; fire prevention and control; and civil disturbances.

Commissioner Naito was especially influential in leading her committee's endeavors in developing solid NACo policy affecting counties during my 2007-2008 term as NACo President. Notably, she represented NACo at President Bush's April 9 signing of H.R. 1593, the Second Chance Act, a top priority for NACo for several years. The bill authorizes $165 million per year in federal grants to local governments and states to provide ex-offenders with education, job training, substance abuse and aftercare treatment, and assist them with finding housing and employment upon release from jail and prison. The law is designed to help reduce recidivism, increase public safety and save local taxpayers money.

I believe with conviction that Commissioner Naito's strong leadership as the chair of the Justice and Public Safety Steering Committee has been of immeasurable benefit to the residents of Multnomah County. I hope she will continue to actively participate in NACo's efforts in Washington, D.C. to guarantee that all 3,068 counties in the nation have the tools, programs and information essential to achieving their goals.

Sincerely,

Eric Coleman, President

National Association of Counties

Eric Coleman is a county commissioner representing Oakland County, Mich.

Note: Reprinted with permission of Eric Coleman

solution to a problem, or state the best reasons for the organization and the public to show continued concern about an issue.

Exhibit 12.2 is an excellent example of an op-ed piece, written by the CEO of NRG Energy, Inc., a power company in New Jersey. It has an attention-getting opening and quickly gets into the main message: carbon dioxide emissions must be regulated by Congress. The writer supports his opinion with solid arguments presented in a persuasive writing style that is personable and easy to understand. The main point is reiterated at the closing—"Global warming should be at the top of Congress's agenda."

While most op-ed pieces have a news angle that reflects current events, organizations also distribute op-ed pieces to coincide with timely events such as a national day, week, or month. A university professor of social work, for instance, wrote an op-ed piece published during Hispanic Heritage Month to comment on the growing influence of the Hispanic/Latino community in the United States.

Like media pitches, op-ed pieces tend to work best when they are submitted to one publication at a time. In fact, some national publications, such as the *New York Times* and *Washington Post*, require that submissions be exclusive, so you want to make sure the publication you choose will best reach your target public. You might want to talk with the appropriate contact at the publication and gauge his interest in publishing the op-ed piece before taking the time to write it. Monitor possible publications and become familiar with the types of op-ed they run to increase your chances of success. You should pay close attention to the publication's submission guidelines, which will include the preferred length of an op-ed (the average length is 600–800 words) and information on how to submit your piece. There are no guarantees that your piece will be published, even if someone has shown interest or agreed to do so by phone or in an e-mail message. After submitting the piece, you should follow up to make sure it has been received, ask if there are any questions or if the piece could be improved in any way, and get a better sense of the intention to publish and when the article might be used.

Position Statements

Position statements are similar in their approach to letters to the editor and op-ed commentaries; however, they are more formal and represent official positions that have been adopted by an organization's governing body. In fact, they often include a statement in the heading or in the beginning paragraph that identifies who adopted the position and when.

Ranging in length from a paragraph to multiple pages, position statements deal with important, sometimes controversial, issues facing an organization and its publics and are often utilized by nonprofit organizations, especially professional associations. They may be distributed to the media, government officials, and other target publics, or posted online. The National Association for the Education of Young Children has issued position statements on topics such as curriculum, school readiness, and child abuse. The American Association of School Librarians has written a position statement on the confidentiality of library records, and the National Association of the Deaf has taken an official position on cochlear implants.

Position papers have many elements of a research paper (outlined in chapter 11) in that they identify an issue, provide a history of the issue, present data, and make recommendations.

Exhibit 12.2

Op-ed: NRG Energy

We're Carboholics. Make Us Stop.

Advertisement

By David Crane
Sunday, October 14, 2007; B07

I am a carboholic. As Americans, we are all carboholics, but I am more so than most. The company I run, NRG Energy, emits more than 64 million tons of carbon dioxide (CO_2) into the atmosphere each year — more than the total man-made greenhouse gas emissions of Norway.

And we are only the 10th-largest American power generation company. Imagine the CO_2 emissions of Nos. 1 through 9.

Why do we do it? Why does America's power industry emit such a stunning amount of greenhouse gases into the atmosphere in this age of climate change?

We do so because CO_2 emissions are free. And in a world where CO_2 has no price, removing CO_2 before or after the combustion process is vastly more expensive and problematic than just venting it into the atmosphere.

Congress needs to act now to change our ways. Lawmakers should regulate CO_2 and other greenhouse gas emissions by introducing a federal cap-and-trade system, which would put a cap and a market price on CO_2 emissions.

If Congress acts now, the power industry will respond. We will do what America does best; we will react to CO_2 price signals by innovating and commercializing technologies that avoid, prevent and remove CO_2 from the atmosphere.

I emphasize the word "now." We are not running out of time; we *have* run out of time. Decisions we make today in the U.S. power industry will have a significant impact on the size of the problem we bequeath to our children.

Without a price on CO_2, our industry will build a veritable tidal wave of traditional coal-fired power-generation facilities. Traditional coal plants are, and will be for some time to come, the least expensive and most reliable way to generate electricity on a large scale in the United States, China, India and much of the rest of the world -- that is, so long as the CO_2 emissions associated with burning coal in these countries remain free.

We absolutely need to use coal for power-generation purposes. We probably even need to build a few more traditional coal plants in fast-growing parts of the country where there is no practical alternative. But we need to move as quickly as possible toward implementing the low-emissions ways of combusting coal that are under development or, in the case of "coal gasification" technology, are ready for commercial deployment.

A federal cap-and-trade system would push the power and coal industries toward deployment of CO_2 capture and sequestration technology, which is essential to reducing our domestic emissions and, ultimately, to weaning China and the rest of the fast-growing (and emitting) developing world off traditional coal technology. Effective incentives for these new technologies could easily and readily be included in a cap-and-trade regimen. Lawmakers need to provide both the carrot and the stick to get the CO_2 out of coal.

Energy legislation under consideration in Congress focuses almost exclusively on renewables and conservation; both are worthy initiatives that deserve our support. But in a world where a CO_2-emitting traditional coal plant is built every week, renewables and conservation are a sideshow at best.

continued . . .

Exhibit 12.2

Op-ed: NRG Energy . . . *continued*

The vast amount of CO_2 being emitted worldwide by coal-fired power plants is the heart of the global warming issue. Progress against those emissions depends on three critical initiatives: replacing traditional coal with "clean coal" plants, displacing additional traditional coal plants with new zero-carbon-emissions nuclear plants and implementing a federal cap-and-trade system on greenhouse gases.

Global warming should be at the top of Congress's agenda — because action by this Congress will turn the tide of climate change around the world. Never before have we faced the prospect of fundamentally damaging our global ecosystem by the day-to-day activities of each and every one of us. A cap-and-trade system is the place to start. America must act now to protect our future.

David Crane is chief executive of Princeton, N.J.-based NRG Energy Inc., a wholesale power generator. NRG, which owns power plants capable of serving 19 million households, recently filed for a license to build two nuclear reactors in South Texas.

Note: Courtesy of David Crane, president and CEO, NRG Energy, Inc.

When writing a position paper, begin with a clear, objective statement of the issue, followed by background on the issue to provide context. The background should be thorough enough to offer readers who are not familiar with the issue an understanding of the subject matter. This paves the way for the writer to then state the organization's position, or opinion, on the issue. Position papers are persuasive pieces, so the position must be supported by logos appeals, such as facts, statistics, and scientific evidence, and pathos appeals, such as compassion, patriotism, or fear. It is also wise to address any opposition to your position; it is better to address opponents head on and refute their arguments, than to ignore them.

Writing a position paper presents a special challenge to the public relations practitioner. Not only is it a time-consuming project because of the research involved, but the practitioner must also take care to present information that can often be complex in a way the target public will understand.

Talking Points and Speeches

Public relations professionals also help organizations and their people express their points of view through the creation of *talking points* and *speeches*.

Answers.com defines a talking point as, "Something, such as an especially persuasive point, that helps to support an argument or a discussion." Often, talking points are developed to ensure that consistent messages are delivered when organizations deal with difficult decisions and situations. For example, to explain a decision to implement lay-offs, talking points are crafted and provided to senior executives and others who communicate this news to stakeholders. These talking points are core messages that a company wants to repeat and deliver in the same way, using the same language, to help people understand why lay-offs are happening and to justify the company's course of action. If stakeholders hear differing messages, this can cause confusion and make people question the decisions, eroding trust. A talking point in this instance could be as simple as, "We need to take this action now to protect the long-term financial health of the company," emphasizing the importance of this decision as it relates to survival and future success.

Talking points help organizations in their efforts to increase public awareness of an issue and to build support around a cause. Blue Ribbons for Kids, a campaign aimed at community education and prevention of child abuse, offers several brief talking points on its Web site that could be used in presentations and conversations, or to generally guide thinking in the community about this subject. These talking points include:

- Everyone can do something to prevent child abuse. When you see an adult losing patience with a child, intervene but keep it positive. If a child is in danger, offer assistance or call for help.
- Get to know the children in your life, so they feel comfortable talking to you if they feel unsafe. Pay attention to changes in their behavior; this may indicate something is wrong.

Another advocacy-writing role you might be asked to play is that of speechwriter. Speeches take many forms: from brief remarks given at an awards presentation or to introduce another speaker at an event that are fully written for someone or delivered using a series of talking points; to longer scripts read word-for-word by executives who are asked to give keynote presentations at industry conferences or to speak at a commencement ceremony.

In either case, good speechwriting should always follow certain guidelines: know your audience in advance and understand what they expect or want to hear; establish a central theme and main idea that you want to communicate, and repeat that idea throughout the speech; and write an opening that will grab the audience's attention right away, a body that avoids trying to convey too much and focuses on just a few key points, and an ending that comes back to your central idea and leaves people with something provocative or encourages them to think differently.

As the speechwriter, of course, you also need to know the person who is delivering the remarks—how does she present herself, think, and talk? Speeches are meant to be heard, not read or seen, so the language and tone need to be conversational. Ask the person you are writing the speech for to talk through her ideas, and write down what she says. As you're writing, read aloud what's been written and ask yourself if it sounds natural or has the voice of the speaker. In the end, you want the audience to listen and be absorbed in the speech. If people are not engaged and entertained, then it's likely that the message will get lost, and the speech will fall flat.

Some public relations professionals can move through their careers and never write a speech. It's likely, though, that there will be occasions when someone asks for help coming up with brief remarks. Bill Cole, founder and CEO of Procoach Systems, says on the Procoach Web site that the writing for short speeches has to be even better than for longer ones, since you have "less time to get your critical message across." Other tips include:

- You must make sure the audience gets the central core theme and message right away. You don't have the luxury of "warming up" your audience. Get to the point quickly and "make the first impression the best." Keep the message to the point and on target.

- The logical flow of the talk must be tighter than in a longer talk, or the speaker risks being perceived as a "five-minute blatherer."
- If the speech is part of a series of brief remarks by other presenters, you need to "play off" the speaker before you to get the audience's attention quickly, or you might get tuned out. On the other hand, look for ways to write the remarks so that they stand out from the others and leave a memorable impression.

Public Service Announcements

It's a television image that many people remember. The shot opens on a frying pan. No sound. Then you see an egg and hear a voice saying, "This is your brain." The egg is cracked into the pan, you hear a sizzling sound for a few seconds, and the voice comes in again to say, "This is your brain on drugs." The egg continues to cook, followed by a brief closing remark: "Any questions?" This is an example of a classic *public service announcement*, or PSA. It uses simple visuals, minimal voice-over, and the element of surprise to communicate a single, powerful message—drugs can "fry" your brain.

Not-for-profit organizations create PSAs to inform and educate audiences about important health, social, and public interest issues. Although the Federal Communication Commission no longer mandates stations to provide a certain amount of airtime to PSAs, the media still donate time to air these spots as a public service. Many stations have public service directors to coordinate PSAs and public service programming. Competition for PSA placement is stiff. A station may only air a few PSAs a day out of the many it receives each week. Attention to some fundamentals can help your PSAs succeed with the media and your target audiences:

- Come up with a strategic plan for your public service campaign that includes research of the issue, public attitudes, and media interest in the subject; goal setting and targeted message development; production techniques and costs; and distribution and evaluation methods.
- Create and send a variety of formats and lengths—:10, :15, :20, :30, and :60 spots. For radio, you can create prerecorded spots with voice-overs and sound effects, as well as simple announcer scripts that cost nothing to produce and can be read on the air by deejays between songs to fill time.
- Focus on one main idea and reinforce that idea a few times in the spot. Use a memorable theme line (e.g., Friends don't let friends drive drunk). Do something at the start of the spot using voice, visuals, or sound that will get the audience interested and make them ask, "What's coming next?"
- Include a call to action such as a phone number or Web site where people can get more information or make a donation.
- Incorporate a local angle, such as a local phone number to call or a statistic that relates to the geographic area targeted. Many nationally prepared PSAs provide room at the end to include local information. Keep minority audiences in mind, and prepare targeted versions or scripts with content that will appeal to diverse groups and ethnic media.

- Track PSA usage. As with VNRs, SIGMA encoding can be used. Send reminder cards or make follow-up phone calls to the media to build interest.

The Ad Council, founded in 1942, has produced numerous memorable public service ads, many of which have become part of popular culture. Its campaigns have included "Only You Can Prevent Forest Fires," "Take a Bite Out of Crime," and "A Mind is a Terrible Thing to Waste." The council conducts campaigns on health and safety, community, and education by bringing together advertising agencies and the media; ad agencies donate their time to create the spots, and media donate advertising space. The award-winning "Think Before You Speak" campaign sponsored by the Ad Council and the Gay, Lesbian and Straight Education Network includes three television PSAs, three radio PSAs, and six print PSAs. See Exhibits 12.3 and 12.4 for examples from the campaign, which is aimed at reducing and preventing homophobic language among teenagers.

Public Relations Advertising

Organizations wishing to take a public stand on an issue or express a point of view in the media can also create *public relations* or *institutional advertising*. Editors can choose to print your op-ed letters and articles, or they can reject them completely. The advantage of running an ad is that you pay for the space, which means your message will appear in print exactly as you want it to. Ads produced by Anheuser-Busch and other beer companies asking you to drink responsibly and to use designated drivers are public relations ads. They advocate a corporate point of view, not the product.

Public relations advertising is produced in much the same way as a public service announcement. When creating copy for public relations ads:

- Put some thought into the headline. Raise a provocative question or recommend that the reader think a certain way or do something specific about an issue. Some ad headlines have impact when written more like news headlines. Whatever the case, make the headline strong and catchy. A public relations ad placed by Verizon carried the headline: "When One Million People Get Together, a Million Good Things Happen." The ad promoted Verizon's $1 million donation to five major charities in celebration of the company's one millionth long-distance phone service customer.
- Make the first paragraph an extension of the headline. That first sentence in the body of the ad needs to build off of the idea presented in the headline.
- Write simple body copy, use active voice, and keep sentences and paragraphs short. It is acceptable to use incomplete sentences in ad copy for emphasis.
- Recap the main point at the end. Effective ads do that creatively, and bring the reader back to the key idea raised in the headline and first paragraph. Some ads include a final statement that asks the reader to take a desired action. The Verizon ad concluded by informing customers about a letter being sent to them about the company's $1 million charitable donations and encouraging visits to its Web site to learn more about the campaign.

Exhibit 12.3

PSA Print Ad: Gay, Lesbian, and Straight Education Network

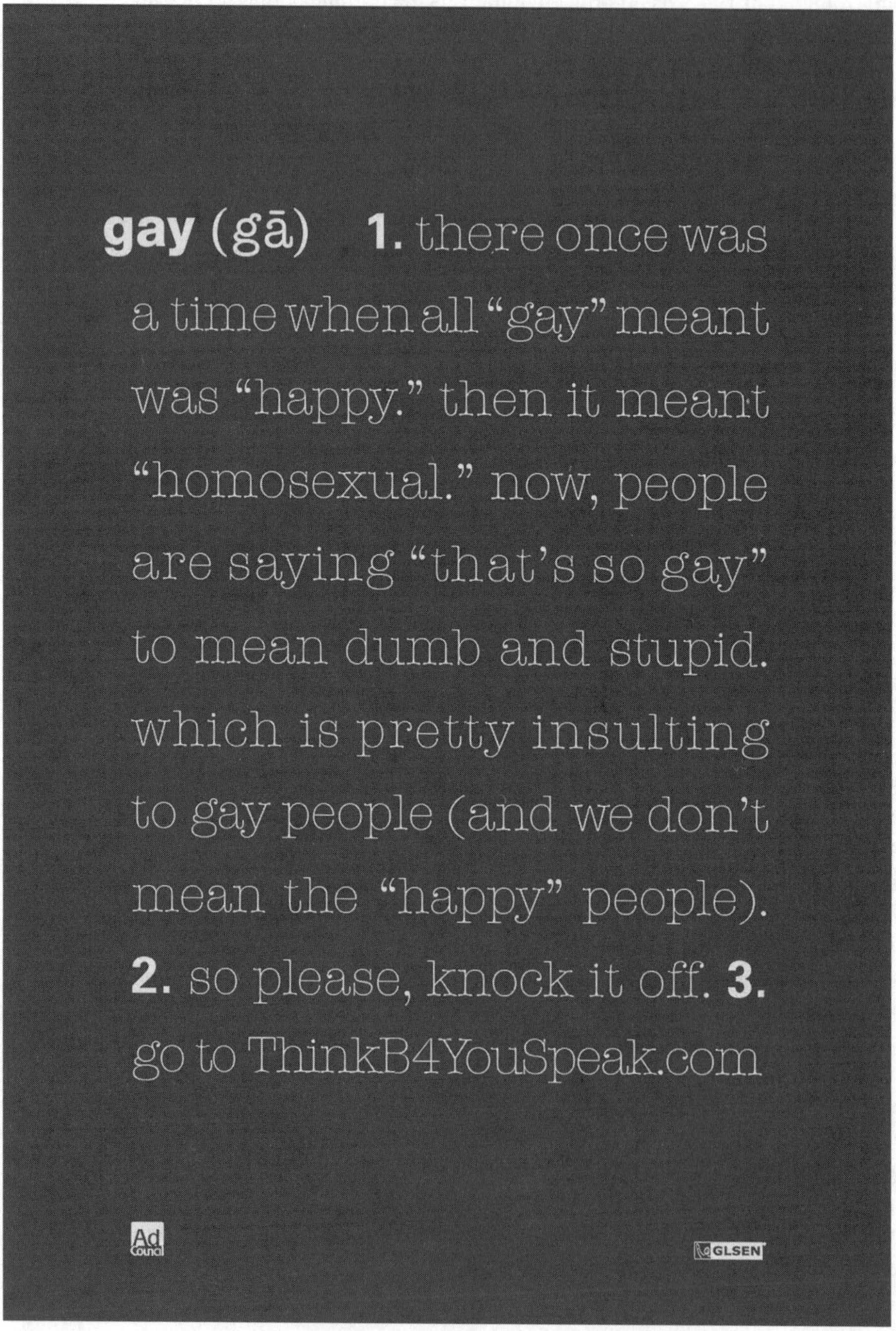

gay (gā)   **1.** there once was a time when all "gay" meant was "happy." then it meant "homosexual." now, people are saying "that's so gay" to mean dumb and stupid. which is pretty insulting to gay people (and we don't mean the "happy" people). **2.** so please, knock it off. **3.** go to ThinkB4YouSpeak.com

Ad
Council

GLSEN

Note: Courtesy Think Before You Speak campaign, created pro bono by ArnoldNYC on behalf of GLSEN and the Ad Council

Exhibit 12.4

PSA TV Script: Gay, Lesbian, and Straight Education Network

HILARY DUFF
AD COUNCIL/GLSEN
"FITTING ROOM"
TV: 30

OPEN INSIDE A CLOTHING STORE FITTING ROOM. TWO TEEN-AGE GIRLS
ARE TRYING ON CLOTHES.

GIRL 1: Do you like this top?

GIRL 2: Ugh. That's so gay.

GIRL 1: Really?

GIRL 2: It's totally gay.

CUT TO SEE HILARY DUFF IS ALSO IN THE DRESSING ROOM. SHE'S
HOLDING SOME CLOTHES ON HANGERS IN HER HANDS, LIKE SHE'S
ABOUT TO TRY THEM ON.

HILARY: You know, you really shouldn't say that.

GIRL 2: Say what?

HILARY. Say that something is "gay" when you mean something is bad.

It's insulting.

THE GIRLS LOOK AT EACH OTHER, NOT QUITE UNDERSTANDING. SO
HILARY CONTINUES.

I mean, imagine if every time something was bad, everybody said "Wow. That's
so "girl wearing a skirt as a top."

THE GIRLS THINK ABOUT THIS FOR A MOMENT AS HILARY ADDS…

HILARY: Those are cute jeans though.

CUT TO TITLE CARDS AS WE HEAR HILARY SAY…

HILARY VOICE OVER: When you say "that's so gay," do you realize what you
say?

Knock it off.

ThinkB4YouSpeak.com

Note: Courtesy Think Before You Speak campaign, created pro bono by ArnoldNYC on behalf of GLSEN and the Ad Council

Advertising is very expensive. To make sure your dollars are spent wisely, media outlets should be chosen based on: your target public; *reach*, which refers to how many people are exposed to the medium during a specific time period (such as "sweeps weeks," certain times of the year when television and radio stations are measured for viewership and listenership in order to establish their ratings in the market); and *frequency*, which refers to the number of times those people were exposed to the message.

ASSIGNMENTS

Assignment 12.1—Primo Pizza Advocates Safer Driving

According to the Centers for Disease Control and Prevention, "Motor vehicle crashes are the leading cause of death for U.S. teens, accounting for more than one in three deaths in this age group." The risk of being in a car accident is higher for 16–19-year-old drivers than it is for any other age group, and the risk of a crash is much higher during the first year teenagers are able to drive. For each mile driven, teen drivers ages 16–19 are about four times more likely than other drivers to crash.

Your state has enacted a graduated driver licensing system. Graduated licensing is designed to delay full licensure; it allows beginning drivers to get their initial experience under lower-risk conditions in three phases. Under this system, full driving privileges are given to young drivers after meeting age and other requirements that demonstrate safe driving ability.

Primo Pizza, a chain of more than 50 pizza shops operated exclusively in your state, also has a special interest in teen driving and safety on the roads, since many of its delivery people are older teens. Anthony Roe, the president of Primo Pizza, has asked to meet with you, the company's new public affairs and community relations manager, to talk about ways in which the company can align with this issue.

"As you know, Primo has a special interest in teen driving and safety on the roads. We hire many younger drivers, and if they come to us with well-developed driving habits, that would certainly benefit our business," Roe says. "As we move into the winter months, when driving can be a lot trickier, I think it would be good for us to publicly say something about safe driving and how critical it is for people and to the way we do business."

"What's also really great about this is the fact that we've become known for our concerns about safe driving, so there's a genuine interest on our part," you say. "But, of course, it does bring with it some public relations and marketing benefits, there's no question about that. Can you refresh my memory about some of the steps we take to promote safe driving?"

"Sure. We start by looking closely at people's driving records before we hire them, and new drivers never start driving right away," Roe explains. "We usually have them go out with another, more experienced driver for the first week or so. Then, after that, a manager or a senior driver goes out on a delivery with a newer driver every few weeks for a two-month period to monitor how well that person is doing behind the wheel."

"Don't the drivers have to attend some courses, as well?" you ask.

"Yes, we call them safe-driving workshops. We sponsor a few of those during the year and all of our drivers are required to attend. Those are interesting because they expose our drivers to real-life driving problems they might encounter on the road, and ask them to act out how they would respond to certain hazardous situations. Local police and AAA staff run those for us in each town or city where we have shops," Roe says.

"I definitely see some opportunities for us to get some positive media exposure around this issue. I know the company was a big advocate for the passage of the graduated licensing system laws, so we could weave that into any messaging, too. I did some research, and it looks like those laws have been contributing to a drop in auto accidents that involve teens."

Exercises

1. Write a letter to the editor for distribution to statewide print media. Your focus should be the importance of safe driving during the winter months and Primo's position on teens and safe driving. The letter should be about 300 words and be signed by Anthony Roe, president of Primo Pizza.

2. Write copy for a Primo Pizza public relations advertisement that establishes the company's position on teens and safe driving and the importance of this issue to the company. Your ad copy should begin with a creative headline and a brief description of any appropriate visuals. Limit the copy to no more than three or four short paragraphs.

Assignment 12.2—The Humane Society's PSA Campaign

With more than 10 million members and constituents, the Humane Society of the United States (HSUS) is the nation's largest and most effective animal protection organization. The HSUS serves the animal population in many ways. It advocates for public policies to reduce animal suffering, investigates animal cruelty and works to enforce existing laws, and helps educate the public about animal issues, among other programs and services. The HSUS provides direct care for thousands of animals at sanctuaries and rescue facilities, wildlife rehabilitation centers and mobile veterinary clinics.

You work as a public relations specialist for the HSUS and have been speaking with staff members in the organization's regional offices about their public relations needs. You share feedback received from regional staff with your supervisor, Mary DeFreitas.

"The regional operations are saying that they're getting more requests from individuals and local shelters for information on animal cruelty," DeFreitas says. "It seems that many of the local communities have seen an increase in cases involving pet owners who have seriously neglected their animals. There are more reports of malicious attacks on animals—cats that have been set on fire by kids who said they were playing a practical joke, dogs beaten and left for dead. The regional offices told me that they would like to have some new materials to help better educate people about animal cruelty, in hopes that more people will report abuse and neglect and discourage others from committing these acts."

"We've been thinking about creating some new public service announcements," you add. "This might be a subject we could focus on. There's an interesting tie-in here, too, with the increase in youth violence that we've seen lately. We know that young people who have been involved in violent acts, like school shootings, often have a history of being cruel to animals. On some level, maybe our efforts could contribute positively to a more serious social problem."

"PSAs are a good idea," DeFreitas says. "The local media in these areas have covered many of these animal cruelty cases, and in some instances that coverage got residents to rally around this issue and take a stand. It would be great to bring even more visibility to this issue."

DeFreitas continues. "While you're here, I wanted to talk to you about another project. I've been asked to give some brief remarks at the opening of the new animal shelter in town. I'd like to make a few key points about the importance of shelters, but also about the work we do, in general. The Pet Smart store has donated some food products and toys for the shelter, so I should say something about that in my remarks. The overall remarks don't need to be too long. Besides HSUS staff, we're inviting volunteers and donors, and we'll see if we can get a few local government officials to show up."

Exercises

1. Prepare scripts for the following HSUS public service announcements. At the top of each script, state the goal of the spot and the audience targeted.

    *   20- and 30-second versions of an announcer-only radio PSA on animal cruelty;
    *   a 30-second produced radio PSA on animal cruelty;
    *   a 60-second television PSA on animal cruelty.

2. Prepare DeFreitas's remarks for the opening of the new animal shelter. Her remarks should be at least three but no more than five minutes in length.

Assignment 12.3—Defending Home Health Care

You handle public relations for PersonalCare, the oldest home health care agency in a medium-sized city. PersonalCare offers three levels of service: companions, who assist the elderly and disabled with dressing and personal hygiene and handle household activities such as light housecleaning, meal preparation, and shopping; home health aides, who perform household activities, but who also have the training to take vital signs and assist with patient exercise routines; and registered and licensed practical nurses, who can provide more involved medical care for those recuperating from major surgery or others with chronic illnesses, such as cancer and Alzheimer's disease. All of PersonalCare's companions and aides are supervised and trained by registered nurses. The person receiving home health care enjoys the comfort and security of his or her own home, which can have emotional benefits and speed the healing process.

Recently, the morning daily newspaper ran a story on the front page of its local section with the headline, "Home health care aide convicted of stealing from elderly woman." This led to a few more stories on the risks of hiring home health aides to care for the elderly and disabled in their private homes. After reading these negative stories, you approach Luke Shaw, the agency's executive director, to discuss the impact of this media coverage.

"Even though this incident didn't involve us, I feel like we have a responsibility to respond to all the negative press," you say. "If people start perceiving that it's dangerous to bring a home health aide into their homes, and that all people who work as home health aides are criminals and can't be trusted, it could hurt our business. Unfortunately, that's the picture that the local media have been painting, and it's an undeserved stereotype that we need to correct, since most home health aides are responsible people."

"So far, we haven't had any problems with aides committing thefts. But I see what you mean. The average person will not necessarily separate one home health agency from another. It gives all of us a bad name. What do you think we should do?" Shaw asks.

"I'd like us to put together a public information program that informs people in our community about the value of home health care, but also helps them to become smart consumers when it comes to selecting a home health care agency. People might not know, for instance, that many agencies, like ours, are licensed by the state, and that all employees are required to go through an intensive screening, and their references are carefully checked. We screen employees to see if there is any criminal activity in their background before anyone is placed in a person's home. It's also pretty easy to get information on an agency's reputation by checking with the Better Business Bureau or a chamber of commerce. Consumers should find out if the agency is insured for general and professional liability and how that protects them. Those are some of the tips we could offer."

"I like this idea and I like the fact you're suggesting we be proactive and take a leadership role on this issue. We can provide an important service to the community and strengthen the agency's reputation in the community and in the home health care industry at the same time. It might even bring us some new clients," Shaw says.

"True. I think we have an excellent opportunity to show people just how critical home health care has become, and how it will be even more critical as the elderly population grows in size. We do a lot of good for people. Many sons and daughters tell us that they don't know what they would have done without this service and the companionship it provides day-to-day for their elderly parents. That's a story we need to tell," you say.

Exercises

Prepare the following pieces for the PersonalCare public information program:

- A fact sheet that outlines 10 tips for selecting a reputable home health care agency. Do research to gather information for the fact sheet.

- A 500-word op-ed article to be sent to the local media that explains the positive aspects of home health care and dispels negative images of home health care workers. It should be signed by Luke Shaw, PersonalCare's executive director.

- A three-page feature/human-interest story on the important role of home health care and the benefits it provides to home health care users and their families.

References and Suggested Reading

About Ad Council (n.d.). Retrieved December 11, 2008 from http://www.adcouncil.org/default.aspx?id=68.

Bivins, T. H. (2007). *Public relations writing: The essentials of style and format* (6th ed.). New York: McGraw Hill.

Fink, C. C. (2004). *Writing opinion for impact.* Ames, IA: Wiley-Blackwell.

Newsom, D. & Haynes, J. (2007). *Public relations writing form & style* (8th ed.). Belmont, CA: Thomson & Wadsworth.

Public Service Advertising Research Center, www.psaresearch.com.

Sample talking points (n.d.). Retrieved January 16, 2009 from http://blueribbonsonline.wi.gov/Download% 20resources/WI_talking %20points.pdf.

Shipley, D. And now a word from op-ed. (2004, February 1). *The Washington Post.*

Smith, R. D. (2007). *Becoming a public relations writer* (3rd ed.). Mahwah, NJ: Lawrence Erlbaum Associates.

Top ten tips for writing and delivering very brief speeches: Be good, be brief and be seated (2005). Retrieved January 16, 2009 from http://www.mentalgamecoach.com/articles/BriefSpeeches. html.

Wilcox, D. L. (2008). *Public relations writing and media techniques* (6th ed.). New York: Allyn & Bacon.

Writing for writers: Speechwriting (n.d.) Retrieved January 16, 2009 from http://teacher.scholastic.com/ writewit/speech/index.htm.

13

Promotional Publications

"What we have here is a failure to communicate." That classic line from 1967's *Cool Hand Luke,* with legendary actor Paul Newman, has gone down in movie history. Organizations that fail to communicate with their internal and external publics could become history themselves. Promotional publications such as newsletters, magazines, and brochures can help keep communication channels open.

Newsletters

Some public relations historians trace the origins of the newsletter back to the days of Julius Caesar. Today, it serves much the same purpose as it did centuries ago—to communicate news and useful information to a well-defined group of people. Good newsletters are like good newspapers, in that their main purpose is to report important happenings to their target publics. Newsletters publish news; they are not promotional vehicles for senior managers to brag about the great job they do or how wonderful their company is.

In addition, newsletters target readers who have special interests rather than a mass audience. News releases sent to the mass media can be rewritten, whereas you, the public relations professional, control the content of newsletter articles. A newsletter has the qualities of a personal letter; it talks directly to individual readers and their specialized interests. Because readers receive newsletters at regular, planned intervals—weekly, monthly, or quarterly—they come to rely on them as news sources, if they are well written and executed. Newsletters share the traits of other well-developed public relations tools in that they need a sense of purpose, publics, and strategy; their success depends upon many other factors, such as good timing, targeted content, crisp writing, and reader-friendly design.

Newsletter Goals, Publics, and Strategy

Newsletters are used for many reasons and target both internal and external publics. Organizations publish internal newsletters to keep employees informed and updated on company developments and management decisions. This is important, since employees are an organization's best spokespeople. Professional associations, such as the American Medical Association, send newsletters to their members to help them stay in touch with association and industry news. Companies develop external newsletters to attract and retain customers, inform them about new products and services, and build and maintain customer relationships.

Robert F. Abbott, author of *A Manager's Guide to Newsletters: Communicating for Results*, says that effective newsletters are strategic publications that must be planned with four critical questions in mind:

- Should we use a newsletter?
- What do we want (organization's goals) from the newsletter?
- What do our readers or members (target publics) want?
- What is our strategy statement?

To begin, ask yourself if a newsletter is a worthwhile investment. The public you are targeting may have grown so large or become so spread out geographically that it is hard for members to maintain personal communication, and difficult for senior management to have frequent and direct contact with them. Know going in, however, that producing a newsletter can require a major commitment of time, staff resources, and money. Examine the costs and potential impact of other methods for communicating with the designated audience before committing to a newsletter. These days, an e-newsletter format is a popular option, and that can be much more cost effective than a printed version. You should weigh the pros and cons of print vs. electronic in the early planning stages and then make a decision on format, with audience preferences and cost in mind (more on e-newsletters and e-zines later in this chapter).

After you decide to do a newsletter, be clear about its goals. The purpose of an internal corporate newsletter could be to support top management's desire to have open communication with employees and acknowledge their value to the company, which can help strengthen morale and build employee trust. It would make sense to include straightforward information about the company's profits and performance, as well as stories that recognize the positive contributions of employees (actually, employee newsletters should usually include those kinds of story). A product manufacturer's customer newsletter might aim to strengthen relationships with readers and strive to keep them loyal to the company and its products. Content could include new product stories, with a focus on the customer benefits of those products. See Exhibit 13.1 for more on writing effective customer newsletters.

These examples illustrate the third point, that newsletters must be written with the public's interests and information needs firmly in mind. Newsletters are most effective with publics that already have a relationship with an organization. Talk to potential readers, conduct focus groups, and do surveys to find out what they want to know, and to uncover issues and subjects that are important to them before you start writing. Balance their needs with your goals. Once you have addressed these first three questions, create a ***mission statement***, like this one for the IMPACT electronic newsletter, distributed by the American Cancer Society:

> The IMPACT e-newsletter has been designed to recognize and support the efforts of corporations engaged with the American Cancer Society [*target publics*]. The focus of this newsletter is from

Exhibit 13.1

Writing an Effective Customer Newsletter

Good customer newsletters do more than focus on the benefits of your company's products and services. The southeast-based Publix Super Markets, one of the largest grocery store chains in the United States, produces several newsletters, including the Publix Baby Club® newsletter, for its customers. While the newsletter does include store-specific articles, recipes, and coupons, much of it focuses on advice and practical tips about baby care and parenting. Publix's newsletters have strengthened loyalty to the store and its brand.

Product manufacturers should avoid the hard sell in customer newsletters and include informative articles that have value to customers and their businesses such as:

- a regular column by your CEO that focuses on significant business and industry trends and shares the CEO's insights about where customer industries are heading;
- by-lined articles written by other experts in your company that provide customers with information on manufacturing processes, emerging technologies, market development, and other subjects related to workplace productivity and profitability;
- case studies and application features that show how a customer used one of your products or services to successfully solve a business problem;
- profiles that humanize executives and highlight their expertise, which builds credibility and reinforces customer confidence in your company and its people.

the perspective of the employer, using quotes and interviews to share insight into the decision-making process and the business impact on offering the American Cancer Society's Workplace Solutions [*organization's goals*]. Published quarterly, the newsletter will profile the work of corporations in the following areas [*readers' needs*]:

- Community Involvement
- Employee Wellness
- Policy & Benefits
- Workplace Giving.

Developing the Newsletter and Its Content

With goals, target readers, and strategy in place, the next step is to begin developing the newsletter and its content. Before any writing is done:

- Select an editor. No matter how many people are involved in the process, you need one person to oversee the newsletter and keep it on track. The editor may assemble a group of contributors—staff members from various departments who submit news from their area.
- Decide on the frequency of distribution. High-involvement audiences, those more willing to respond to your messages, such as college alumni, can receive the newsletter quarterly, in the winter, spring, summer, and fall. Low-involvement audiences, such

as potential customers, should be targeted on a monthly basis, if there is enough legitimate information to share and adequate staff and money to do the job. Employee newsletters generally circulate weekly, bi-weekly or monthly, depending on the size of the organization, the amount of information that needs to get to them on a regular basis, and reader interest. Some organizations distribute e-updates on a daily basis.

- Establish a budget. Printing and mailing costs are the main budget items. Small quantities (a few hundred) can be photocopied in-house or for a reasonable price using high-quality photocopy machines such as those at a quick copy center. For large quantities with color and complex designs, it's more cost effective to hire an offset printing company. Additional funds may be needed for freelance writers and design, although desktop publishing systems make it possible to do the typesetting and layout in-house at little or no cost. You also can think about creating a design template. For a one-time cost, or investment of time if you or someone on your staff has some basic design skills, you can produce a design "shell" that provides a format and layout to follow for each issue. You can simply "drop in" the written text and visuals without having to completely redesign pages each time. Using templates can help you reduce your design costs.

- Determine the length and format. Many newsletters are four pages—one 11" × 17" sheet of paper folded to four 8½" × 11" pages—or eight pages (two folded 11" × 17" sheets) in length. You might be tempted to publish longer newsletters if you circulate them less frequently. But the average reader spends just a few minutes reading a newsletter and may not read a long newsletter as thoroughly as a shorter one. Therefore, a better option to consider is distributing shorter versions more often. You may need a bigger budget to do this, if you're producing a printed vs. an e-newsletter, but it could produce greater returns from the newsletter in the long run.

- Develop the content. Many employee newsletters include stories on subjects such as the organization's future plans, company policies and procedures, and financial performance. Include other stories on topics such as:

  - employee benefits and human resources matters;
  - staff additions and promotions;
  - advice on improving job performance (e.g., "10 tips for dealing with criticism on the job") and on dealing with family and life outside of work (e.g., "A checklist for choosing a child daycare center");
  - new products and services, promotions, and campaigns;
  - profiles of employees and how their jobs benefit the organization;
  - regular and guest columns from the CEO and other executives, who comment on important new advancements, industry trends affecting the organization, the organization's competitive position, etc.;
  - company/employee involvement in the community and charitable activities.

- You might consider creating a ***content formula*** to follow for each issue to ensure a balanced publication. This entails outlining the percentage of space that should be devoted to each type of article. For example, a content formula based on the above examples might look like this:

- company news: 30%;
- CEO column: 10%;
- program or product feature: 20%;
- human resource issues: 15%;
- new staff and promotions: 10%;
- employee or customer profile: 15%.

Writing Newsletter Articles

Newsletter writers need something specific to write about. Where do you find good story ideas? Attend department meetings. Review internal documents such as reports and proposals, summaries of company-sponsored research studies, executive speeches, and news releases. Talk to department heads and other internal decision makers. Professional and trade associations involved in your industry, government agencies that establish regulations affecting your business, and stories published in other print and electronic media are also sources of news. Be sensitive to copyright law when using published materials. Always make an effort to write in a way that will foster two-way communication between employees and senior management by providing a mechanism for feedback. So, if you are writing an article about a new employee program or a controversial issue, include a name and phone number of someone who can provide more information or to whom readers can direct opinions and comments.

When crafting effective newsletter content and articles:

- Write strong headlines, subheads, and captions. These draw readers into stories, and, sometimes, they are all the reader sees. Headlines should use active verbs and emphasize reader benefits or state problems for which readers want solutions, for example:
  - New MIS Classroom Simplifies Computer Training
  - Reorganization to Benefit Chapter Members
  - Focus on Skin Cancer: Tanning Beds Have Darker Consequences
- Keep in mind that the higher a headline is placed on a page, the more important the story will be perceived to be by the reader.
- Use the appropriate writing style based on the article. Hard news stories (e.g., XYZ Company Reports Record Earnings) use straight news leads and inverted pyramid style, and should always explain the subject in simple language. Features are less rigid. They can take a chronological approach. Consider a profile of a long-time employee. The story could lead with an interesting fact about how she joined the company and then trace her time with the company from the early years to the present. Personalize stories by using words such as "our" and "you," and by using conversational phrasing throughout.
- Write with busy people in mind. Concise stories with short sentences and paragraphs are best. Rewrite and edit carefully, so that each story is complete and appears in full on one page. If you continue a story on a following page, the reader may not finish it. In that case, make sure the most crucial information is presented within the first page of the article.

- Write articles in different formats. Complex subjects are easy to explain in a Q & A format. How-to articles, written with subheads and bulleted items, present advice in a clear, easy-to-follow manner. A how-to article focusing on how college students can obtain internships may begin with a few introductory paragraphs, followed by key subheads that lay out the steps involved: "Determining Eligibility," "Finding Internships," "Applying for Positions," and "How to Get Credit." The text under each subhead is a series of bulleted suggestions. For example, under "Applying for Positions," students might be advised to "develop effective résumés" and "polish interviewing skills."

Other Newsletter Considerations

One of the first items that the newsletter reader sees is the title, or *nameplate*, of the newsletter at the top of the first page. The Ragan Report, a weekly newsletter that publishes news and research of interest to corporate communications and public relations professionals, recommends a simple nameplate that includes the company name followed by one or two words (e.g., "River Reach," the newsletter of the San Antonio River Authority, or "Inside Children's," published by Akron Children's Hospital). If it suits the nature and content of the publication, use a cute or clever name that reflects the organization, making it easy for readers to remember, such as the Make-A-Wish Foundation's "Wishmaker®" newsletter or Mountain Area Safety Taskforce's "The Lookout," named for the forest rangers who keep an eye out for forest fires.

The title of your newsletter will attract readers, but it's the content and substance that will get people to read it and motivate them to keep reading. Here are some other design and writing tips:

- Make sure the overall "look and feel" of the newsletter are consistent with how you want the organization perceived. As stated earlier in this chapter, there are many newsletter styles and formats from which to choose. Select one that is reflective of your organization's character. Not-for-profit organizations need to think about producing newsletters that don't look too expensive. Otherwise, donors might question whether the organization really needs financial support if it can afford to produce such elaborate materials.
- Create an attractive cover page that draws the reader into each issue. Feature a cover story of major interest to readers, and a strong photo or some other visual element. Include a partial listing of a few notable stories published inside, to draw readers into the publication.
- Use "pull quotes" and sidebars. A *pull quote* is a comment taken, or pulled, from a story and highlighted in large, bold, or italic type. Pull quotes are placed in boxes or surrounded by extra white space within the text of the story; they break up the text of longer stories and add visual appeal. Look for interesting or provocative pull quotes that will get the readers' attention, give them a sense of the story's subject matter, and entice them to read further. *Sidebars* are short pieces that expand on an aspect of a larger story. They are presented as a boxed item on the same page as the main

story, with their own short headline. An article about employee charitable activities during the holidays could have a sidebar focusing on one employee helping people in need in a special way. By including a sidebar, you can cut down on the amount of detail presented in a single story. The result is two shorter, easier-to-read pieces. The page from NorthBay Healthcare's "Wellspring" newsletter shown in Exhibit 13.2 illustrates a main story, "Lifestyle Change Can Offer Success at All Ages," accompanied by a sidebar.

- Use 10- or 12-point text type and a clean, highly readable typeface such as Times Roman or Courier. It's best to select separate typefaces for the body and headlines. Too much type printed in bold, italics, and all capital letters is hard to read, so use these techniques primarily for emphasis and to single out names or key ideas. Try to include a photo or illustration on each page, and make sure your newsletter has the same graphic look for each issue.

- Include a masthead. **Mastheads** are small, boxed items that include the name of the publication; the volume and/or issue number and date; the names of the newsletter editor, staff, and contributors; information on how to contact the editor; and the newsletter's mission or editorial statement (based on the strategy statement). Some mastheads also include the names of the organization's president/CEO and board of directors. The masthead often appears on the first inside page of the newsletter.

Exhibit 13.3 is an example of a well-designed newsletter that contains an interesting nameplate, strong headline, prominent photo, and table of contents on the front page.

Exhibit 13.2
Newsletter: NorthBay Healthcare

Note: Courtesy of NorthBay Healthcare, Department of Public Affairs

Exhibit 13.3

Newsletter: Susan G. Komen for the Cure

frontline

The Susan G. Komen Breast Cancer Foundation's Newsletter Fall 2006

Cancer Stem Cell Research Shows Promise

Still in the very early stages of development, cancer stem cell research is a growing area of interest in the scientific world. Due to continuing developments in this relatively new field, it's important to understand cancer stem cells and why researchers are anxious to study and perhaps use them for medical purposes.

Stem cells have some special properties:
• They can remain as a stem cell and make more stem cells (known as undifferentiated). These cells, through self-renewal, can survive for very long periods of time.
• They can develop along several pathways: they can divide, duplicate or become specialized into specific tissues, such as cells that produce insulin.
• When they reproduce more stem cells in large numbers, the result is called a stem cell line.

Embryonic stem cells (derived from embryos that develop from eggs that have been fertilized in vitro and then donated for research purposes) have the potential to give rise to many different types of tissue. Because of this, embryonic stem cells are currently considered to have the most potential for use in the regeneration of diseased or injured tissues. Another potential role is providing a better understanding of cancer development.

Adult stem cells (sometimes called somatic stem cells) are different from embryonic stem cells. They are found in all humans at birth and exist throughout life. Adult stem cells are few in number and are hard to isolate. Their role is to maintain and repair the tissues where they are located. For example, liver stem cells might repair damage to the liver.

The fact that adult stem cells have the potential to replace and maintain tissues has led to research into other possible roles of adult stem cells. The theory that abnormal adult stem cells may play a role in the development, growth and spread of cancer is an active area of research.

It is thought that a tumor could start from cancer stem cells (normal adult stem cells that somehow become cancer stem cells). In fact, in early research on acute myeloid leukemia, cancer stem cells were shown to be the only cells that could reproduce the cancer when transferred during laboratory testing. The interest in cancer stem cells has been fueled further by the identification of cancer stem cells in brain and breast cancers. Similar results to those seen in myeloid leukemia have been found in these cancers' ability to regrow from stem cells located in the tumor. Other tumor cells that were not cancer stem cells did not demonstrate this ability to regrow.

We know that sometimes, even when we treat cancer and it can no longer be found, it can come back or spread. One theory is that current therapies that target cancer and cause the tumor to get smaller might only be killing certain tumor cells (the differentiated ones), but leaving the cancer stem cells unharmed and able to produce more cancer cells later. If this proves to be true, it can change the way we understand and treat breast cancer in the future because we will have the cancer stem cell as a target. It might be possible to recognize these extremely early changes (from normal stem cells to cancer stem cells) and treat them before a tumor or metastatic disease ever exists.

(continued on page 5)

Note: Courtesy of Susan G. Komen for the Cure®

Magazines

Magazines share many characteristics of newsletters, except they have more pages, include in-depth articles, and feature an enhanced design. While newsletters feature articles on their front page, magazine covers typically feature a prominent photo or graphic and selected headlines of articles that can be found within that issue. The longer length and more complex graphics of magazines mean that they are generally more expensive to produce than newsletters, so public relations practitioners should carefully consider whether the benefits of a magazine will outweigh the cost.

Publix Super Markets, the largest and fastest-growing employee-owned supermarket chain in the United States, produces newsletters, as well as several quarterly magazines aimed at various publics:

- The *Publix FamilyStyle®* magazine includes ideas for family fun, parenting advice, and coupons.
- *Publix GreenWise Market®* magazine is aimed at people who choose a natural organic lifestyle.
- *Publix Grape™* magazine offers articles about wine, recipes, and entertaining tips.

E-zines

The explosion of the Internet and increasing focus on electronic communication have led more organizations to launch e-zines. Wikipedia defines an e-zine as a "periodic publication distributed by email or posted on a website." An e-zine can take the form of a printed magazine that also appears online, a magazine that is strictly published in electronic form, or an electronic newsletter. Thousands of e-zines are now available on the Web, and many of them share the same purpose: to build and maintain relationships with important publics. The main advantages of an e-zine are:

- People can read about new developments shortly after they happen, instead of having to wait weeks and months to get the printed, hard-copy newsletter. Timely, consistent information helps builds public trust and loyalty, increases brand recognition, and positions the organization as "the" source of information.
- They can help an organization build a list of prospective clients. Many companies provide free access to e-publications with a registration or "subscription."
- E-zines save organizations money on printing and postage costs and are easily distributed.
- E-zines can be e-mailed to subscribers or housed on an organization's Web site. In the latter case, subscribers receive an e-mail with the e-zine's table of contents or list of headlines that will then link them directly to the Web site. Once there, they can read more complete articles and be exposed to other information on the site, including any special promotions or discount offers.

These benefits create challenges, as well. Online newsletters require continual updates and a regular distribution schedule to keep news fresh. Stories must be written with even greater attention to brevity and to the special needs of online readers. The Make-A-Wish Foundation® distributes a monthly e-zine called *Wishnews*® to keep subscribers informed of the organization's latest news, activities, and wish stories. Each issue features several one-paragraph stories, each with a headline, news lead, and a link to the full text of that story on a Web site page. Because e-zine articles should be brief, the news leads get right to the point, like this one written for an article titled "Macy's *Thanks for Sharing* Raises $5.8 Million":

> Thanks to Macy's and Make-A-Wish supporters, the holiday campaign hit a new fundraising record and will help grant more than 800 wishes.

Karl Walinskas, a professional writer, speaker, and trainer, offers these additional tips for developing a productive and informative e-zine:

- Lead with substance, not promotion. The e-zine should be a relationship-building tool, not an advertisement for an organization's products and services. Just like a print newsletter, the e-zine must not focus on the organization, but rather its publics (e.g., customers, employees, donors) and the type of information they will find interesting and helpful. Include material that will be valuable to the reader, such as:

  - how-to articles
  - industry news
  - useful Web sites and links.

  Walinskas suggests limiting the promotional aspect of your e-zine to 20% of its content.
- Keep it short. Internet users are usually looking for specific information, which they want fast. Write five or six brief articles (each consisting of a few lines to one or two short paragraphs), include helpful tips, and use bulleted lists. You also might consider placing a table of contents at the beginning that outlines information included in each issue and links the titles to longer articles. That way, readers don't need to scroll through information of little interest to them.
- Respect your subscribers. The easiest way to start building a subscriber list is by including a "subscription submit" button on your home page. Receiving your e-zine should be completely voluntary. E-zines should not be distributed unsolicited, unless you know for sure that your audience will be open to receiving your e-zine. Every issue of the e-zine should include an "opt out" statement near the top that tells the reader how to unsubscribe to the e-zine, if he or she no longer wants to receive it.
- When distributing the e-zine, make sure to protect the privacy of your subscribers. Suppress the distribution list so that individual e-mail addresses do not appear. This will also alleviate the need for readers to scroll through a list of addresses before they reach the articles, and prevent other people (including the e-zine's readers) from looking for names with which to build their own e-mail list.

Promote your e-zine by featuring it prominently on your Web site. List the reasons why visitors should subscribe to the e-zine—give examples of the type of information they will receive, offer testimonials from satisfied subscribers, offer "freebies" or special behind-the-scenes "sneak peeks." Archive old issues of the e-zine on the Web site so new visitors can get an idea of how it will benefit them. You may also want to consider registering the publication with a specialized search engine such as "The Ezine Directory."

Brochures

Pop megastar Madonna once said, "I've written my best things when I'm upset. What's the point of sitting down and notating your happiness?" That's probably not the best way for public relations professionals to approach brochure writing, since it is best to "think positive" when creating these important communication tools.

The goal of most brochures is to encourage the reader to consider doing something—purchasing a product or service, getting involved in an event, or taking a certain stand on an issue. That means brochures are written in a more persuasive and promotional tone than other public relations pieces, such as news releases and backgrounders.

Brochures don't "make the sale" on their own; they are normally used as one tool in a coordinated program of communication activities. Businesses mail brochures to prospective customers to make them aware of a new product and to pave the way for a future sales call. Fundraising professionals leave brochures behind after meetings with would-be donors as a reminder of the most important reasons to give money to their cause, and also so the information can be shared with other decision makers who didn't attend the meeting. All kinds of organization send brochures to consumers who call 800 numbers and make requests via Web sites for information on products and services.

Brochure Format, Content, and Writing

A popular brochure format is the ***pamphlet***, often printed as a single sheet folded twice (like a business letter) and inserted into an envelope or mailed by itself. This common-size pamphlet is printed on both sides and has six pages or panels; each panel is 8½" long by 3⅜" wide. If you held a standard pamphlet in front of you and opened it up to see each panel, this is what it might look like and how content might be organized:

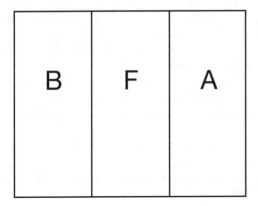

- Front cover (A)—a headline, a photo, or illustration, with the organization's name and logo. Try to place the most important information in the top third of the cover panel.
- Back right panel (B)—this is folded over and is the first panel you see on your inside right after opening the pamphlet. It can include background information on the organization, or additional information about the product, service, or issue that you want to highlight.
- Inside panels (C, D, E)—introductory copy (and possibly a visual) on the inside left panel; subheads and a few paragraphs of copy under each subhead, on the inside center and right panels, that further explain the subject, along with visuals. The simplest pamphlets might not include any photos or visuals, but they can still have a clean, interesting look using just an attractive presentation of text along with graphic elements and some color.
- Back center panel (F)—brief text that reinforces the main idea or selling point; contact information (mailing address, phone numbers, Web site address) and the organization's logo.

Many product brochures are printed in color, with larger individual panels and more folds than the traditional pamphlet. Some informational brochures are produced in booklet form, with many bound pages. You can package a brochure in many ways. Your approach to developing brochure content and writing effective copy, however, should not vary too much from brochure to brochure:

- Outline your key messages. Identify a single, main message that you want readers to comprehend. Additional messages should focus on other important product features and benefits, or on common questions about an issue to which your reader needs answers. The main message in a brochure produced by PR Newswire is positioned by asking three questions important to public relations practitioners: "Who's Looking? Who's Reporting? Who's Talking?" These three questions, which appear on the cover, provide the basis for the main text and appear as subheads inside the printed brochure.
- Make graphic design a priority. Involve graphic designers early in the process. Make sure they understand the purpose of the brochure, who it targets and what their reading habits are, and what distribution methods will be used. A fundraising brochure sent to a busy corporate executive, for instance, has to be special to demand attention. That executive might decide to take a second look at your piece because its design made a positive first impression. That was the case with Loaves & Fishes, a Charlotte, NC, emergency food assistance program. The oversized "Making Ends Meet" piece resembled a brown grocery bag, and it was cleverly bound with a mock grocery store receipt listing some of the basic items that many families in the area could not afford to buy. The creative design made people take notice and helped generate a 24% increase in donations.
- Establish benefits on the cover. The cover headline immediately lets your readers know why this subject is important to them and gives them a good reason to open the brochure and continue reading. Headlines might ask a question, provide advice, make an intriguing statement, or offer a promise. Some examples:

A brochure for i-SAFE, a nonprofit organization dedicated to Internet safety education:

> *Headline:* "It's midnight somewhere on the Internet . . . do you know who you're talking to?"

A pamphlet on date rape published by the San Diego District Attorney's Office:

> *Headline:* "Staying in control. How to avoid date rape drugs."

An Automobile Association of America Mid-Atlantic publication promoting a member discount on a GPS system:

> *Headline*: "Put a BIG screen in your car."

A credit score brochure distributed by TRW Credit Group:

> *Headline*: "How To Raise Your Credit Score 120–200 Points in As Little As 90 to 180 days!"

As these examples show, effective headlines talk directly to the reader by using personal terms such as "you" and "your." They indicate that there is valuable information inside targeted to the reader's interests. More advice on writing good headlines is offered in Exhibit 13.4.

Exhibit 13.4
Writing Brochure Headlines that Sell

How do you write brochure headlines that make your audience take notice and motivate them to keep reading? Tony L. Callahan, an expert on Web site promotion, has these suggestions:

- Include dynamic headline words that get the audience's attention such as "advice," "save," "rewards," "security," and "protect."

- Use the direct approach. Write in first and second person. Don't write that a product will help "customers" save money; write that it will help "you" save money. Use active, present-tense verbs for greater immediacy and impact.

- Make it believable. Too many adjectives and superlatives (e.g., great, sensational, superior) in the headline can lead the reader to think your product is too good to be true.

- Keep headlines short—no more than 15 words—and present them in simple, easy-to-read type.

- When creating a headline, write as many different headlines as you can and write variations of the same headline. Evaluate each headline based on three primary criteria—is it honest, does it grab the reader's attention, and does it state a clear benefit for the reader?

- Test market headlines. Get reactions from co-workers, friends, and family. Run a few versions of a free classified ad, with each one featuring a different headline. Track the response you get to each ad. Did one ad and headline prompt more phone calls, requests for information, or sales than the others?

- Introduce the subject. After you hook the reader, begin with some copy that sets the tone and builds reader interest. The creative headlines on the cover and information printed on the back right panel often are written so that they work together to convey one idea. The inside panel of the date rape brochure lists four startling statistics, such as "four out of five rape victims know their attacker." The content then focuses on how women can reduce their risk of being drugged and sexually assaulted, and what do to if they think they have been raped. Here's another example from a Department of Transportation brochure:

  Cover headline: "Childproof your flight."

  Inside headline: "Play it safe when flying with your child."

  The cover and inside headlines introduce the main message of the brochure. The body copy that follows the inside headline then sets the stage for the rest of the brochure: "Parents go to great lengths to keep children safe at home and on the road. But what about in the air?" After explaining the importance of properly restraining children when flying in case of turbulence, the brochure offers a checklist under the heading, "Make sure you're cleared for take-off." Throughout the brochure, the focus stays on the main message and the interests of the reader.

- Feature testimonials. Support your product's claims or convince readers that your program is making a difference. One way to do that is by including favorable comments—testimonials—from other satisfied customers or program participants. Professional organizations include testimonials from longtime and well-regarded members in recruitment brochures that emphasize the networking activities that membership provides and how these activities contribute to professional and personal growth.

- Tell the reader more about you and your history. Devote a panel of your brochure to a description of your organization, how long it has been in existence, what it does, and who it serves. Emphasize achievements and results. A not-for-profit group can mention how many people the organization has helped since its founding and the critical services it provides to make lives better. A manufacturing firm could note some of the well-known companies that use its products and highlight how its products help customers save money and achieve their goals. Brochures do more than sell a product, service, or issue; they sell the organization and its capabilities and reputation.

- End with a key selling point, and request reader action. Leave the reader with a final, motivating thought. The Department of Transportation brochure concludes with the following paragraph:

  It's a good idea to bring this brochure with you when you travel. For more information, visit www.faa.gov. And remember that adults should wear their seat belts at all times while on board, too, because *turbulence happens*!

This closing text is effective for several reasons: it suggests keeping the brochure, it provides a Web site for more information, and it reinforces the key safety message.

Some brochures include tear-off cards that can be sent back to the company, requesting more information. Make sure street addresses, 800 numbers, e-mail addresses, and Web sites are printed on the piece.

Write in "brochure style." Brochure copy needs to do more than just relay information in a matter-of-fact way. It should have some flair and promotional style. It needs to stress targeted benefits and tell readers how your product, service, or company stands apart from the competition:

> *Okay brochure style:* Our company has been in business for 30 years and manufactures several medical products used by doctors and health care providers.

> *Better brochure style:* Our company has served the medical community for 30 years by providing a variety of products that improve efficiency and respond to the changing needs of physicians and health-care providers.

Also, make sure your copy is written in a way your public can appreciate. Use words and expressions, in moderation, that are part of their everyday vocabulary, and indicate in the copy that you understand their interests and lifestyle. An increasing number of organizations are distributing their brochures in more than one language. Exhibit 13.5 is an interesting example of how one organization used two languages in one brochure.

Exhibit 13.5
Brochure: Monterey County Health Department

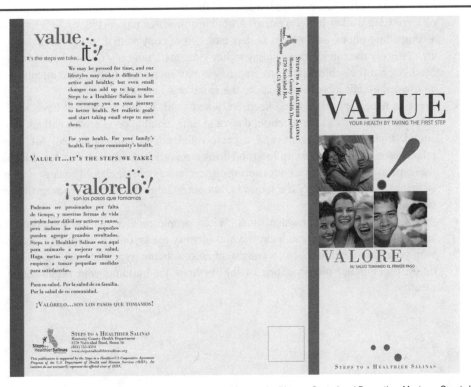

Note: Courtesy of Centers for Disease Control and Prevention, Monterey County Health Department

Brochures should be designed and written to stand alone; however, they may be part of a series. If an organization provides several services, you might consider developing a separate brochure for each one. In this case, make sure that each brochure has information specific to that one service, while at the same time sharing a similar design and core messages about the organization with the others in the series. The consistent look will reinforce the organization's corporate identity.

Fliers and Posters

Fliers and posters are informational pieces used to announce and promote meetings and public events, rally support for a cause, or get someone to think more carefully about an important issue. Fliers and posters are single sheets, with type and visuals printed on one side of the page only. Many fliers and posters are put up on bulletin boards or displayed in other high-traffic areas, such as store entrances and hallways. More and more, fliers are being sent via e-mail. A typical flier is 8½" × 11" in size, while posters tend to be larger. Here are some writing and design tips:

- Use a large headline and a single visual. The message has to jump out quickly to readers and catch their attention instantly. This is especially true of fliers and posters that a passerby has just a second to see, and that are surrounded by many other pieces on a crowded wall or bulletin board. A bold headline that targets the reader's interest, a compelling photo, and a short sentence or two of copy with a strong call to action are generally the rule. When sending a flier via e-mail, not only do you need a strong headline, but the subject line—as with any e-mail message—has to grab attention in a crowded e-mail inbox and speak to the receiver's interests.
- Mention necessary details and keep body text brief. Event fliers must have all the relevant facts, such as the location, date, and time, notable people who will speak or attend, topics of discussion, and a person and phone number to call for more information. If complimentary food and drink are available, mention that, too. Include the name(s) and logo(s) of the sponsoring organization(s); these should be large enough so that readers can identify the sponsors, but not so large that they overpower the key message.
- Adopt a familiar and consistent look. When people receive one of your fliers or see one of your posters, you want them to identify the layout and copy presentation with your organization. Using a consistent color scheme, typeface, logo, and slogan on all promotional pieces is one of the methods for building your organization's identity.

ASSIGNMENTS

Assignment 13.1—The Big Brothers Big Sisters Brochure

Your public relations firm and its employees are actively involved with nonprofit groups and charities in the community. Several senior executives serve on the local boards of directors of major human service organizations such as Big Brothers Big Sisters of America (BBBSA), and employees regularly take part in events to raise money for cancer research and other worthy causes. The agency also "gives back" by donating its professional services and expertise. This includes writing, designing, and producing public relations materials free of charge for BBBSA.

Today, at the request of your supervisor who serves on the BBBSA board, you are meeting with Claudia Rivera, executive director of the local BBBSA agency. Founded in 1904, BBBSA matches adult volunteers with youth between the ages of 6 and 18 who are looking for an older person with whom to spend time. The adult volunteers, known as Big Brothers and Big Sisters, develop one-on-one mentoring relationships with these youths. Many of the Little Brothers and Little Sisters are young people from single-parent families who have lost a parent to death, or who no longer have contact with a parent due to divorce, separation, or abuse. A Big Brother/Big Sister becomes a positive adult role model and brings balance to a young person's life to help keep him or her on track.

In talking with Rivera on the telephone prior to your meeting, you learn that the local BBBSA agency wants to enhance its efforts aimed at recruiting new adult mentors. Currently, the agency has a waiting list of youth requesting a Big Brother or Big Sister, and it does not have enough adult volunteers to meet that demand. As your meeting begins, Rivera gives you more background on the volunteer shortage and additional details about the brochure project.

"We haven't updated our recruitment brochure in some time, and we thought this would be a good time to do it," Rivera says. "As I told you, there's a real need to get more adults on board as mentors. We're hoping a new, attractive brochure targeted to the right kinds of audiences will help us build our volunteer base. We'll probably mail some of them and hand others out at events, but we'll also post it on our Web site and drive people to it that way."

"Is there a certain kind of person you look for? Can anybody be a Big Brother or Sister? Are there specific requirements?" you ask.

"All good questions. We need men and women of all ages and backgrounds. Some of our Big Brothers and Big Sisters are young professionals, some are older people who have their own kids or grandchildren, and some are college students. We do have an increasing need for young male professionals and African Americans, based on the requests we are getting," Rivera says.

"So, how does this work? Once you get a volunteer, how do you decide with whom that person should be matched?"

"First of all, any potential volunteer is carefully screened by professionals on our staff. We get a lot of information about the adult, and then we make a match based on the child's needs and interests and the interests and characteristics of the volunteer. This is a thoughtful process."

"I would guess that one of the common objections you hear from potential volunteers is that they are busy and they don't have enough time to spend with someone."

"That's true," Rivera replies. "But we stress that you only have to spend a few hours a week. And what you do together is really up to you. It can be as simple as just taking a walk in a park or grabbing a bite to eat. The important thing is being there for young people, and letting them know that you are an adult they can count on."

You then ask a few more questions about the preferred design and format of the piece. Rivera tells you that the piece could be designed as an 8½" × 11" pamphlet with six panels, but she's open to other suggestions. She also says that BBBSA has many good-quality photographs to choose from, but that she welcomes your thoughts on specific photos or artwork that could be included in the new brochure. Before she leaves, Rivera asks you to get back to her shortly with a project time line.

Exercises

1. Prepare a brief memorandum for Rivera that includes the following:

   - goals of the BBSA brochure and key message points to include in the brochure copy;

   - a recommended cover headline that could serve as a recruitment campaign theme, along with a proposed visual element. Justify your copy and visual choices;

   - suggestions for other photo/visual ideas that you think will enhance the piece;

   - a time line for producing the finished recruitment piece. List the activities in the order that they should occur, and indicate the estimated number of days (or weeks) needed to complete each activity.

2. Using the information provided in this case and any additional information compiled from your own research, write the copy for the BBBSA recruitment brochure. Limit your copy to two to three pages, double-spaced. Indicate where subheads and copy blocks should appear in the brochure (e.g., cover, inside right fold, inside spread, back panel).

3. Write the copy for a BBBSA poster to be distributed on college campuses. The goal of the poster is to interest college-age men and women in becoming Big Brothers and Big Sisters. Your copy should include an attention-getting headline and a few sentences of body copy that convey key messages. Begin the copy draft with a brief description of a proposed design concept (what visuals would you use, color scheme, etc.).

Assignment 13.2—A Hospital's Public Relations Challenge (B)

As a communications professional working for Mercy Hospital (Assignment 3.3), you were asked by Charles Kepner, the hospital's vice president of marketing communications, to design a public relations program aimed at building awareness of Mercy's services among young parents 25–40, in an effort to increase usage of hospital services by this critical public.

During the program planning process, you learned that more people in your community and in the hospital's service area are indicating an interest in e-communication, especially those in the 25–40 age group. Many say they use the Internet and Web sites more frequently to get information about health services, and close to 60% said they have visited Mercy Hospital's Web site.

In addition, you learned that readership of the hospital's external magazine, *Life Lines*, is high among older patients. The magazine includes some hospital-specific news, but puts a lot of its focus on important health issues and preventative care stories. One third of those aged 25–40 say they spend some time reading the magazine, but the rest say they "skim through" or don't read it, due to time constraints and a sense that the content isn't all that relevant.

You have talked to Kepner about the hospital's marketing communications budget and the increasing need to find ways to be more efficient and cut costs. This includes an ongoing debate about scrapping the printed version of the magazine in favor of an electronic version or e-zine, which would reduce printing costs.

Exercises

Write a report that presents your recommendations on the hospital's *Life Lines* magazine, the pros and cons of doing an e-version versus a printed version, and your suggestion on what to do with the *Life Lines* publication moving forward. Propose any changes that could be implemented, especially to have greater impact on parents aged 25–40.

As part of your report, map out and justify an editorial framework for an issue of *Life Lines* magazine. Explain the kind of content you would suggest including in the magazine, and how you would organize the content. Recommend specific story ideas and features. ∎

Assignment 13.3—Creating the PRSA Chapter E-Newsletter

Brad McCully recently graduated from college with a degree in public relations. McCully was an active member of the PRSSA chapter at his college. Soon after graduation, he joined the PRSA chapter in his city as an associate member. Graduating PRSSA members may join the professional society at a lower rate than full members.

PRSA, the largest professional association for public relations practitioners in the world, provides its members with professional development support, regional and national conferences, publications, networking opportunities, and other benefits. PRSA members can also take an exam and earn accreditation, or APR, which is a designation that indicates a member has achieved a high level of experience and competence. Each PRSA member also becomes a member of one of the society's local chapters; there are PRSA chapters in major cities and areas throughout the United States. Local chapters have their own boards of directors and sponsor professional development activities and other programs for the benefit of local members.

At a monthly program sponsored by his local PRSA chapter, McCully strikes up a conversation with Michelle Wu, one of the chapter's officers.

"This is my third PRSA program, so I haven't been connected to the chapter all that long," McCully says. "I wondered if the chapter communicates with members on a regular basis, outside of the e-fliers we get that announce the monthly programs."

"We had a monthly newsletter and we used that to keep members up-to-date on chapter programs and developments," Wu says. "Our members also told us they wanted to see more information in the newsletter that would help them in their careers, or help them to do their jobs better, so we started including those kinds of stories as well. But we haven't put out a regular newsletter for about two years now. It takes some effort to get a newsletter together, as you probably well know, and you really need to have someone who can take the lead on it and keep it going month to month. This time around, we want to do this as an e-newsletter, since we've heard from our members that they would prefer to receive it electronically rather than in printed form."

McCully responds: "I know I'm new to the chapter, but I do have some pretty good newsletter experience. In one of my internships, I wrote most of the stories for three or four issues of an employee newsletter, and did most of the layout. I'd be willing to take this project on, if I can get the support of a few other members to help do the writing. Maybe the chapter secretary could help with proofreading and distribution."

"I bet the board would jump at the idea," Wu replies. "Here's what I would suggest. Let's start giving more thought to the newsletter's goals and content. We should also decide how we want to do this e-newsletter. Should we write and design a newsletter that appears on our chapter's Web pages, and send out an e-mail with headlines and links that pushes people to that online newsletter, or should we do it some other way. We'll plan to have you come to the next board meeting, so you can meet the other board members and share your ideas for the newsletter. I'm sure they'll have thoughts, too. Since many of them may not know you, be prepared to sell yourself and emphasize your ability to carry through on this project."

Exercises

1. Working alone or with a partner, prepare a memorandum for Wu and the board that presents your approach to the PRSA chapter e-newsletter. Include:

   - Goals/format. An introduction that explains the goals of the newsletter and the approach/format you would recommend.

   - Content. Suggest some of the general types of story that could be published in the newsletter, as well as any ideas for regular monthly features. Include 10 story ideas that could be considered for the first issue. List, briefly explain, and justify each idea.

   - Evaluation. Ideas for evaluating the effectiveness of the e-newsletter.

2. Select one of the story ideas presented in your memo, and write a 250-word article on that topic.

References and Suggested Reading

AAA Mid-Atlantic. (n.d.). *Put a big screen in your car.* [Brochure]. Wilmington, DE: Author.

Abbott, R. F. (2001). *A manager's guide to newsletters: Communicating for results.* Airdrie, Alberta, Canada: Word Engines Press.

Carter, D. E. (1999). *Brochures that work.* New York: Hearst Books International.

Department of Transportation. (n.d.). *Childproof your flight.* [Brochure].

Gedney, K., & Fultz, P. (1988). *The complete guide to creating successful brochures.* Brentwood, NY: Asher-Gallant Press.

Hudson, H. P. (1998). *Publishing newsletters* (Rev. ed.). Rhinebeck, NY: H & M Publishing.

Madonna (n.d.). Madonna. In *80s rock star quotes.* Retrieved September 7, 2003 from http://80music.about.com/library/weekly/aa070198.htm.

Harris, C. (2005). *Producing successful magazines, newsletters and e-zines.* Oxford: How To Books.

Increasing ezine subscriptions for maximum success (n.d.). Retrieved December 8, 2008 from http://www.joetracy.com/articles/newsletter/increase-ezine-subscriptions.html.

Publix Baby Club® newsletter (2008). Retrieved December 5, 2008 from http://www.publix.com/babyclub.

Ragan Communications. http://www.ragan.com.

San Diego District Attorney's Office. (n.d.). *Staying in control. How to avoid date rape drugs.* [Brochure]. San Diego, CA: Author.

Walinskas, K. (2000, April). *The art of the e-zine.* Retrieved January 19, 2003 from http://www.speakingconnection.com/Communication_Articles/E-zines_4–00-B.html.

Part Five

EVALUATION

14

Evaluation

As a preface to this final chapter, here are two quotes worth pondering, from Socrates, the ancient Greek philosopher, and talk-show host and celebrity Oprah Winfrey, who some might call a modern-day prophet: "The unexamined life is not worth living," Socrates once said. And according to Winfrey, "Luck is a matter of preparation meeting opportunity."

How do these words of wisdom fit into a chapter on public relations evaluation and measurement, you might ask? Because like an unexamined life, a public relations program that is not examined and evaluated has little value to an organization. And, you can't leave the success of a program to chance or luck, although you do need to prepare. You need to think about how you will measure success during the initial stages of campaign planning, not as an afterthought once the campaign has ended.

Because public relations involves a broad range of activities and many different approaches, there isn't "one right way" to measure public relations effectiveness. As this chapter points out, you measure public relations success by using a number of techniques that consider the specific public relations objectives you establish, the exposure created by communications tools and public relations activities, and the influence your work had in changing public perception or motivating people to do something that supports your organization and its mission.

The Components of Public Relations Measurement

A 2006 report published by the Institute for Public Relations, titled *Public Relations Research for Planning and Evaluation* (Lindenmann, 2006), recommends that public relations professionals consider four components of the evaluation process:

- Setting specific, measurable public relations goals and objectives—have specific goals and objectives been established at the start? After a project is implemented, you can measure its success against predetermined goals and objectives. When goals and objectives are stated in specific terms, they are much easier to measure. For example, a public information campaign can aim to generate 1,000 phone calls or requests for information within a certain time period. The goal of an annual fundraiser might be to increase donations by 10% as compared with the previous year. Or, a professional organization hopes to double the number of attendees at its national conference.

- Measuring communications outputs—what public relations materials did you produce and what activities did you execute, and how much exposure or attention did you get as a result? Outputs also look at how well an organization presents itself to its publics. Outputs are the most immediate and most visible results of a public relations program. Typical public relations outputs include quantities of brochures and other printed materials produced and distributed, and the extent and content of media coverage gained through publicity.

- Measuring communications outtakes and outcomes—what impact did your public relations programming have on target publics' awareness, understanding, attitudes, behaviors, and actions? While outputs are short-term in nature, outcomes relate to the more lasting effect that public relations efforts had on your publics. Focus groups, audits, and other scientific research techniques are used to measure if a public received and understood messages contained within internal and external communications tools, or if a public felt more positively about an organization or situation following a public relations campaign. Also, consider changes in behavior that led to a desired action, such as endorsing a new organizational policy.

- Measuring institutional outcomes—how did public relations programming support the mission and profitability of the organization? Public relations programs that contribute on some level to increased sales or a better market share will carry more weight than those that don't. Public relations efforts alone cannot often be tied directly to improved sales. But the number of new business leads generated by a direct-mail brochure produced by the public relations department, and the number of those leads that turned into new clients or customers, are valid measures of public relations' impact on the bottom line.

Goals and objectives were discussed in detail in chapter 4; however, we should take a closer look at measuring awareness, acceptance, and action.

Awareness

Most public relations materials are aimed at creating awareness, which in turn will hopefully lead to acceptance and ultimately action. The first step in evaluating awareness is looking at whether the target publics were exposed to an organization's message. A common way of measuring the quantity and quality of exposure is analyzing media coverage. Other techniques include looking at statistics related to Web sites and blogs, and conducting readership surveys.

Media Coverage

- If your organization generates extensive media coverage, you may want to hire a ***media clipping service*** to handle this for you. Clipping services monitor print, electronic, and Internet coverage based on your search criteria. Some of the more popular clipping services include BurrellesLuce, VMS, Cision, and WebClipping.com.

- Clipping services can also analyze the coverage they compile for you, or you can conduct a ***content analysis*** yourself. As outlined in chapter 4, this type of research generally looks at how many media placements you received and the types of medium (i.e., print, broadcast, online) in which those stories appeared; how many people potentially read, heard, or viewed those stories; and how effectively those media placements conveyed your organization's key messages. Tracking the source of each story will help you assess the effectiveness of specific publicity tools in generating media interest and make adjustments when developing future media campaigns.

  - When conducting a content analysis for evaluation purposes, record the name of the media outlet and date of coverage, the reach and frequency of the outlet's distribution, type of placement (i.e., news or feature article, op-ed piece, blog) and length of each story in total column inches, paragraphs, pages or seconds/minutes of air time. Look at the source of each story. For example, did it result from a news release or media pitch you sent?
  - Subject, tone, and key message points: summarize the editorial focus of the story and total mentions of your organization by name in the headline and body copy. Identify individuals from your organization quoted or referred to in the story. Look at how often your organization and its officials are mentioned in comparison with your competitors. Also, determine if the story portrays your organization and positions company officials in a favorable way. The tone of a piece can be open to interpretation. What some view as a positive story, others may see as a neutral or even slightly negative piece. You should, however, examine how clearly and accurately the story conveys your key message points and attempts to give a balanced view of the topic.

- Consider figuring out how much the coverage you received would have cost if it had appeared as advertising. ***Advertising equivalency*** is commonly used in evaluating public relations campaigns. This can be computed by looking at how much the media coverage would have cost if the same newspaper space or television time had been purchased as an advertisement. Because publicity is filtered through a third party and thus seen as more credible than advertising, some organizations use a "credibility factor," multiplying the advertising cost by 2, 5, or even 10.
- Another common evaluation technique is counting ***media impressions***, the total circulation of a newspaper or magazine, or the total number of people listening to or watching a radio or television program. If a daily newspaper has a circulation of 500,000 readers, and two stories are published in that newspaper, then that coverage produces 1 million impressions. Like advertising equivalency, such large numbers can be impressive, but don't mistake impressions with impact. Impressions represent the number of people who may have been exposed to your message at a given time.

Internet Statistics

One way to measure how well your Web site or blog is doing is to monitor the site's ***traffic***— that is, the number of people who make daily visits to your site. Count how many people have used RSS to subscribe to your site in order to be notified when updates are made. Monitor the pages or posts that are visited most and least often, and adjust the site content accordingly. As with media impressions, the number of hits will be large numbers, but don't be fooled. They don't tell you if desirable target groups received the message, understood it, or acted on it.

It is also helpful to find out how people are arriving at your site. Monitor how people are finding out about you, for example, through search engines or other blogs. This information is available automatically in most blogging software.

If overall traffic is low, you may need to expand your promotional strategies or rethink the content of the site to make it more appealing. Always include a "Feedback," "E-Mail Us" or "Tell Us" section for visitors to give you suggestions for improving the site to make it more useful and more user-friendly. Respond quickly to people and let them know you've received their e-mail and that you appreciate their feedback.

Readership Surveys

You should do more than simply look at how many newsletters, e-zines, and brochures are distributed and to whom they are being sent. For example, conduct periodic readership studies to find out if your target publics are taking the time to read your newsletter, what content they are reading most often, and the kinds of story they would like to see, in comparison with the types of article you are publishing. A simple questionnaire can assess readership preferences, while interviews and focus groups are good techniques for examining readership and Web habits in more depth.

Some key points regarding awareness objectives: While they are often the easiest to execute, their success is much harder to measure. You can't just assume that extensive media coverage of an issue made your target public more aware. Evaluating media exposure, Internet statistics, and readership helps you to see if your communications materials and activities have been received, and if a target public took notice of what you had to say. But it is critical to go further to find out if the information you shared increased audience understanding, led to a change in their thinking, or inspired them to take action.

You cannot assume that people became more aware of something based on the number of stories they may have read in the media, nor that they have become more supportive of an issue because a few of them wrote positive letters to the editor. *Benchmarking* is used to help accurately measure changes in awareness levels or changes in public opinion. Before implementing a public relations program, conduct interviews, focus groups, or surveys to clearly identify what people know or think about an issue. This provides a benchmark or a point of reference at the start of the campaign. After the campaign concludes, do follow-up focus groups or surveys and compare your findings at that time with previous research results. If awareness levels are higher or public opinion has shifted more in your favor, then you can say more definitely that your public relations programming elevated awareness or influenced opinion.

Acceptance

Benchmarking will also help to evaluate acceptance objectives that deal with shifts in attitude. Receiving feedback from your target public is another common evaluation technique.

When producing printed materials, make sure to build in response mechanisms such as reply cards, toll-free numbers, and Web site addresses. On the Internet, offer coupons or other items that can be downloaded. The key is to be able to measure how many people sought out additional information based on your awareness message. Track how many brochure reply cards you receive requesting more information. Tabulate the number of phone calls and Web site visits you get as a result of a newsletter or news release. Always ask new customers if they received a printed piece that prompted them to call your company or visit its Web site. Track the number of people who registered for an event online as a result of a targeted e-mail campaign.

The Department of Health Services for the State of California wanted to reduce the escalating costs incurred by state and local governments for emergency health care provided to uninsured children. It launched the "Healthy Families/Medi-Cal for Children" public relations campaign to deliver preventive, low-cost health care to uninsured Californian children. Working with Hill & Knowlton in Los Angeles, the department set up a toll-free phone line. The hotline made it possible for callers to get information on low-cost health care and to be put in touch with community-based organizations in the state that could assist them in securing this coverage. The hotline, which handled calls in more than 10 different languages, received more than 270,000 calls, and 60,000 of those callers got referrals to local "Healthy Families" enrollment sites.

Action

While awareness objectives are the easiest to achieve, but the most difficult to measure, action objectives are the opposite: they are the easiest to measure, but the hardest to achieve. A few examples of action measurements are adoption of a new policy; sales figures, market share, and the number of new customers; and the number of dollars raised for a fundraising project. When we measure acceptance, we are looking at how many people have responded to our awareness message. When we measure action, we are looking at how many of the people who expressed interest in the message actually acted upon it.

The "Healthy Families/Medi-Cal for Children" public relations campaign was credited with enrolling more than 90,000 uninsured children in the "Healthy Families" program. Public relations strategies, then, had a positive impact because they motivated the target public to take a desired action—to call the hotline (acceptance) and enroll in the program (action)—but they also contributed significantly to the organization's goals of providing low-cost health care to uninsured children, reducing government spending on health care, and improving the overall health care of California residents.

References and Suggested Reading

Alexander, J. E., & Tate, M. A. (1999). *Web wisdom: How to evaluate and create information quality on the web*. Mahwah, NJ: Lawrence Erlbaum Associates.

Anderson, F. W., & Hadley, L. (1999). *Guidelines for setting measurable PR objectives*. Gainesville, FL: Institute for Public Relations Research and Education.

Daymon, C., & Holloway, I. (2002). *Qualitative research methods in public relations and marketing communications*. New York: Routledge.

Li, Hairong (2002). Advertising media. *Encyclopedia of advertising.* Chicago: Fitzroy Dearborn Publishers.

Lindenmann, W. K. (2003). *Guidelines and standards for measuring and evaluating PR effectiveness.* Gainesville, FL: Institute for Public Relations Research and Education.

Lindenmann, W. K. (2006). *Public relations research for planning and evaluation.* Gainesville, FL: Institute for Public Relations Research and Education.

Patterson, J. G. (1996). *Benchmarking basics: Looking for a better way.* Menlo Park, CA: Crisp Publications.

Socrates (n.d.). Retrieved December 15, 2002 from http://www.yokemonster.com/quotes/quotes/s/q101168.html.

Winfrey, Oprah (n.d.). *Quotes worth repeating.* Retrieved December 15, 2002 from http://www.womenwhonetwork.com/Quote.asp.

Appendix A

Planning Outline

Type of Project:
Situation:
Objectives: Awareness: Acceptance: Action:
Key Public(s):
WIN Analysis of Key Public(s):
Specific Appeal(s) to be Used: Logos: Pathos: Ethos:
Core Message:
Communication Channel:
Evaluation Methods: Awareness: Acceptance: Action:

Checklists

The Public Relations Process

Research

- ☐ Conduct primary research
- ☐ Review secondary sources
- ☐ Include situation analysis

Planning

- ☐ Identify goal(s)
- ☐ Identify target publics
- ☐ Write measurable objectives
- ☐ Develop strategies
- ☐ Outline tactics
- ☐ Develop budget
- ☐ Establish timetable

Execution

- ☐ Develop message(s)
- ☐ Determine channel(s) of distribution

Evaluation

- ☐ Measure communication output
- ☐ Measure communication outgrowths and outcomes
- ☐ Measure institutional output
- ☐ Compare measurements to objectives

Interviews

Before

- ☐ Make appointment
- ☐ Confirm time, place, and purpose
- ☐ Provide prep questions to interviewee
- ☐ Research interviewee and topic
- ☐ Prepare questions
- ☐ Get permission to tape record interview
- ☐ Check tape recorder for batteries and adequate tape
- ☐ Bring notepad and extra pens

Conducting the Interview

- ☐ To start, find a general topic unrelated to interview
- ☐ Restate goal of interview
- ☐ Ask questions from prepared list
- ☐ Listen
- ☐ Stray from the script, if necessary
- ☐ Make sure important questions are answered

After

- ☐ Review notes immediately
- ☐ Send thank you
- ☐ Confirm next steps

Case Analysis

- ☐ Determine what needs to be measured
- ☐ Carefully define terms
- ☐ Identify sources of communications
- ☐ Develop coding sheet
- ☐ Train coders

News Release

Format

- ☐ Company letterhead
- ☐ Minimum 1" margin on all sides
- ☐ 1½- to 2-line spacing between sentences; no double spacing between paragraphs
- ☐ Indent paragraphs
- ☐ Contact information: name, title, phone number, e-mail
- ☐ Date release is distributed
- ☐ Release information
- ☐ Headline
- ☐ Dateline
- ☐ End mark
- ☐ For additional pages: "more" and slug

Content

- ☐ Lead with news
- ☐ Emphasize local angle
- ☐ State why news is significant
- ☐ Include details: who, what, where, how, when
- ☐ Provide background information
- ☐ Include boilerplate
- ☐ Use strong quotes that are not obvious or too self-serving

Writing

- ☐ Short sentences and paragraphs
- ☐ Objective
- ☐ Active voice
- ☐ Few adjectives
- ☐ AP style

Broadcast Version

- ☐ Avoid hard news or details in first sentence
- ☐ Use simple, one-subject, one-verb sentences
- ☐ Avoid clauses that begin with "who," "which," or "where"
- ☐ Write for the ear
- ☐ Use conversational tone
- ☐ Use active voice
- ☐ Attribute information up front
- ☐ Use pronouncers (phonetic spellings)
- ☐ Mirror broadcast style (e.g., all caps, double spaces)
- ☐ Radio: consider including actuality (8–12 seconds)
- ☐ TV: consider a-roll (90 seconds) and b-roll

Social Media Version

- ☐ Carefully select keywords for searches
- ☐ Use bullets to list facts
- ☐ Use links to relevant sources within copy
- ☐ Include multimedia
- ☐ Put quotes and boilerplate under separate headings

E-mail Version

- ☐ Address individually (avoid group mailings)
- ☐ Include strong subject line
- ☐ Include headline
- ☐ Include contact information
- ☐ Summarize important information
- ☐ Direct reader to full release on the Web

Media Alert

Print Format

☐ Company letterhead

☐ Minimum 1" margin on all sides

☐ 1½- to 2-line spacing between sentences; no double spacing between paragraphs

☐ Indent paragraphs

☐ "Media Advisory" label

☐ Contact information: name, title, phone number, e-mail

☐ Headline

Content

☐ Summarize why event is newsworthy

☐ Include only necessary details: who, what, where, when

☐ Avoid too much information

Writing

☐ Brief

☐ Clear and concise

☐ AP style

E-mail Version

☐ Address individually (avoid group mailings)

☐ Include strong subject line

☐ Include headline

☐ Include contact information

☐ Summarize important information

Media Pitch

Print Format

- [ ] Company letterhead
- [ ] Heading (date; recipient's name, title, company, and address)
- [ ] Salutation
- [ ] Closing and signature
- [ ] Single space between lines; double space between paragraphs

Content

- [ ] Begin with attention-getting first paragraph
- [ ] Introduce story angle
- [ ] Suggest credible sources
- [ ] Share key facts, statistics, anecdotes, and details that legitimize story
- [ ] Clearly state what you want (interview, feature coverage, etc.)
- [ ] Indicate follow-up plans
- [ ] Reinforce willingness to provide additional information
- [ ] Include contact information: name, title, phone number, e-mail

Writing

- [ ] Creative
- [ ] Address editor's interest
- [ ] Avoid being self-serving
- [ ] Avoid being pushy
- [ ] Brief

E-mail Version

- [ ] Include strong subject line
- [ ] Include headline
- [ ] Include contact information
- [ ] Summarize important information
- [ ] Keep it brief

Photo Caption

Photos

- [ ] Show action
- [ ] Look natural
- [ ] Avoid clutter
- [ ] Avoid overly promoting the company
- [ ] Ensure high-quality/high-resolution
- [ ] Use preferred format for media

Format

- [ ] Company letterhead
- [ ] Contact information: name, title, phone number, e-mail
- [ ] Date being sent
- [ ] Headline
- [ ] Dateline

Content

- [ ] Describe action in photo in first sentence
- [ ] Write first sentence in present tense
- [ ] Use past tense for rest of caption
- [ ] Refer to company only once
- [ ] Identify people based on action

Writing

- [ ] Avoid "obvious" references
- [ ] Brief
- [ ] Straightforward

Fact Sheet/Backgrounder

Format

- ☐ Name of company
- ☐ Contact information: name, title, phone number, e-mail
- ☐ Headline
- ☐ Subheadings
- ☐ Q & A, bullet, narrative

Content

- ☐ Summarize important information
- ☐ Highlight interesting, provocative facts

Writing

- ☐ Factual and informative
- ☐ Objective

Organizational History

Format

☐ Name of company

☐ Contact information: name, title, phone number, e-mail

☐ Headline

☐ Q & A, bullet, narrative

Content

☐ Introduce history in first one or two paragraphs

☐ Provide chronological account

☐ Highlight significant years and notable achievements

Writing

☐ Factual

☐ Objective

Biography

Format

- ☐ Name of company
- ☐ Name and title of person
- ☐ Photo (optional)

Content

- ☐ State job description in first paragraph
- ☐ Provide specifics of job duties and activities
- ☐ Include special knowledge or practice areas
- ☐ Summarize career history
- ☐ Highlight professional activities
- ☐ Summarize education
- ☐ Include community/public service work
- ☐ Include personal information, if appropriate

Writing

- ☐ Factual
- ☐ Objective

Feature

Format

- ☐ Name of company
- ☐ Headline

Content

- ☐ Begin with attention-getting lead
- ☐ Clearly state focus of story
- ☐ Include colorful details
- ☐ Use revealing quotes
- ☐ End with strong conclusion that reconnects with focus of story

Writing

- ☐ Imaginative
- ☐ Descriptive language

By-lined Article

Format

☐ By-line

☐ Headline

Content

☐ Offer general advice

☐ Support claims and/or predictions

☐ Attribute statistics

☐ Avoid promotion of company or products

☐ Mention company name with brief author description at the end

Writing

☐ Factual

☐ Objective

Case Study

Format

- ☐ Headline

Content

- ☐ Present problem
- ☐ Present possible solutions
- ☐ Position product/service as best solution

Writing

- ☐ Factual
- ☐ Objective

Web Site

Planning

- ☐ Establish goals
- ☐ Target specific audience
- ☐ Monitor competition
- ☐ Develop site map
- ☐ Create short, easy-to-remember Web address
- ☐ Determine how site will be evaluated

Designing

- ☐ Reflect character of organization
- ☐ Create strong home page
- ☐ Develop creative, efficient toolbars
- ☐ Develop short, easy-to-read sections
- ☐ Include headlines and subheads
- ☐ Avoid small type, all caps, reverse type, and multiple typefaces
- ☐ Consider podcasts and vodcasts
- ☐ Include online media room

Writing

- ☐ Short sentences and paragraphs
- ☐ Aim for minimal scrolling
- ☐ Direct, conversational tone

Blog

Planning

- ☐ Pick name that reflects organization
- ☐ Decide who will author blog
- ☐ Determine how often postings will be made
- ☐ Consider how comments will be handled

Designing

- ☐ Complement corporate Web site
- ☐ Include RSS
- ☐ Set up archive for posts
- ☐ Include blogroll

Format

- ☐ Include tags, categories
- ☐ Incorporate trackbacks

Writing

- ☐ Use conversational tone
- ☐ Let personality shine through
- ☐ Use personal language
- ☐ Determine length by how much needs to be said
- ☐ Be transparent
- ☐ Protect privacy
- ☐ Disclose possible conflict of interest
- ☐ Give credit where due

Memo

Format

- ☐ Company letterhead
- ☐ Heading (to, from, date, subject)
- ☐ Single space between lines; double space between paragraphs

Content

- ☐ Clearly state purpose in first sentence
- ☐ Include important points in body
- ☐ Suggest follow-up action in closing

Writing

- ☐ Brief
- ☐ Short sentences and paragraphs
- ☐ Personal language ("I," "you," "we")

Planning Memo

Format

☐ Company letterhead

☐ Heading (to, from, date, subject)

☐ Subheads

☐ Single space between lines; double space between paragraphs

☐ Numbered items

☐ Graphics

Content

☐ Introduce plan

☐ Summarize research

☐ Include situation analysis

☐ Identify goal(s)

☐ Identify target publics

☐ Include measurable objectives

☐ Outline strategies and tactics

☐ Include budget

☐ Include timetable

☐ Explain evaluation methods to be used

☐ Reinforce strengths and benefits of plan in conclusion

Writing

☐ Easy to read

☐ Informative but persuasive

☐ Use section headings, numbers, and bullets

Business Letter

Format

- ☐ Company letterhead
- ☐ Heading (date; recipient's name, title, company, and address)
- ☐ Salutation
- ☐ Closing and signature
- ☐ Single space between lines; double space between paragraphs

Content

- ☐ Clearly state reason for letter in first paragraph
- ☐ Present key ideas in subsequent paragraphs

Writing

- ☐ Brief
- ☐ Personal language ("I," "you," "we")

Sales Letter

Format

- ☐ Company letterhead
- ☐ Heading (date; recipient's name, title, company, and address)
- ☐ Salutation
- ☐ Closing and signature
- ☐ Single space between lines; double space between paragraphs

Content

- ☐ Specialize letter to customer's preferences
- ☐ Include testimonials/endorsements
- ☐ Present credentials
- ☐ Add useful information
- ☐ Include call to action
- ☐ Include incentive
- ☐ Pay attention to visual aspect

Writing

- ☐ Brief, but persuasive
- ☐ Personal language ("I," "you," "we")

Response to Complaint Letter

Format

- ☐ Company letterhead
- ☐ Heading (date; recipient's name, title, company, and address)
- ☐ Salutation
- ☐ Closing and signature
- ☐ Single space between lines; double space between paragraphs

Content

- ☐ Acknowledge complaint in first paragraph
- ☐ Don't make accusations
- ☐ Show concern
- ☐ Outline specific steps to correct problem
- ☐ Offer apologies, if appropriate and cleared by legal counsel
- ☐ Stress value of customer and his/her business

Writing

- ☐ Brief
- ☐ Personal language ("I," "you," "we")

E-mail

Format

- ☐ Strong subject line
- ☐ Include salutation
- ☐ Formal closing (sender's name, title, company, phone, fax, e-mail, Web site)
- ☐ Check to see if attachments are welcomed by recipient

Content

- ☐ Clearly state purpose in first paragraph

Writing

- ☐ Brief
- ☐ Short paragraphs (one or two sentences)
- ☐ Personal language ("I," "you," "we")
- ☐ E-mail etiquette used (proper use of capitalization, no smiley faces, etc.)

Research Report

Format

- ☐ Cover page (title, names, date)
- ☐ Table of contents
- ☐ Executive summary
- ☐ Introduction
- ☐ Narrative
- ☐ Supporting information
- ☐ Charts/graphs/graphics
- ☐ Bibliography

Content

- ☐ Detail findings
- ☐ Interpret and analyze data
- ☐ Discuss implications
- ☐ Propose recommendations

Writing

- ☐ Short sentences and paragraphs

Annual Report

Format

- ☐ Theme
- ☐ CEO letter to shareholders
- ☐ Detailed financial facts, figures, and statements
- ☐ Company information
- ☐ Photos, charts, or other visuals

Content

- ☐ Review previous year
- ☐ Examine current or potential critical issues
- ☐ Show connection with company goals

Writing

- ☐ Factual, straightforward, honest
- ☐ Positive tone
- ☐ Simple, easy-to-understand language
- ☐ Avoid technical terms
- ☐ Active voice
- ☐ Visually creative and interesting

New Business Proposal

Format

- ☐ Cover page (title, names, date)
- ☐ Table of contents
- ☐ Executive summary
- ☐ Introduction
- ☐ Narrative
- ☐ Supporting information
- ☐ Charts/graphs/graphics
- ☐ Bibliography

Content

- ☐ Detail findings
- ☐ Interpret and analyze data
- ☐ Discuss implications
- ☐ Make recommendations
- ☐ Consider including sample creative materials
- ☐ Ask for sale

Writing

- ☐ Short sentences and paragraphs

Grant Proposal

Format

- ☐ Narrative
- ☐ Supporting information
- ☐ Budget
- ☐ Timetable
- ☐ Credentials of key staff
- ☐ Authorized signatures

Content

- ☐ Clearly state proposal at beginning of narrative
- ☐ Present background on problem
- ☐ Use statistics and hard evidence
- ☐ Connect the funding need to the funder's mission
- ☐ Include reasons why proposal should be funded
- ☐ Address short- and long-term benefits
- ☐ Identify target publics
- ☐ Include goals and measurable objectives
- ☐ Include budget
- ☐ Include timetable
- ☐ Explain evaluation methods to be used
- ☐ Emphasize cost efficiency
- ☐ Express confidence in idea

Writing

- ☐ Concise, persuasive language
- ☐ Appeal to self-interest of all parties
- ☐ Tailor to reader

Letter to the Editor

Format

☐ Company letterhead

☐ Salutation ("Dear Editor" or "To the Editor")

☐ Signed (name, title)

☐ Follow other guidelines provided by newspaper

Content

☐ Refer to issue or specific article (headline and date) in first paragraph

☐ Identify why issue is important and timely

☐ Provide background on subject

☐ Use facts and statistics

☐ Express opinion

☐ Summarize main point

Writing

☐ Brief (250–300 words)

☐ Maintain positive tone

☐ Avoid name-calling and harsh criticism

Op-ed Article

Format

- [ ] By-line
- [ ] Follow other guidelines provided by newspaper

Content

- [ ] Identify key points or arguments
- [ ] Include facts, statistics, and other supporting evidence
- [ ] Summarize main points
- [ ] Offer solutions without blatantly trying to promote your own company
- [ ] Provide reason why solution should be enacted or supported

Writing

- [ ] Concise (600–800 words)
- [ ] Persuasive language

Position Statement

Format

- ☐ Title
- ☐ Statement of formal adoption

Content

- ☐ Identify issue
- ☐ Provide history of issue
- ☐ Present data
- ☐ State opinion
- ☐ Discuss implications
- ☐ Refute opposing arguments
- ☐ Propose recommendations

Writing

- ☐ Short sentences and paragraphs
- ☐ Be persuasive

Speeches

Content

- ☐ Know audience in advance
- ☐ Understand what they expect
- ☐ Write attention-grabbing opening
- ☐ Establish central theme/main idea
- ☐ Repeat idea throughout speech
- ☐ Put key points in body
- ☐ Avoid conveying too much information in body
- ☐ Return to central idea in ending
- ☐ Leave people thinking

Public Service Announcement/Public Relations Advertisement

Format

☐ Creative headline

☐ Simple body copy

☐ Variety of formats and lengths

Content

☐ Expand on headline in first paragraph

☐ Focus on one idea in body

☐ Use supporting information

☐ Recap main point at end

☐ Emphasize desired action

Writing

☐ Memorable theme

☐ Short sentences and paragraphs

☐ Active voice

☐ Simple language

Newsletter

Planning

- [ ] Identify purpose
- [ ] Create mission statement
- [ ] Select editor and contributors
- [ ] Determine frequency of distribution
- [ ] Establish budget
- [ ] Determine length and format
- [ ] Develop content formula
- [ ] Choose "look and feel" that reflects organization
- [ ] Create attractive cover page

Format

- [ ] Nameplate
- [ ] Strong headlines, subheadings, and captions
- [ ] Masthead
- [ ] Clean, highly readable fonts
- [ ] Reader-friendly design
- [ ] Photo/graphic on each page

Content

- [ ] Follow content formula
- [ ] Use a variety of writing formats and styles (news, feature, etc.)
- [ ] Keep consistent with mission statement
- [ ] Focus on news, not promotion
- [ ] Emphasize reader benefits
- [ ] Provide two-way communication and encourage feedback
- [ ] Be aware of copyright infringement

Writing

- [ ] Reader-focused
- [ ] Simple language
- [ ] Concise and crisp
- [ ] Short sentences and paragraphs

E-zines

Format

- ☐ Table of contents
- ☐ Strong headlines
- ☐ Links to full text

Content

- ☐ Lead with substance, not promotion
- ☐ Include helpful tips
- ☐ Use bulleted lists

Writing

- ☐ Brief articles

Brochure

Format

☐ Enticing cover (focus on top third)

☐ Strong graphic design

☐ Visuals on each panel if possible

☐ Reflect organization

Content

☐ Focus on benefits to reader

☐ Highlight key points

☐ Explain features and benefits

☐ Use testimonials or other supporting information

☐ Include background information on organization, product, or service

☐ End with selling point

☐ Request action from reader

☐ Include contact information

☐ Include company mailing and Web address, phone, fax, e-mail, and logo

☐ Information should be inclusive so brochure can "stand alone"

Writing

☐ Persuasive and promotional

☐ Writing should have flair, promotional style

☐ Personal language ("I," "you," "we")

☐ Copy should set tone to build reader interest

☐ Easy to understand

Flier/Poster

Format

☐ One-sided, single sheet

☐ Large headline

☐ Single visual

Content

☐ Focus on important details only

☐ Include call to action

☐ Identify sponsor(s) by name and logo

Writing

☐ Brief

Appendix C

Special Events

In many instances, public relations practitioners prepare written materials as part of special events, so it is fitting that information on planning events be included in this book. This appendix focuses on events that public relations people arrange and coordinate, from news conferences and media parties to major special events that celebrate history, enhance a company's image, and advance marketing goals. You will also get more information on the critical factors that planners need to consider before, during, and after events, as well as suggestions for publicizing events to maximize your media exposure. Public relations professionals who plan events (that's most of them at some point in their careers) are aware of the need for detailed checklists; sample checklists are at the end of the appendix.

Media Events

Because public relations practitioners are often sharing information with the mass media, media events are among the most common events you will be arranging:

- *News conferences* are held to make news announcements that have great impact on a community or an industry, or that have significant public interest. A company planning a major expansion might hold news conferences in its hometown and in expansion cities, to announce this development and talk about its positive effect on the job market. Unfortunately, there are no strict rules or formulas to follow when deciding if a news conference is appropriate. There are some considerations, however, that provide a good rationale for your decision:

  - Is this a major, immediate story that has widespread importance?
  - Will the media want to hear directly from our CEO and other senior officials, and ask them questions about this development?
  - Will reporters be allowed to ask questions or will only a statement be made?

- Does our announcement present many possible story angles, and will the reporter who attends have a chance to discuss some of these angles and, therefore, develop an individualized story?
- Are visuals or demonstrations central to our news announcement?

If your answer to these questions is "yes," then holding a news conference that media contacts will come to is a pretty good bet. But, if reporters show up at your news conference and walk away saying, "That was a waste of time, why didn't they just e-mail or fax me a news release?", it may be impossible to ever get them back to another media event.

- *Press parties* use a more informal, party-like atmosphere to generate publicity and to build relationships with key reporters and editors. Media parties are common in the entertainment industry. Motion picture previews, held a day or two before the first public screening, are followed by a lavish party featuring cocktails, hors d'oeuvres, or a dinner. Media attending the party can interview the film's actors and other invited celebrity guests, which gives them time to prepare timely stories about the film that can be published or aired the day the movie opens. Press parties are often done in combination with news conferences when an organization opens a new facility or launches a new product.
- If news announcements must reach multiple audiences in several different locations at the same time, in those cases it may be best to do a *teleconference*, or a *videoconference* using satellite technology. Reporters can participate in teleconferences and videoconferences without having to travel to your location, which saves time and adds convenience. For teleconferences, reporters are asked to call a specific telephone number to log in to the conference; for videoconferences, they are asked to go to a designated site in their city equipped with satellite technology and with phone lines to call in questions. The cost of teleconferences and videoconferences can be expensive, depending on the size and length of the event, the number of locations involved, and the technical complexity. Many video news conferences use *one-way video* (reporters see your spokespeople, but the spokespeople don't see the reporters) and *two-way audio* (both sides can ask and receive questions). Two-way video is available but for a much greater cost.
- Another technique that will allow you to reach multiple audiences while enhancing your online media relations and publicity efforts is the *Webcast* or *Internet videoconference*. Webcasts make it possible for journalists, investors, or other key audiences to attend videoconferences without having to leave their desks. Technology allows for live video to be converted into a digital signal as the event is taking place. The video is then "streamed" on the Internet, so media contacts can view the conference on personal computers as it happens. A special Web site is created for Webcasts, and passwords can be provided if there are security concerns. Those viewing the Webcast will need a sufficient modem or Internet connection, and a multimedia player such as RealOne™ Player. Give reporters access to the player, which costs nothing to download, on the Webcast's Web site. You can hire a specialty company, such as Medialink Worldwide, West Glen Communications, or Orbis Broadcast Group, to

plan, execute, and coordinate Webcasts. Most video production companies that arrange videoconferences can add a Webcast for a reasonable cost. Webcasts can be stored on the Web site after the event, too. Individuals who couldn't log on at the time of the event can go to the Web site at their leisure and see and hear recorded video and audio.

- Although they can cost twice as much to do, **satellite media tours** (SMTs) have a clear advantage over VNRs. They make it possible to ask questions of a spokesperson live, via satellite hookup. Each station that takes part in the SMT can choose to pick up the satellite feed and do an exclusive interview with a designated spokesperson during a pre-arranged timeframe. Celebrities, CEOs, and national experts who are not easy for producers to book on their own are excellent choices for SMT spokespersons. Media contacts typically receive a b-roll package as well, so they can have additional footage to air during the interview or prepare a background piece in advance of the SMT. The simplest form of SMT involves a spokesperson sitting in a television studio doing the interviews. More companies are opting to take their spokespeople out of the studio and put them in a visually interesting location that has relevance to the story. Most of the companies that can arrange a Webcast can also accommodate SMTs.
- *Media tours* take clients or an organization's spokesperson "on the road"—in town or out of town—to visit media outlets. During a media tour, spokespersons do a series of prearranged interviews and make appearances, or simply get better acquainted with media contacts to lay the groundwork for future publicity opportunities. Another type of media visit is an "ed-board" or editorial board meeting. This involves executives from your organization sitting down with a publication's editorial board to explain policies or procedures or to discuss a timely issue in more detail. The result can be more balanced coverage of a news subject related to your organization, or favorable editorial support or endorsement of an initiative or project.

Before planning any media event, consider the appropriateness of doing so and make sure that the event does not violate any ethical standards of the public relations or media professions. The PRSA's Member Code of Ethics uses the following examples of such violations:

- A public relations practitioner entertains a government official beyond legal limits or in violation of government reporting requirements.
- A public relations representative for a ski manufacturer gives a pair of expensive racing skis to a sports magazine columnist in an effort to influence a positive review of the equipment.

Once you are sure the media event is appropriate, you can start planning. Each media event you plan has several common elements that are critical to its success: location; timing; budget; invitations; program; media kit; and follow-up activities.

First, select an appropriate *location* for the event. The nature of the event may dictate the site you choose. Your organization's main offices are one possibility for news conferences, parties, and briefings, but many media events are scheduled at hotels and conference centers that have ample facilities the media are familiar with and can get to easily. Those facilities book events months to a year in advance, so have some alternate sites in mind in case your first choice is unavailable. In addition, the nature of the event can present logical and, in some cases, more creative location possibilities. If you are planning a media event around the grand opening of a store or some other building, it makes sense to hold the event at the site, so reporters can see the new facility. For videoconferences and SMTs, select an appropriate central location for the media that can accommodate the necessary telephone or satellite hookups.

As with most publicity activities, good *timing* will help boost turnout at your media event. If your news announcement relates to a major, breaking story, your goal is to arrange the media event as quickly as possible. If you have more flexibility with your timing, such as introducing a new product, do some research first to find out if other events are planned that may draw media attention away from your event. Consult the chamber of commerce in the area where your event will take place and access city Web sites to get information about scheduled events. The best day of the week and time of day for a media event really depend on the media you most want to attend your event and what their deadlines are. A mid-to-late morning news conference, for example, gives TV crews adequate time to prepare their stories for evening newscasts. Many public relations professionals say that midweek and even Sundays can be good days for media events, but again, let your media's needs drive the selection of the best day and time.

When planning the *budget*, there are obvious costs to consider. Hotels, conference centers, and other non-company-owned facilities may charge room rental fees. There will also be expenses for food and drink and the use and set-up of audio-visual equipment supplied by the site. Don't forget to factor in tax and gratuities to your food costs. You may need to cover travel costs for non-company experts who agree to speak at your event, not to mention airline and other travel expenses for company personnel, if the event is held in a location away from the organization's main headquarters city.

Budget monies might need to be allocated for printed *invitations*. Invitations to your media event can take many forms. When your event focuses on important hard news, a media alert sent via e-mail will suffice. But for other events, such as media parties, you may want to make the invitation more formal or creative to capture the media's interest. All invitations, regardless of form and format, should be individually addressed and include the date, time, and location of the event, and a brief explanation of the event and its news value. Include the names of dignitaries and other top officials who will be available to answer questions, and let the media know how long the event is expected to last so they can plan their day accordingly. For teleconferences, make sure you include the information on how to get connected to the conference; for Webcasts, let reporters know the Web site address they will need to access and how they can download any software needed to view the Webcast.

The media event *program* is the itinerary that outlines who will speak and in what order, what each person will say and how long each person will talk, and any other activities. The program for a basic news conference or briefing can be simple: a brief welcome and introduction by a company official (sometimes this is a public relations person), followed by prepared statements from a designated spokesperson and a Q & A period with reporters. Media parties are usually less rigid in their program approach, although time should be set aside for someone from the sponsoring organization to make remarks, and provisions should be made for the media to conduct group or one-on-one interviews. Refreshments should be available at all media events. Coffee, pastries, and bagels are often served at morning news conferences, while elaborate media parties require more extensive catering.

When reporters arrive at a media event, especially news conferences, give them some background material that will help them better understand the subject and write their stories. This material can be as simple as a news release, or it can be organized into a larger packet of information known as a *media kit*. Prior to the start of a news conference, a busy reporter who had little time to prepare for your event can look through the media kit and get a quick overview of the subject and formulate some questions for your spokespeople. The media kit also allows you to make sure media contacts receive your key messages in writing. Facts, statistics, and historical data included in the media kit prove valuable to reporters who may have to return to their offices and file their stories under pressing deadlines. Among the standard elements of a media kit:

- a general news release summarizing the main news announcement;
- backgrounders and fact sheets that further explain the subject and offer more information on the organization sponsoring the event;
- sidebars and features that focus on specific newsworthy aspects of the subject in more detail; sidebars can give reporters ideas for possible story angles;
- biographical sketches and head shots of key company personnel who participated in the media event;
- visual aids such as architectural designs, maps, charts and graphs, and photographs.

At the conclusion of your media event, there are several *follow-up activities* that bring closure to the event and help you measure its success. These include:

- Getting back to reporters who had questions that require more complete answers. It is important to brief your spokespeople before the event and anticipate questions, but there are going to be times when a question pops up for which you aren't totally prepared. Right after the event, get the answer and call the reporter back as soon as you can.
- Making follow-up calls to media contacts who didn't attend, and delivering or sending media materials by fax or e-mail at their request. You can also include those materials on your Web site, and refer media contacts to that site.
- Paying site and catering fees and taking care of any other expenses.
- Tracking media coverage. For local media events, make sure someone from your staff is assigned to collect newspaper clippings and tape broadcast stories. You may want to hire a clipping service for events expected to generate more widespread media coverage.
- Compiling a final report that summarizes the media coverage received and assesses the planning and execution of the event. Note those aspects of the event that went smoothly and not so smoothly, and suggest any new approaches that would make similar media events run more efficiently in the future.

Broadcast Promotional Events

Promotional opportunities through broadcast media, especially radio, also take on aspects of special events and can extend your publicity in original ways. Organizations that sell tickets for sports events, concerts, shows, and other activities, for example, can do *giveaways* with radio stations. The sponsoring group donates tickets to give away on the air prior to the event. The prospect of winning tickets is an incentive for listeners to tune in, and stations are receptive to getting free items that their listeners would want. In return, the station's deejays make repeated mentions of the group and its event when giving away the tickets, which helps build public awareness of the event.

Stores and businesses celebrating an anniversary or grand opening, and not-for-profit organizations sponsoring popular charitable events might arrange for a radio or TV station to do a *remote broadcast*. During remotes, radio and TV personalities broadcast live from the site of the event and publicize the remote's sponsor during commercial breaks. This helps build traffic at the remote location and gives the media good exposure to passersby who see the station's signage, banners, and mobile vans. Remotes can be expensive because they are considered advertising time; however, a station may occasionally reduce or waive the price for frequent advertisers and charitable organizations. A *trade* may also be arranged, where the remote sponsor trades its product or services for the remote.

Another possibility is *media sponsorship* of an event. Media sponsors can help fund the event, but their primary role is often to create and air announcements and provide publicity support, in exchange for visibility at the event and the goodwill this kind of community sponsorship creates.

Contests are another creative way to reach key audiences. Regardless of which type of media promotion you choose, make sure the demographics of the radio or TV station match your target audience.

Other Public Relations Events

Public relations professionals organize many other types of special event, including:

- celebrations such as company anniversaries, employee recognition dinners, and holiday parties;
- marketing communications events such as trade shows;
- fundraising and public service events;
- informational events such as conferences, workshops, and presentations to community groups.

These types of event may require much more in-depth planning than a media or broadcast promotional event. Practitioners know that, when organizing events, you should have a disciplined planning team, ample time and resources to do the event well, the ability to think quickly on your feet, and backup plans since something is bound to go wrong. While each event has its own unique set of challenges, most require attention to some general planning principles before, during, and after:

Before the Event

- Develop a plan, including goals and objectives, target publics, strategies and tactics for organizing and promoting the event, a budget, and a timetable of activity. Assemble an event planning team, delegate responsibilities, and assign weekly deadlines. As mentioned, research the market to make sure your event doesn't go head-to-head with others that could be of interest to your target public.
- Start promoting the event to the target publics right away; send a print or e-postcard announcing the upcoming event to prospective attendees several months in advance, so they can mark their calendars early. Follow up with regular, strategically timed mailings, e-mail, and other personalized communication to continue building interest.

  In addition, some events have news value and the potential to receive media coverage. The media will likely cover your event, for example, if it features an appearance or speech by a well-known person; focuses on a timely issue that people are talking about; involves a notable business advancement; is designed to help the less fortunate in your community; or has a unique theme.

  Let's say you are a business association and you are planning a conference for business professionals in your area that spotlights a keynote speech by an internationally known corporation president. The smart public relations person knows that, in a situation like this, there's more to publicizing the event than just sending out a single news release a few weeks before the event. A better strategy is to supply the media with information about the event in several stages to get media exposure:

  - Send a general announcement release six weeks (or so) before the event to inform the business community about the upcoming conference and its focus, when and where it will be held, and how people can register.
  - Send a second news release announcing your keynote speaker, a few weeks before the event and registration deadline. This gives you a second opportunity to share details about the event and boost registrations, while giving the media another legitimate news hook.
  - Distribute a media alert a few days before the event that invites the media to a news conference with the industry leader, or that invites them to attend the news conference or briefing and cover the speech.

- Maintain activity checklists, have weekly meetings to discuss progress and obstacles, and adjust timetables as needed. A template of an activity checklist is located in this appendix.
- Anticipate problems and establish backup plans. When planning outdoor functions, event planners should secure a tent or indoor site in case of bad weather. Conference planners need to think about guest speakers or presenters canceling at the last minute and identify others in advance who could speak in their place. Fundraising events that involve running or some other physical activity by participants require on-site medical care.
- Confirm final attendance and make sure there are adequate space, food, and parking for the expected crowd. Hotels and caterers want to know the expected attendance several days to a week before the event, and they will bill you for that number, even if that minimum number of people doesn't show.

Day of the Event

- Do a final walk-through of the space you are using and check on details such as room setup (are there enough chairs, and are they arranged properly?), sound and lighting (do microphones work?), and equipment (do PowerPoint slides or computer programs operate without difficulty?).
- Make sure there is adequate and visible signage to direct people to the event site.
- Have a formal registration area set up and adequately staffed for people to officially check in. Have name tags, extra pens and pencils, and notepads available.
- Distribute a brief survey or comment card at the end of the event to get feedback from participants.

After the Event

- If the event had news value, send out a follow-up news release or photo release to the appropriate media later that day or the day after the event.
- Hold a meeting with your planning team to assess the event and critique the event plan. Did you achieve your goals and get the desired response from the target audience? If problems came up, were they handled efficiently? What lessons did you learn from planning this event?
- Compile participant survey results and gather any media clippings.
- Send thank you letters to participants, guests, speakers, vendors, and any others who contributed to the success of the event.
- Prepare a final report for clients and senior managers summarizing all the information above; attach a summary of participants' survey responses.

References and Suggested Reading

Armstrong, J. S. (2001). *Planning special events*. San Francisco: Jossey Bass.

Coons, P. (1999). *Gala!: The special event planner for professionals and volunteers*. Dulles, VA: Capital Books.

Hoyle, L. H. (2002). *Event marketing: How to successfully promote events, festivals, conventions, and expositions*. Hoboken, NJ: John Wiley & Sons.

Levy, B. R., & Mairon, B. (1997). *Successful special events: Planning, hosting and evaluating*. New York: Aspen Publishers.

PRSA member code of ethics 2000. (2000). Retrieved January 9, 2009 from http://www.prsa.org/aboutUs/ethics/preamble_en.html.

Salzman, J. (1998). *Making the news: A guide for nonprofits and activists*. Boulder, CO: Westview Press.

Skinner, B. E., & Rukavina, V. (2002). *Event sponsorship*. Hoboken, NJ: John Wiley & Sons. *Special events magazine*. www.specialevents.com.

News Conference

Before

- [ ] Select location
- [ ] Determine best date and time
- [ ] Develop budget
- [ ] Prepare/distribute invitations or media alerts (include connection information for videoconferences and audioconferences)
- [ ] Outline program
- [ ] Draft welcome and introductions
- [ ] Write opening news statement/announcement
- [ ] Brief speakers; anticipate questions and prepare answers
- [ ] Assemble media kit
- [ ] Arrange for refreshments
- [ ] Prepare background visuals
- [ ] Provide media with access to multimedia player (for Webcasts only)

After

- [ ] Provide any follow-up information that is requested
- [ ] Contact media that were not in attendance
- [ ] Track media coverage
- [ ] Write final evaluation report

Special Events

Initial Planning

- [ ] Set goals and objectives
- [ ] Identify target publics
- [ ] Select theme
- [ ] Develop strategies and tactics
- [ ] Develop budget
- [ ] Develop timetable
- [ ] Check for competing events
- [ ] Assemble event planning team
- [ ] Delegate responsibilities

Logistics

- [ ] Visit potential sites; check for:
  - [ ] Handicapped accessibility
  - [ ] Kitchen access
  - [ ] Bathrooms
  - [ ] Parking area
  - [ ] Coat check
- [ ] Confirm floor plan
- [ ] Book valet service
- [ ] Book caterer
- [ ] Select menu
- [ ] Arrange for bar service
- [ ] Rent tables, chairs, linens, dishes, flatware, stemware, serving dishes, tent
- [ ] Arrange for security
- [ ] Arrange for insurance
- [ ] Obtain permits (e.g., parking, hanging outside banners)
- [ ] Determine type of music (band, deejay, "piped" in) and book

- [ ] Determine audio/visual needs; arrange for:
  - [ ] microphones and speakers
  - [ ] podium
  - [ ] projectors and screens
  - [ ] lighting
  - [ ] staging or risers
  - [ ] Internet connection
- [ ] Conduct final walk-through on day of event to check on details, if AV equipment is working, etc.

Special Considerations

- [ ] Hire décor consultant
- [ ] Order centerpieces, corsages/boutonnières, and decorative arrangements
- [ ] Order balloons
- [ ] Buy candles
- [ ] Book photographer
- [ ] Order table favors
- [ ] Order "goody bags" for guests
- [ ] Assemble hospitality baskets for bathrooms

Program

- [ ] Arrange transportation, accommodations, and meals for speaker/emcee
- [ ] Order gift/awards for speaker/award recipients
- [ ] Obtain guest list from award recipients
- [ ] Write script
- [ ] Prepare visual presentation and test all A/V equipment beforehand

Special Events ... *continued*

Publicity

- [ ] Send news release announcing event
- [ ] Send news release announcing speaker or award recipient
- [ ] Send media alert inviting media to cover the event

Printing

- [ ] Hire graphic designer
- [ ] Select printer
- [ ] Assemble mailing list
- [ ] "Save this Date" card
- [ ] Invitations
- [ ] Program
- [ ] Signage (directional, registration, recognition, tables)
- [ ] Banners

Staffing

- [ ] Recruit and train volunteers
- [ ] Assign someone to be the "go to" person on day of event
- [ ] Assign someone to take care of writing any checks at event (e.g., caterer, musicians)
- [ ] Assign people to work at the registration table
- [ ] Assign greeters
- [ ] Assign an escort for speaker/emcee
- [ ] Arrange for help to set up/clean up
- [ ] Order or make special nametags
- [ ] Arrange for snacks
- [ ] Arrange for "thank you" gifts

Registration Table

- [ ] Arrange for table, chairs, linens, décor, etc.
- [ ] Easel
- [ ] Wastebasket
- [ ] Printed nametags
- [ ] Blank nametags
- [ ] Pens/markers
- [ ] Reservation list
- [ ] Table diagram/seating arrangements
- [ ] Cash box/change

Follow Up

- [ ] Send thank you notes to:
  - [ ] Speaker/emcee
  - [ ] Sponsors
  - [ ] Volunteers
  - [ ] Event planning team
- [ ] Send follow-up news release
- [ ] Evaluate and write summary report

Index

Note: page numbers in *italics* refer to information contained in the Exhibits.